The Treasure Divers

THE
TREASURE DIVERS

Kendall McDonald

PELHAM BOOKS
London

Pelham Books Ltd
52 Bedford Square, London WC1B 3EF

ISBN 0 7207 1048 0

Phototypeset in V.I.P. Palatino by
Western Printing Services Ltd, Bristol and
printed in Great Britain by
Billing & Sons Limited,
Guildford, London and Worcester

Contents

Illustrations

Foreword

by H.R.H. The Prince of Wales,
K.G., K.T., P.C., G.C.B.

There is no doubt about it. There is something irresistibly fascinating and tempting about wrecks and the possibility of sunken treasure. We are all basically treasure hunters and I often think that even the most serious and dedicated archaeologists have to suppress, to a certain extent, the urge to dig for 'treasure' and to concentrate instead on piecing together the jigsaw puzzle of the past.

I have experienced the excitement myself of diving on a wreck in the Virgin Islands and of searching the seabed (on the site of a 17th century wreck) off Cartagena in Colombia for Spanish coins and musket balls, but when I think about it I was really behaving like a submerged vandal. That was in the days before I became President of the British Sub-Aqua Club!

All those divers who wish to search for specific wrecks would do well to follow the excellent example (described in this book) of the Plymouth Sound divers who found a ship's bell a hundred feet down, and instead of surfacing with the bell, as most people are normally tempted to, they tied their surface marker buoy to it and came up to take very accurate transit bearings of the exact location. As a result a most useful and interesting archaeological project ensued, which might otherwise have been lost.

Underwater archaeology is still basically in its infancy, but there is obviously a great deal of fascinating material in the waters round our coasts which may one day add considerably to our knowledge of the past. The current excavation of Henry VIII's warship the *Mary Rose* is an example of the kind of project being undertaken by a team of dedicated divers and, having dived on the wreck myself, I can only express the hope that one day it may prove possible to raise her from the seabed – if she is still reasonably intact.

Kendall McDonald has written a most fascinating and entertaining book, at once informative and eminently readable, which should serve to inspire all British Sub-Aqua Club members with new-found enthusiasm to become responsible treasure divers and not just underwater vandals!

Introduction

'I am the Duke of Cornwall'

Lost at sea	On land
10 December 1786	*George III reigns*
Die Fraumetta Catherina von	*Trial of Warren Hastings*
Flensburgh	
Christian Hendrick	

The ship's bell sat on the top of the top table with all the very top people. Despite the fact that it was completely covered by napkins so that no one could see it, that bell was closer to the light than it had been for most of the past two hundred years; it had spent nearly two centuries a hundred feet down under the sea in the mud of Plymouth Sound. The occasion when the ship's bell was to see the light again was the twenty-first anniversary banquet of the British Sub-Aqua Club, in London's historic Guildhall on 18 November 1974.

But the bell's big moment had not yet come. First it almost rang as gusts of laughter swept through Guildhall over Harry Secombe's speech proposing the toast of the BS-AC:

I have been made a BS-AC trainee – the world's biggest sub-aqua club now has the world's biggest diver. . . . I have been reading about all the exciting things to do down there, like finding the wreck of Henry VIII's *Mary Rose* – a tall thin girl with glasses. . . . Take the dolphin. After only three weeks in captivity, it can train a man to stand on the very edge of its pool and throw it fishes three times a day.

Those and other jokes flowed free, until it came to the moment for Harry Secombe to hand over to the BS-AC's president, HRH Prince Charles, the Prince of Wales. Harry Secombe did it with a poem of his own. It went like this:

We have a Prince for President,
Well-known to one and all,
Because he is a noble gent,
And nearly six feet tall.

He's always touring foreign lands,
His life is not his own,
And if he's spotted holding hands,
She's going to share the throne.

The only place that I can see,
Where he'll find peace and quiet,
Is down beneath the deep blue sea,
With haddock, bream and mullet.

But, Sir, when following fishy trails,
Just heed these few remarks,
That though you may be Prince of Wales,
It don't apply to sharks!

Prince Charles replied in like vein giving as good as he got, but
he then became more serious and spoke of the ship which had
carried the bell, which was still incognito under its napkin covering. This ship, said Prince Charles, was blown into the Sound in
December 1786 and struck Drake's Island – 'something I nearly
did the other day when I tried to navigate'. Wrecks found in
certain areas in the West Country were the property of the Duchy
of Cornwall – 'and', said the Prince, 'I am the Duke of Cornwall!'
He then presented the bell to the B S-A C. At that moment he
pulled the napkin covering off the bell and the bell heard a roar of
applause – which dwarfed even that it had heard at the launching
of the ship that carried it in 1782.

In the 1700s – indeed at any time before the Plymouth Break-
water was completed in 1841 – any gale from the south-
south-east or south-south-west was a wind to be feared in Plymouth. A direct southerly gale was worse. It bore disaster for
shipping on each and every gust.

The night of the tenth of December 1786 was such a night. The
gale swung from south-west to south-south-west and then full
south. On that day two ships had put into Plymouth for shelter in
view of the obviously worsening weather. Both were outward
bound. The *Christian Hendrick* had come from Rotterdam with
wheat and cheese for Barcelona. The ship called *Die Fraumetta*

Catherina von Flensburgh was on her way from St Petersburg (which we now call Leningrad) to Genoa, with a cargo of hemp and leather. She had already had a long voyage, working her way through the Gulf of Finland, across the Baltic, then out of the Kattegat around the top of Denmark, through the Skagerrak and out into the North Sea. Her course had then taken her through the Straits of Dover into the channel and finally, out of the obviously deteriorating weather, into the shelter of Plymouth.

It was to prove no shelter at all. By eight o'clock that night the *Catherina* was snubbing hard against her anchor rope as the wind increased in violence from the south-west. At 10 pm a full gale was howling into what would normally be a sheltered anchorage. First to go was the *Christian*, which broke free and was driven ashore in Deadman's Bay in the Cattewater; all the crew were saved. But then it was the *Catherina's* turn. The fifty-three-ton brigantine was torn from her shelter, struck Drake's Island with what those on board knew was a death-blow, and was then whirled in spray and gale-driven foam across the narrows towards Mount Edgcumbe before sinking in the darkness somewhere under the Raven's Cliffs on the Cornwall side of Plymouth Sound. Somehow the crew got ashore, but the ship was gone.

Her passing did not go unrecorded, unlike that of so many other ships of her time which sank in the night somewhere out in the dark and only their non-arrival at some port or other merited a line in a port agent's letter. *The Times* of 14 December 1786 reported her loss and that of the *Christian*: 'Same night was drove on shore the Motte Catherina of Flansberg bound from Petersburgh for Genoa laden with hemp and leather. Vessel and cargo entirely lost, crew saved.' The *Sherbourne Mercury* of 18 December the same year added: 'on Drake's Island the Motte Catherina . . . from Petersburgh for Grenada and ship and cargo totally lost; the crew lost'.

Even allowing for some divergence of views about the health of the crew and the destination of the ship, she was lucky to have her passing recorded at all. She was lucky too that in 1973 the divers of Plymouth Sound branch of the B S-A C started looking for another ship. If they had not done so, the *Fraumetta Catherina von Flensburgh* would be completely forgotten, her bell would never have attended a Guildhall banquet, nor would it be on view to the public today in Plymouth City Museum.

The dive that was to bring her back to the land of the living started out as a search for another well-documented wreck, that of HMS *Harwich* (which was the victim of an earlier gale in 1691 – see chapter 7). At first the divers' searches revealed no trace of the wreckage of the *Harwich* which they expected to find on the sloping sea-bed in the water under the Battery Buoy. These underwater slopes lead down to a prehistoric river gorge which forms the deep channel in the Sound to the west of Drake's Island. Two divers, Chris Holwill, who is the BS-AC regional coach for the south-west, and Colin Hannaford in their turn pushed deeper down to the foot of the gorge. There in the twilight a hundred feet down they literally bumped into a complete ship's bell.

It was now that the Plymouth Sound divers showed their expertise. Instead of surfacing with the bell as most people have been tempted to, they tied their surface marker buoy to it and came up to make sure that very accurate transit bearings were taken of the location. Once this had been done, a careful search in the vicinity of the bell located a large iron ring, which they guessed was an anchor ring, and masses of what looked like peculiar dead kelp. Only after this search did they raise the bell.

So far the divers had behaved impeccably. And they got a bonus. The bell was obviously very old, but the name of the vessel, *Die Fraumetta Catherina von Flensburgh*, was still discernible. An immediate identification of a ship just like that happens very rarely to any wreck diver. The bell was kept wet in sea-water and contact was made with Mrs Mary Greenacre of Bristol City Museum, who is the archaeological technician for the area. She advised drying the bell, and shipping it immediately to her department. This was done. In fact when the bell attended the banquet at which Prince Charles presented it to the BS-AC, it was on a very short leave from the conservation process it was still undergoing.

Plymouth Sound branch realized that they had a first-class archaeological project on their hands and set to work to find out more about the ship, starting diving operations to investigate her present condition. The director of operations is Ian Skelton, the chairman of the nautical archaeological section of Plymouth Sound branch, whose idea it was to dive in the area in the first place. Describing the site of the wreck, Chris Holwill says:

The average depth is about thirty metres and it lies at the base of an underwater cliff face. The sea-bed consists of thick mud. The visibility is usually poor, at least in the upper portion of the tidal stream, the lower depths sometimes are clearer but rapid light cut-off makes it into a simulated night-dive! The tides here are quite strong and we have found, with experience, that the stream on the surface can be running in the reverse direction to that on the bottom and indeed with a surface run there may not be any bottom movement. This is important when you bear in mind the nature of the sea-bed and the need for some movement to remove disturbed silt during our work on site. It is impossible to dive the site on spring-tides and even on neaps there is only a short 'slack-water' period.

We were able to use the large, substantial ring as our datum point and so we laid out the first site-lines for our initial archaeological survey. At about this time we sampled the rather concentrated masses of dead 'kelp' and found, to our astonishment, that it was leather!

A sample of the bales of leather was brought to the surface and found to be a complete hide, with the animal's tail and whiskers still attached. in a remarkable state of preservation. We treated some hides with alcohol, xylene and paraffin wax and obtained reasonable results. However, we found that washing well with fresh water and then drying and treating with neat's-foot oil produced remarkable results. A small sample was sent to the British Leather Manufacturers Research Association for examination and they wrote back: 'cattle hide, vegetable tanned . . . grain surface lightly boarded or embossed . . . no indication of age or origin'.

Another expert living locally gave this pleasing description:

'The lovely scent of this leather is caused by the age old Russian method of tanning with willow bark and currying with birch oil. Calf leather tanned by this method was much favoured in the seventeenth/eighteenth century and I have always known that it was astonishingly long standing, but for it to be so strong after nearly 200 years immersion is amazing. I think the leather is probably reindeer but this can only be proved by expert microscopic examination.'

This was not the only leather recovered. Diving and probing the silt revealed more bales of leather.

The divers' first major set-back came in the Spring of 1975 after over two months of winter gales. On their eventual return to the site, they found no anchor ring or site-lines. The site was clear, apart from one solitary probe with a small length of line still attached. They suspected sabotage initially but it was more likely that a boat innocently anchoring over the site had hooked the lines and removed them together with the anchor ring. So they started marking the site again.

Now a 150-kg cast-iron radiator painted white serves as the divers' underwater site-marker. Their surface transits are so good that in 'bombing' the site with a shot weight and buoy they have never missed the radiator by more than two metres. Sometimes they swear they can hear the 'clunk' as the shot weight hits the radiator a hundred feet below! Says Chris Holwill:

Our next task was to systematically probe the site which would ordinarily require a traditional grid-line to be laid over the site. However, it was decided that such a grid would be an unacceptable risk to the divers on this site, in view of the depth, darkness and poor visibility. We came up with yet another approach. By triangulation and not least a little help from Pythagoras, we set up lines east and west of the north datum line, labelled A to P at metre intervals. The probe is used along this line, at numbered 1 metre intervals.

A positive probe point was subsequently core-sampled and found to be wood, in fact identified as oak. We fervently hope that it is not the figure-head's nose, or other anatomical protrusion, that we have sampled!

At this point the branch purchased a Pegson 100 gall/min petrol-driven pump, to be used as a water-dredge. With the exceedingly unmanageable length of fireman's hose and the instantaneous low visibility achieved by the jet action it was not a success. Nor was there enough power to deal with the thick mud of the sea-bed.

I wrote a begging letter to Messrs ComAir of Camborne, Cornwall on the off-chance that they had a second-hand compressor they could let us have. This firm has responded magnificently. We have received on long-term loan a 100 psi 150 cu ft/min air compressor. This monster will be of great help in uncovering the wreck and I am confident that we will reveal her, much as she went down.

The divers now plan to complete the survey of the ship and uncover as much of the site as seems practical. All artefacts found are to be donated to the Plymouth City Museum. The Plymouth Sound divers are realists. They know that in the ship they found they do not have a *Mary Rose* or a *Vasa* (see chapter 3) which can be raised and put on show to the public. Nor is their ship historically all that important. Nor is she a treasure wreck. But she is revealing to them the joy of learning from a disciplined, careful excavation all sorts of things about the way people lived – and died – on board ships of long ago. Like the bell, they have seen the light!

Though the Plymouth Sound wreck is perhaps not of the greatest importance to our knowledge of history, it is important in this book about wreck divers. Not because it has had its glamorous moments with the bell at the banquet, but simply because here you have a group of amateur divers who are prepared to make great personal sacrifices in their leisure diving – no one can really think that probing in a cloud of silt at a hundred feet is fun – for the *greatest* pleasure to be had in all modern treasure hunts, the satisfaction of finding out about the past.

This book is not simply about treasure hunting. Nor is it a complete record of underwater archaeology. It is about the people, mostly amateurs under expert guidance, who make underwater archaeology happen. This book is literally about the people who go down to the ships in the sea. Some it is true come up with a profit. But most take part in controlled excavations of the ships they discover and find their satisfaction not in pieces of eight and golden crowns, but in seeing those discoveries displayed in museums or described in print for all to see. This book is about them, and for them.

ONE

'So you've joined the lunatic fringe!'

Lost at sea	On land
5000 BC to AD 480	*Mesolithic Man sets up stone*
A Bronze Age arms-trader	*idols*
Roman ships	*Romans conquer Britain*
	Saxons win bridgehead at Selsey,
	Sussex

Two thousand years before the first stone was raised at Stonehenge, a group of hunter-fisherfolk were setting up their own stone monuments along the edge of the sea near what we now call Selsey Bill in Sussex. And if you wonder what a book about wrecks and diving is doing wandering about in the Mesolithic Age around ten to four thousand years before the birth of Christ, then you should know that part of the thrill of diving down to the wrecks around the coast of Britain is that you never know what is going to loom up at you through the grey-green mists of the waters around our shores. In fact it was a dive in the sea off Selsey Bill which led to discoveries that may well tell us a great deal more about life in Britain's Stone Age.

The area of sea in which divers have made the earliest known underwater discovery of man in Britain is marked by the Mixon Beacon, a modern metal pencil warning of danger some two miles off the single-fringe promontory of Selsey Bill. The iron basket on the top never held a beacon and as you approach it in a small boat, the pencil effect widens into iron-work, streaked white with the droppings of cormorants, which perch there to rest between fishing expeditions.

The purpose of the beacon is not of course to mark an underwater site in use by early man in perhaps 5000 BC, but to keep modern ships away from the dangerous rock and shingle banks of the Mixon, which emerge at low tide. This is no place for modern super-tankers drawing some ninety feet of water and only inches clear of the sea-bed in mid-channel. Nor is it the place for modern coaster, though many have, despite the beacon, come to grief on surrounding shifting shingle. Most have got off; some are still there in very small and twisted pieces (for the seas around the Mixon can be terrifyingly wild).

Even on calm, still days the narrow channel near the beacon boils and spits as though raining from the underside up. I find it a sad place even on the brightest day. I respect it as a dangerous place. For here professional fishermen have drowned, swept overboard entangled in their pot ropes. Here too is the place where an amateur diver died, caught in the treachery of the sudden rush of the tide. It is this sudden movement of vast weights of water that makes the Mixon as dangerous as it is, and makes it a diving area only for the experienced.

One man understands the underwater landscape of the Mixon better than any other. This man is Major Hume Wallace, former administrative agent of the B S-A C, who now lives at Selsey and is one of the few diving geologists that Britain has so far produced. Hume Wallace has scientifically proved the first explanation of the odd outline of the sea-bed under water off Selsey. He was the first to realize – by means of aerial survey and allied underwater exploration – that the area he canoed over as a boy in the 1930s was in fact a river estuary of ancient times. This could be the mouth of the river which Ptolemy considered important enough to name and list with its latitude and longitude in his *Geography* of about 150 AD. This was the 'thrice-blessed river' – one of five river mouths that Ptolemy listed on the south coast of Britain, including the Fal, Tamar and Exe.

Hume Wallace's geological underwater studies of the area have resulted in his production of a map of the probable coastline in Roman times (see figure 1). And for a time his underwater researches concentrated on the Mixon Hole, a strange slash in the sea-bed reaching depths of nearly a hundred feet in places. The sea-level in ancient times must have made this exit of the river to the sea something like a Norwegian fjord.

If you can imagine that, it makes Hume Wallace's next discovery much more understandable. For Hume, on dives in and around the Mixon Hole, found there the remains of a Roman fortress (at the Mixon Beacon of today) which would have guarded the entrance to the lost estuary. This fortress would have complete control over ships coming in or out. The deep navigable

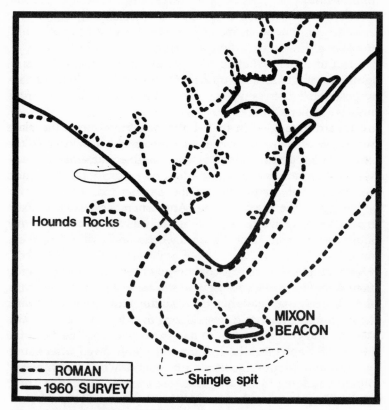

Fig. 1.　Map of area around Mixon Beacon in Roman times

channel must have passed almost underneath the fortress walls and the Romans did not rely on bow or sling to enforce that control.

While diving with members of Kingston branch of the B S-A C, Hume Wallace found a large number of round stone *ballista*, or catapult balls, though there is so far no sign of the exact location of the giant machine that must have been required to fire these aerial monsters. It is interesting to note that the way that these are scattered over the sea-bed of the hole suggests that they were fired rather than that they rolled down to the depths of the Mixon when the fortress walls collapsed.

In fact on dives I have made there myself I found two such round stone balls, each two feet in diameter, at least 250 to 300 yards from the probable catapult site. Interestingly too, on the area on figure 1 opposite the fort site which Hume has marked as probably a shingle spit, there are big cut square blocks in forty-five feet of water. Whether these blocks are all that is left of a lighthouse to guide ships in to shelter or whether there was an outpost of the fortress on the other side of the entrance we shall probably never know.

It is of course possible that all the missiles were fired during training, because we know that the Roman army was insistent on regular target practice. But it is also possible that some missiles were fired in anger and found a target, since Saxon and other German raiders were active in the English Channel from the beginning of the third century. And when the end of Roman Britain came, soon after AD 450, Selsey was the place where the South Saxons won their first bridgehead and established their kings.

But if Hume Wallace's discoveries in the Mixon area up to that point were fascinating, his next was to be sensational. And I am pleased to say that I gave him the first clue. It came when my wife Penny, my son Kevin and I were diving the Mixon Hole with John Messent and Geoff Bowden from John's boat *Pisces*. The date was Sunday, 5 September 1971. John and Geoff dived first, being swept to the west during their dive by the tide which was running strongly, judging by the movement of the surface marker buoy attached to John's arm by a hundred feet of buoyant rope. In fact during our cover of the two divers with the boat following the buoy, the westward run of the tide was almost too strong for comfort. It was a strange day, cloudy, with no wind. Yet the Mixon tides that day did not behave as the tide-tables thought they should. Instead of getting the normal period of slack water – the only time the Mixon is really diveable – when our turn to dive came, the movement of water seemed to swing back to the east run with no break in between.

Because of this quick change of tide we were in a hurry after recovering John and Geoff to get our dive in before matters got worse. Even so we did not get into the water until 5 pm. Hurried diving is bad diving, and can be dangerous diving. The very nature of the sport requires a calm, unhurried approach to the water. Fortunately all that went wrong with this dive was that, instead of landing on the top of the south bank shingle in forty-five feet of water and making a leisurely descent down the side of the Mixon Hole, we missed the bank and landed some sixty feet down at a point where the slope levelled out on its way to the bottom. Even there the sea-bed was shingle and I was annoyed. I know I was because I even noted it in my diving log. I had hoped to take some underwater pictures of the prolific life higher on the walls of the hole. Where we were there was a visibility of only plus or minus seven feet.

I mumbled my fury in clouds of bubbles through the mouth-piece at Penny and Kevin and, because they are used to me making strange noises when discontented under water, they took not the slightest notice. We were now, I thought, almost at the bottom of the hole and being swept gently to the east. I tried to guide the three of us across the flow to regain the south bank. It was at this moment that we all saw it. The first of them.

In my diving log for that day I said that at first it looked like a great cannon-shell, or mortar, or intact amphora. But whatever it was there was not the slightest doubt in any of our minds on first sight that it was man-made. Penny thought it was an amphora with the base pointing to the west, but a closer examination proved it to be solid stone. There was some small growth on it and the surface was pitted with marine worm holes. And what had led Penny to think it was an amphora was the fact that the end opposite to the point at first appeared to be the mouth of some kind of vessel. In fact the 'mouth' proved to be only a shallow depression, perfectly even all round, in the base of the 'projectile'.

I am sorry to use words like 'projectile' and 'cannon-shell', but I want to convey to you our first impressions. Both those words fit well. The thing was approximately four feet long, came to a distinct point and was bellied in the centre. With some effort from all of us we could lift it enough to see that the shape was sym-metrical and that the object was not part of a bigger structure continuing under the sea-bed.

All the time we were examining the stone, I was worried about the tide, which seemed to be increasing by the second. That is the only explanation that I can give for failing to use the camera round my neck. In truth I had forgotten all about it. After a few minutes we let go of the stone and drifted with the tide to the east. And within twenty-five feet, give or take a few feet because calculating distance over a featureless shingle bed in low visibility is almost impossible, there were two more of the stones. Exactly the same shape, but smaller by a foot. These two were closer together, within ten feet of each other. Then a few feet further on was a fourth stone. It looked smaller, but this may have been because it was deeper in the shingle. I calculated that this was only two feet in length with only the curve of the side showing. We stopped long enough to scrape the growth away with a diving knife to satisfy ourselves once again that it was solid stone. Scraped down, the stone looked the same yellowy colour as the others.

Within seconds of leaving this one, we hit the foot of the rubble bank of the south side of the Mixon and were able to work upwards to finish off the dive among the teeming life of the forty-five foot level at the top of the bank. I knew that what we had found was important and sketched out what we had seen as soon as I could. After that I rang Hume Wallace, told him and then wrote to him including copies of my sketches (see figure 2).

Hume was interested, but sceptical. People do see, or imagine

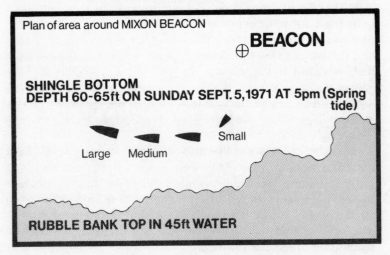

Fig. 2.   Sketch plan of finds near Mixon Beacon

they see, strange things under water and for the time being I felt that Hume had put our discoveries firmly into the non-proven category. But he was interested enough to arrange to meet on a dive within three weeks to see if he and Kingston branch divers of the B S-A C could locate the stones again. We met and Hume showed me some rocks that he thought might be the stones, but they were totally different and I thought definitely natural formations. There for a while the matter rested.

Then Hume telephoned. His scepticism had now completely disappeared. He and the Kingston divers had found the stones. Or very similar ones. He had consulted with archaeologists and experts and he now believed that these stones could well be mooring posts from ancient, probably Roman times, which had tumbled down from positions at the top of the banks of the ancient river. I accepted this as a reasonable explanation. After all the bellying of the stones would mean that, if they were used as mooring posts, the belly would stop any loop of rope dropped over them from sliding off. However Hume did add a stray thought during our chat. To him, he said, they looked remarkably like the phallic symbols in stone which were raised along the avenues leading to temples he had visited during his army service in India. Was there a temple under the sea at Selsey? I dismissed the thought almost as soon as it was formed. We laughed and that was that.

But not for long. Very soon Hume and his divers made a sensational discovery. Some of the stones were not just lying on the bottom. They were upright, sixty feet down. Furthermore they were not only upright. They were deliberately upright with stones packed in around the base to keep them so. Stones shaped by man, sixty feet under the sea, upright and deliberately placed like that! It was mind-boggling! The truth is that Hume was right. I have seen one of the upright stones, so has John Messent, so has Geoff Bowden. It is placed, not accidental. So what is the explanation?

Of course one has to be careful. Facts are facts. The stones are there. But explanations can only be theories. The non-diving archaeologist will be the first to dismiss anything else as part of the 'lunatic fringe'. In fact when I told one eminent archaeologist about these discoveries, he laughed and said exactly that – 'So you've joined the lunatic fringe!' Well, I have not and nor have common-sense divers who have seen the stones. So what could be the explanation? First of all you could say at once that these phallic symbols were a freak of nature and are just in the positions they are in because of weathering and the effect of frost during Ice Age times. But it does seem a remarkable coincidence that all these stones came out exactly the same. Then again you could say that these stones were almost the shape they are because of weathering and early man seized on the shape and erected them with only minor adjustments.

But the one thing you cannot get away from is their age – because of the sixty-foot depth of sea over them. Both geologist Hume Wallace and the man who is the greatest British expert on sea-levels, Dr Nic Flemming, agree that the depth must mean that the stones, *if they were erected by man*, would date back to five to six thousand years before the birth of Christ. This is because melting glaciers increased the sea-level and the land was tilted by the weight of ice being removed.

Hume Wallace says that this sort of formation of stone does occur in the geological beds of the area of soft Shelley sand and has even led divers to think that they have found cannon wrecks in the area. So he is inclined to think that the basic shape was natural in origin, but man shaped them off and dragged them up the hillside – they are not down in the middle of the hole – and set them up on little platforms there.

He has found them all along this particular slope, set up, or on the sea-bed lying parallel to the slope as though they have rolled down from earlier positions. He compares them with neolithic standing stones in the Scilly Isles and Cornwall set up as individual clan or family fertility symbols, possibly near tombs. As a result, in all his dives around the Mixon he is looking out for these 'box of stones' tombs. He has already seen flat stones together which might have been such tombs but centuries of anchoring in the area may have pulled such structures into the shape in which he has found them today.

So Hume Wallace carries on his searches in the Selsey area. He may well come up with fresh discoveries about man in Britain in ancient times. But his discoveries at the moment hardly concern wrecks. For evidence discovered by divers of a shipwreck of really ancient times we have to go east from Selsey in Sussex to Dover in Kent.

For many years after the amateur divers of Britain started exploring the sea-bed around our coasts, it was realized that sooner or later they would find traces of the early civilizations which had come to conquer us or to trade with us, but no one was really optimistic about the form those discoveries would take. It was felt likely that what traces there were would be smashed beyond all hope of reconstruction – probably just chips of pottery protected from final destruction in some sheltered gully on the sea-bed. The truth proved to be beyond a marine archaeologist's wildest dreams.

We know that the history of the British Isles was one with the history of shipping. Ships, probably flat-bottomed, with skin sails were travelling from southern Spain to the west of England, Scotland and even Sweden, at the end of the British neolithic period nearly four thousand years ago (around 2000 BC). We know they were seafarers, for their elaborate tombs are on the western sea-routes. Other tomb-builders sailed the seas too, but they came from the Pyrenees and southern France to settle in south-west Scotland, Ulster and the Isle of Man.

But obviously these ancient sailors did not come just to build tombs. They came for the same reasons that ships still enter and leave our ports today – to trade. It seems ridiculous today to think of some Bronze Age continental export manager saying to his equally ancient staff, 'The market we should concentrate on is Britain. . . . Completely new territory. . . . Open it up for our latest line and we'll all be millionaires.' But whether you believe that history repeats itself or not – someone somewhere on the Continent of Europe did think that there was a market for his wares in Britain between 1200 and 1000 BC. And what is more he was an arms-dealer.

The irrefutable evidence of this came when Simon Stevens, Mike Hadlow and Alan Moat of Dover branch of the B S-A C dived in Langdon Bay, east of Dover Harbour on 14 August 1974. It is fair to say that on that dive they penetrated into British pre-history. What they found is so far the earliest definite evidence of a wreck in British waters.

The site of their dive was literally under the towering chalks of the White Cliffs of Dover. It is a dive area well known to the members of Dover S-A C. They dive it often mainly because it is easy to reach by boat and because it has reasonable periods of slack water. And also because the sea-bed is interesting, not flat, but cut by chalk gullies. In the gullies are relics of various wars, from cannon-balls, through arms used in World War I, to bombs and shells of World War II, some of which are obviously still unexploded and dangerous.

When Simon Stevens, Mike Hadlow and Alan Moat set out on their dive from a boat on the eastern side of Langdon Bay on that August day they were still within five hundred yards of the famous White Cliffs when they made their first discovery. Alan Moat, who is diving officer of Dover branch, talking later of that moment, said: 'My first thought was that they were some of those old-fashioned wedges that used to be used to hold railway lines down to the sleepers. Some were in gullies and perhaps protected by that, but others were lying on top of rocks in fine sand deposits. I suspect that they were covered and uncovered by tides and storms.'

Said Simon Stevens: 'They were heavy and because of that we picked up five and surfaced. Once back on board no one really knew what the objects were, though Mike Hadlow suggested they might be ancient tools.'

The following day the objects were taken to Dover Museum and shown to Mrs Rosemary Coveney, the curator. Mrs Coveney to her credit had a good idea of what they were and contacted Mr Brian Philp, director of the Kent Archaeological Rescue Unit and he identified them for certain. What in fact the Dover divers had discovered were Bronze Age winged axes, daggers and spear-heads.

Brian Philp then enlisted the aid of the Dover divers to make a complete and accurate survey of the site and to record any further finds. First of all the divers relocated and marked the site. Within a fortnight they had found another bronze axe. And then another twenty-two bronze objects. The finds mostly came from a narrow gully in the chalk some eighty feet long, which varied from two to ten feet wide and was only about a foot deep into the sea-bed. And on one single dive fifty-eight more bronze weapons were brought to the surface!

During the next year's diving season – all the markers had been swept away by winter gales and it took ten hours of diving on a grid search to relocate the site – more objects were located. A final dive that year using an underwater metal-detector produced

Number of finds made and time in minutes spent underwater by divers working on Dover Wreck.

TABLE 1

	1974 Aug. 14	Aug. 28	Aug. 29	Sept. 10	Sept. 14	1975 May 15	May 18	June 1	June 7	June 8	June 12	June 15	July 19	July 20	July 21	July 27	Total time dived (hrs. mins.)	Total finds
S. Stevens	50	45	85	10	05	—	05	20	30	40	30	30	40	40	50	60	9.40	46
C. Osmond	—	—	—	—	—	—	—	—	—	40	—	30	40	—	50	40	3.20	—
P. Mayes	—	40	—	—	—	—	—	20	30	—	—	—	—	35	60	60	3.10	11
K. Jaynes	—	—	30	10	—	05	—	—	30	—	30	—	—	—	—	40	2.35	—
A. Moat	—	40	65	—	—	—	—	25	—	—	—	—	—	35	—	—	2.25	20
T. Stewart	—	45	—	—	—	—	—	—	30	—	30	—	—	—	—	—	2.15	13
R. Player	50	—	—	—	05	—	—	—	30	—	—	30	—	—	—	—	2.05	—
M. Hadlow	—	—	—	—	—	—	05	—	45	—	—	30	—	—	—	—	1.55	—
D. Leviar	—	45	—	—	—	—	—	—	45	—	—	—	—	—	—	—	1.35	—
T. Dole	—	—	—	—	—	—	—	—	—	—	—	—	—	—	—	60	1.00	—
B. Atkins	—	—	—	—	—	—	—	—	—	30	—	—	—	—	—	—	0.30	—
R. Mosely	—	—	—	—	—	—	—	—	—	30	—	—	—	—	—	—	0.30	—
R. Shelow	—	—	—	—	—	—	—	25	—	—	—	—	—	—	—	—	0.25	—
total time dived (hrs. mins.)	1.40	3.35	3.40	0.20	0.10	0.05	0.10	1.30	2.45	2.20	2.00	2.00	1.20	1.50	3.40	4.20	31.25	
Total finds recovered	5	23	58	—	—	—	—	—	—	—	—	—	—	—	2	2		90

another six, making ninety in all. Thirteen divers had taken part in the work and had spent 31.25 hours on the bottom. Simon Stevens writing his story in the *Kent Archaeological Review* in the spring of 1976 produced the table of the divers' work (see page 19).

It is interesting to note too that he calculated that the cost of these dives was about £40–£70 for the boat and £30 for compressed air. Such a small sum for such an important discovery. I hope that those archaeologists who still spurn the efforts of diving amateurs have taken careful note and compared it with the cost of land excavations!

Brian Philp, while taking the usual care of any professional archaeologist not to commit himself too firmly to unproven dating, is enthusiastic about the divers' finds and their public-spirited attitude in handing them over to Dover Museum. He says that this group of bronzes is a highly important collection and suggests that they come from Middle Bronze Age date, perhaps 1200–1000 BC. He points out that while similar winged axes do occur occasionally in British Bronze Age hoards, they rarely appear in such numbers. He suspects that they come from Central Europe:

At first glance this group appears to be essentially Continental in character and origin. That it was found in the Straits of Dover suggests that the objects were in fact in transit to Britain and had formed a cargo lost at sea. The site, only some five hundred yards from the present white cliffs, strongly suggests a wreck which even allowing for the change in coastline since Bronze Age times must have been offshore. Had any vessel been wrecked at the foot of the cliffs then the bronzes could have been collected at low-water or at least subsequently buried by millions of tons of chalk rubble from the cliffs above. The evidence tends to suggest that a trader or bronzesmith was bringing a cargo of material across the channel in a small craft when, failing to make the shelter of the wide tidal estuary of the Dour (now deeply buried under Castle Street) he was wrecked close to the cliffs one mile further east. Of his vessel or any other cargo there is, apparently and logically, no trace, but his heavy bronze implements became trapped in the gully. Indeed, is this the earliest evidence of a wreck in British waters so far recorded?

Obviously such a valuable hoard must stay in Britain. To protect the group of bronzes from being broken up and sold individually – and possibly going abroad – the British Museum stepped in and bought them. Dover branch of the B S-A C were paid £448 as their share of the proceeds. This is I think without doubt the oldest *shipwreck*, or evidence of a shipwreck discovered by divers around Britain.

Or it *was*, until July 1977 when Phil Baker, the B S-A C coach for Yorkshire and Humberside, and the very experienced diver John Hinchcliffe of Bournemouth branch of the club, were passing on their love of the sport to others by acting as instructors to a six-day adventure diving holiday course run by the Youth Hostels Association at Salcombe in South Devon. What happened on one of those dives is best described first in the words of Phil Baker:

Our motor launch *Kirby* was anchored close to the shore beyond Gammon Head. It was my turn to take Ursula Jurda, a German housewife, down for her second open-water dive. Hand in hand we moved over the kelp covered rocks and shallow gravel bottomed gullies. (It's a good idea to go hand in hand with any beginner but with a nice girl like Ursula it's a very good idea!)

The first few minutes of the dive were uneventful and we reached a depth of twenty feet with excellent visibility and nil current and surge. I squeezed Ursula's hand and got a reassuring double squeeze back. Then I caught sight of what looked like the eye and top half of an angler's lead weight, half hidden behind a weedy rock. When I could see further around the rock the 'weight' grew longer and longer. Its colouring changed from grey to verdigris green and the shape was such as no fisherman would every use!

I paused for a moment, running the available data through my mental computer. . . . Green means copper or brass or something similar. . . . The shape just had to be that of either a sword or a spearhead . . . for I could see the whole of it lying exposed on the brightly lit gravel. Nobody made sword blades of brass or copper . . . but bronze? . . . Nobody's made any bronze blades in yonks. . . . Bronze equals Bronze Age?? I wasted no more time in cogitation but grabbed up the blade and was surprised how sharp the edges were and how clear the decorative pattern remained.

I returned later with another beginner, John Clark of Broadstairs, Kent and we resumed the search. A few minutes later I turned to see him staring unbelievingly at the long thin metal thing he held in his hand. On examination it turned out to be a very badly worn slender bronze blade that we christened the 'dagger'. Repeated searchings failed to locate any other artefacts. Naturally we took a very good fix on the position before leaving the site.

The Doncaster Museum were quite excited by the blades and they put me in touch with Professor Keith Branigan, Head of the Department of Prehistory and Archaeology at the University of Sheffield. Professor Branigan gave it as his opinion that the sword originated in or around Northern Italy, Southern Germany, or what is now Switzerland, in 1200–1100 BC. He also believes that this blade is the earliest known imported blade yet found in this country and is a very significant find. (By 'imported' he means brought into this country during its working life as a sword, not a later import as an antiquity or souvenir.) The 'dagger' remains unidentified and is something of a mystery.

Purists may say that these two artefacts should not have been lifted. However, both were totally exposed and wholly unattached to the sea bed so their position probably bears no relationship to the remainder of the wreck – if wreck there be. The first mild storm could well have buried them again for another three thousand years.

Details of the two Bronze Age finds are as follows: the sword is in very good condition and measures 65 centimetres × 4 centimetres at the widest, and is of flattened diamond section with a round rat-tailed hooked-end tang; the 'dagger' is badly worn by sea action; it measures 34 centimetres × 2 centimetres and retains traces of a flattened diamond section with one point still sharp. This discovery, if it was from a shipwreck, will add strength to the argument of those archaeologists who believe there was a sort of Bronze Age Common Market and disappoint the theories of those who believe we had little contact in those times with the Continent of Europe.

Was the sword part of a small ship-trader's goods for barter in exchange for Cornish tin? We shall of course never know. So far there is no other evidence of a Bronze Age shipwreck there off Salcombe. And there is always the possibility that the presence of the sword in the sea is the result of the contents of a Bronze Age burial being washed down from collapsing cliffs. As the swords were found over two hundred yards from the present cliff line, this would seem to be unlikely. It does suggest that in those very early times small ships were plying along the coasts of Britain carrying goods from Europe for trade.

It is of course not the oldest evidence we have of water-borne activity in Britain. Radio-carbon dating suggests that dug-out canoes like that found at Branthwaite, Workington in Cumberland date back to 1570 BC. Though I doubt if you can really call that discovery a shipwreck. Nor of course can you say that the discovery of a lost anchor necessarily means that the ship was lost. It may well be that many an ancient ship abandoned its anchor for the simple reason that it was stuck or the cable to it broke. Modern anchors are abandoned for identical reasons.

Anchors of ancient times were of course nothing like the ones used by a diving boat today. On second thoughts perhaps that is not strictly accurate. Many a diver's inflatable boat has been held in position over a suspected wreck site simply by means of a heavy stone at the end of the anchor rope. The use of stone anchors goes back a very long way indeed. And certainly common sense tells you that the ancient mariner would use a stone as an anchor long before more complicated devices became available.

A fine example of a stone anchor recovered by divers is already on display at the National Maritime Museum, Greenwich. It weighs about a hundredweight and a half, and it came from the sea-bed just outside Lulworth Cove, Dorset. The discovery of the anchor followed the recovery by Albert Greenland, of Bromley branch of the B s-a c, of a pottery 'cone' in the same area. When this 'cone' was shown to Joan du Plat Taylor, of the Committee for Nautical Archaeology, it was identified as the base of an unguent bottle from the Roman occupation period. Greenland was asked if he would dive again in the area to see if his find was an isolated one. Was the bottle flung overboard from some passing ship because the neck was broken – or was there an ancient wreck in the area? Certainly the bottle was made in the Mediterranean area, but experts said that they had never seen one like it in this country – the nearest place that such a type of bottle had been found was near Cologne, Germany.

Greenland dived again, and was just as surprised as anyone else when he found a large stone, buried under small rocks and shale but with enough of it standing clear for him to see that a hole was bored right through it. He says that he recognized it at once as a stone anchor, as he had recently seen photographs of some found in the Mediterranean. After a great deal of underwater effort, Albert Greenland, together with two other Bromley branch divers, John Humphreys and Mike Greenhough, raised the anchor with the help of a forty-gallon oil-drum, which they filled with compressed air from their aqualungs.

More stone anchors in various parts of the country were to

follow that one to the surface; from Ilfracombe, Dartmouth and Seaford. These are on display at Fort Bovisand, the home of the School for Nautical Archaeology at Plymouth. If you wish to see these relics of our long-forgotten seafaring past, you will be made most welcome if you call at the Fort.

Another stone anchor, heart-shaped with the two-inch hole near the top and weighing sixty-five pounds was recovered at Berry Head, near Brixham by two divers recently. Both came from Bromley branch of the B S-A C; they were chairman Alan Hewitt and diving officer Mike Collins.

The importance of these anchors is great. From the anchors the size of the ship that carried them can be deduced. Diving archaeologist Honor Frost says that the size of most Mediterranean Bronze Age anchors would sink the modern fishing-boat from the same area. It is not uncommon for these to weigh half a ton and from this one can estimate that the Bronze Age ships that carried them were about sixty feet long, and were in the region of two hundred tons.

But the kind of wreck that has not yet been found by divers around Britain is oddly enough an amphora-laden ship of Roman times. I say oddly because, though our waters are subjected to strong tides as opposed to the quieter waters of the Mediterranean, where these wrecks have been found in quantity by divers, the amphora, the wine-jar of ancient days, has proved tough enough to take centuries of immersion under water. And one would have thought that if a wreck laden with these jars had sunk swiftly and deeply enough to avoid shallow disturbance, then British divers might well by now have come across at least one. They have not, but I think they will.

There have been some discoveries of Roman material under water round our coasts in addition to the unguent bottle mentioned earlier. For example John White, a London diver and member of Holborn branch of the B S-A C, was diving off Seaford Head, Sussex in May 1970. He, his brother George and Bob Barrett were finning over the sea-bed at a depth of thirty-five feet when John White spotted the neck of an amphora firmly stuck into the sea-bed. But it was unfortunately just a neck. It was dated to the first or second century AD and possibly made in Spain. Holborn branch carried out a proper survey in the area and found a stone anchor, nearly twenty inches long and fourteen inches wide. Did the anchor, which is one of those on display at Fort Bovisand, mean that this was the site of a wreck? Further diving is going on but so far without result.

Diving around Pudding Pan shoal, off Whitstable, Kent is difficult. But we can be pretty certain that there is a wreck there. We can almost date it to an exact year – AD 160 – because that is the date of the large quantity of Roman pottery that is on show at museums in Whitstable, Herne Bay, Maidstone, Rochester, Canterbury, Leicester, Kingston, Liverpool, Bristol and London. All of it was recovered over centuries by fishermen or dredgers in the Pudding Pan area. There are nearly three hundred items in all and they were all made in the Allier district of France. Divers have searched the area, but visibility is poor and tides are tricky. In recent years fishermen's recoveries have been very few.

Still, divers are not the kind of people who give up easily and I am sure that one day soon we shall read of Britain's amateur divers locating a Roman wreck – or at least finding a great mound of wine-jars to mark the spot where a Roman captain came to grief.

TWO

'Sum say that part of . . . King of Castelle navie was driven toward . . . periculus rokkes'

Lost at sea	On land
17 January 1494	Henry VII reigns
St James of the Croyne	Perkin Warbeck captured
1509 Philip of Castille's two ships	Sebastian Cabot lands in America
A balinger with a cargo of slates	Henry VIII succeeds

Modern air-sea rescue craft are deeper in the water than earlier models. This fact alone led to the discovery of one of the oldest wrecks in Britain. The explanation for that surprising statement is simply this. There is an area of the port of Plymouth called the Cattewater. The Cattewater is the last reach of the River Plym before it flows out through Cobbler Channel into the sound proper (see figure 3). (Incidentally it was into Deadman's Bay at the mouth of the Cattewater that the *Christian Hendrick* from Rotterdam was driven on shore in December 1786. See Introduction.)

The Cattewater, or at least the part of it which lies off Mount Batten, has been used since the beginning of World War II to moor flying boats and air-sea rescue launches. As a result it has never been necessary to dredge the Cattewater anchorage deeply. By the beginning of 1973 however it was clear that the anchorage was no longer suitable for the new breed of high-speed rescue craft.

I do not know that there were any incidents of these new craft grounding, but the Department of the Environment contracted for the anchorage to be dredged more deeply that very summer. I am indebted to Commander Alan Bax, RN Retd, who together with Jim Gill runs the Fort Bovisand Underwater Centre at Ply-

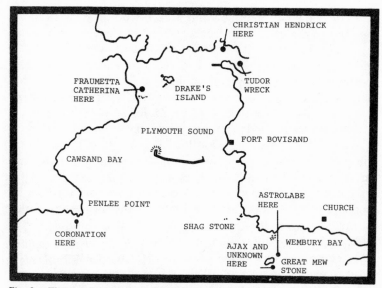

Fig. 3.   The wreck area around Fort Bovisand, Plymouth

mouth – just around the corner from the Cattewater so to speak –
for the story of what happened next. In *The Tudor Shipwreck in the
Cattewater*, which he co-authored with Mary Turner, Alan Bax
writes:

On the morning of June 20th, 1973, an Anglo-Dutch bucket dredger,
Holland XVII, was working in the area off RAF Mountbatten carrying out
this contract. She was on a westerly heading when she was suddenly
halted after bringing up timber wreckage. It appears that what may have
stopped the dredger was the fact that she struck the keelson of a ship
with sufficient force to break a piece from it.

The booklet by Bax and Mary Turner is available from Fort
Bovisand, Plymouth, Devon, P19 0AB.
    It was quite obvious to the dredger crew that the timbers they
had raised were extremely old. It was even more obvious to
archaeologists and when divers went down they knew it too.
Their joint conclusions were that it was a wreck from either the
late fifteenth century or early sixteenth century. It was also obviously of great historical importance and was swiftly protected
under the 1973 act (see appendix III).
    But the dredger had not only brought wood to the surface.

Parts of two small wrought-iron breech-loading guns came up too, and so did other pieces of wood shaped like floors or decking. Later that summer the divers found and raised a third gun and the keelson of the ship. The keelson or kelson is a longitudinal piece of wood placed along the floor-timbers of a ship binding them to the keel. These woods and in particular the guns provided very strong evidence of a Tudor ship.

The Cattewater used to be spelt 'Catwater' and that is the way it is pronounced today. In Tudor times it was certainly a haven for shipping from most strong winds that blew from the south into the sound. 'Cat' in early writings meant either a ship or a fort (which no doubt led to some confusion!) and as there is no evidence of a fort in the area we are left with 'Shipwater', which is probably right. It is interesting to note that the Kattegat or Cattegat is, being translated, the 'Ship-gate' to the Baltic.

However the ship the dredger found was at the entrance to the Cattewater and her position suggests that she was possibly trying to reach shelter when she hit some rock ledges and sank. Commander Eric McKee of the National Maritime Museum searched in Plymouth City archives to see if the ship could be pinpointed. He found several strandings between 1475 and 1575. Finally he narrowed the field down to one ship, the *St James of the Croyne*, a trading ship which was noted as lost 'in great winds' on the night of 17 January 1494. No one of course can say with certainty that this is the ship, but it may be.

No further work was put in on the site until a licence to survey was given in November 1974. Small amateur teams working at weekends started the work and the divers were immediately brought face-mask to face-mask with a rather nasty problem. There was no trace of the wreck. In very poor visibility the divers searched and probed the mud, but there was no sign of any buried timbers at all. At the end of the year one team carried out yet another despairing search and found some stones which might have been ballast, but there was still no sign of the original site.

In the spring of 1975 Professor Robert Farrell of Cornell University and Lieutenant Commander Alan Bax, who had worked together on two major diving expeditions, teamed up once again. Ten volunteers from Guildford and Plymouth Sound branches of the B S-A C and affiliated RAF divers joined in. Finally the divers were successful. Near the mooring known as 'Spitfire', they found timbers on the sea-bed which were almost certainly the result of the blow from the dredger. The diving continues today.

Another very old ship has recently been discovered fifty feet down in the Menai Strait. The discovery was made by Dr Cecil Jones's Marine Archaeological Unit of the University College of North Wales at Bangor during an underwater survey of the area.

The ship – about 54 feet long with a 21-foot beam – is believed to be a 'balinger', a general cargo ship of the late fifteenth or early sixteenth century, which used both oars and sail. And cargo she was certainly carrying. There on the sea-bed are fifteen thousand dressed roofing slates, of triangular shape, still neatly stacked. They were probably intended for roofing the conical towers of castles.

The man trotted his horse across the wooden bridge at Lee Mill in South Devon and stopped at the other side to make a note. The servants who attended him must by now have become used to the man's strange ways. So, when he stopped again a few miles on at the next bridge at Ivybridge and made another note, they probably waited patiently enough.

For the man with the quill was John Leland, Keeper of Henry VIII's Libraries before he was twenty-five. At the time that he was making notes on the back of his horse in South Devon, Leland was probably in his early thirties. We know for sure that it was some time between 1535 and 1541. We know what he wrote at Ivybridge over four hundred years ago because most of his topographical notes for his celebrated *Itinerary* exist today. (Indeed the original manuscript is in the Bodleian Library, Oxford.) It was this: 'From Le bridge to Ivy bridge a 3. miles. The ryver of Arme, or Armine, rennith under this bridge and a 2. miles lower on it is Armington Bridge.'

The problem for wreck divers begins with the next piece of information that John Leland wrote down immediately after noting the distance to the next bridge at Ermington over the Erme (or 'Arme or Armine' as he called it). We do not know who he talked to at the time or who he had recently talked to, but he carefully noted: 'Sum say that part of Philippe King of Castelle navie was driven toward the mouth of this water, wher is no haven, but periculus rokkes. This river risith by north est, and rennith apon great rokky stones with no smaul noise.'

Unfortunately some reports of that note miss out the vital qualifying statement 'Sum say'. Others have failed to read on from folio 25 to folio 26 where Leland records crossing the 'Awne' by a ford and then adds, 'Awne and Arme rivers go to the se at Arme mouthe.' Now the Awne is the Avon and the Arme is the Erme – and they have never gone to the sea together at Erme Mouth, not even four hundred years ago in Leland's time. He got it wrong. The Erme of course comes out at Erme Mouth, but the Avon comes out to the sea at Bantham by Burgh Island. The mouth of the Arme is over three miles away as the crow flies from the mouth of the Avon.

On sheet 2, folio 30, he repeats his mistake:

Arme Haven is a . . . [missing] miles above Saultcombe Haven. The mouth of this lyith ful of flattes and rokkes, and no ship cummith in tempest hither, but in desperation. Too of Philip King of Castelle shippes felle to wrak in this haven when he was dryven into England by tempeste.

Arme Ryver cummith to this haven: And, as I hard say, Aune Ryver likewise.

So you pay your money and you take your choice. I know from speaking to Alan Bax – who with Jim Gill created the magnificent Fort Bovisand Underwater Centre from a decrepit Napoleonic fort built to guard the approaches to Plymouth – that he would not have spent so much time searching under water for those two ships off the mouth of the Erme had he studied the full text of Leland's *Itinerary* in the second edition of 1745. It is fortunate for Alan Bax that the shipwreck of HMS *Coronation* (see chapter 7) and the wreck in Cattewater captured his total underwater attention before he poured even more diving time into the search for those two ships of Philip of Castile lost off the mouth of the Erme.

The story of Leland's mistake and the two missing ships does not end there. All we can surmise from Leland's reports is that, some time prior to 1541 (when Leland finished his travels), there were two Spanish ships wrecked on the South Devon coast, possibly as early as 1509. These shipwrecks were possibly in the mouth of the Erme, possibly at the mouth of the Avon near Bantham in South Devon.

And there the matter seemed to rest until the discovery of the

Challaborough cannon. Challaborough is a little bay in the coastline of South Devon near Burgh Island and the mouth of the Avon. Out of season it is a quiet little place. In tourist time however the caravan site there booms into life. And into one of those caravans each Easter and summer holiday went Roy Wardle, a keen South London diver, and his family. Roy spends as much time as he can during his holiday on and under the usually clear Devon sea.

On Easter Sunday 1974, after the heavy storms of that winter, Roy was diving in sixty feet of water near Challaborough with a group including his son Terry, Terry Bent and Lynn Wise. After twenty minutes Roy drifted away from the other three to the limit of visibility so that he could still just keep them in view. And then he saw it. It was, he says, even at first sight quite obviously a cannon. A small cannon but still a cannon. And he knew that, even though only the muzzle was sticking out from under a piece of flat rock. He lifted the rock off with ease and there it lay, in the sand a green but apparently perfect small cannon. It was only when he tried to lift it that he realized its great weight. Finally he and his son managed to raise it to the surface to the inflatable boat waiting overhead.

When cleaned, the cannon was bronze; it was just under two feet long (23½ inches) and was worn in places though even the lifting dolphins were intact. Unfortunately the crest or coat of arms on the first reinforce was so badly worn that it was inde-cipherable. It was interesting to note that the touchhole or vent had been rebushed or repaired some time during the cannon's active life and, though the latch-cover to protect the vent had gone, the bearings were still there, though badly worn. But the crowning joy of this little bronze cannon must be the cascabel. For, though the other decorations only went half-way round the body, the cascabel was completely circled by beautiful little bronze leaves clustering round the acorn of the handle. (See plate 5.) The bore was 1½ inches in diameter. The perfection of this part of the cannon makes it likely that the piece had been buried in sand for years until heavy storms, possibly those of the winter before Roy Wardle made his discovery, had uprooted it.

What ship lies there? Was there any shipwreck at all? Was the gun lost overboard in a violent storm? That is the point at which research starts. Expert examination of the cannon could at the time of writing only identify it as probably French or Spanish and put the date as possibly in the 1600s and supply the added information that this type of cannon was in manufacture up to 1670.

I tried to help Roy Wardle here and with the assistance of Dick Larn (see chapter 6) combed the records of wrecks in the area. For, though it is just possible that the gun was lost without the ship, it would seem highly unlikely that a gun of that kind, mounted as it must have been on some sort of carriage, would just roll or be dumped overboard unless the ship was in a very parlous state indeed. It is true that Bigbury Bay has always been a trap for the unwary sailing ship – and wrecks galore testify to the effectiveness of the trap. Once inside the bay with an onshore gale blowing, few ships escaped.

In that tragic list are only three ships that we could find that would fit the tentative dating of the cannon. Two are the ones noted by Leland, which we know were wrecked before 1541. The other is merely noted as unidentified by name: 'A Frenchman from St Malo wrecked in Bigbury Bay, neither men nor goods survive.' And the date: 20 February 1637.

So has Roy Wardle discovered a cannon-shaped clue to proving that John Leland's information was wrong and that two Spanish ships were wrecked at the mouth of the Devon Avon? Or is this the first clue to that unidentified Frenchman from St Malo, whose crew can never tell the tale? More research on the cannon and on the sea-bed are the only possible avenues which can give us the answer. So far the sea-bed diving research has not surfaced with any more information. Nothing more has been found, but Roy Wardle goes on diving to find the answer.

THREE

'The more cooks, the worst potage'

Lost at sea	On land
July 1545 Mary Rose *off* *Portsmouth*	*Henry* VIII *reigns* *War with France* *Dissolution of the monasteries*

Almost exactly 430 years to the day after King Henry VIII had seen his great warship *Mary Rose* capsize when sailing out of Portsmouth into battle against the French, Henry's ancestor HRH the Prince of Wales, complete with aqualung and modern diving gear, dived down on to the ship. Hovering over the wreck Prince Charles, heir to the English throne, gently touched the massive Tudor timbers within a few feet of the spot where his ancestor King Henry VIII had stood during his review of the fleet four centuries ago. That moment must rate I think as one of the most extraordinary in the history of diving thoughout the world.

But before we go into the reasons for this royal dive, let us look at how the ship came to be there buried in the Solent mud in the first place. The *Mary Rose* was one of over one hundred ships which had gathered together in Portsmouth Harbour in July 1545 for review by King Henry VIII before they put to sea to fight the French. In fact, by the time King Henry arrived at Portsmouth, beacons were burning to warn that the French fleet, commanded by Admiral d'Anneboult, had assembled and sailed out into the channel, and orders had gone out to all the king's ships within range to join the fleet at Portsmouth.

The *Mary Rose* was a big Tudor wooden battleship of 700 tons and was about 150 feet long and of 50-foot beam. Shortly after his arrival at Portsmouth, Henry appointed Sir George Carewe, one of his particular favourites, to be his vice-admiral aboard *Mary*

Rose (in some documents of the time *Mary Rose* is spelt *'Marye Rose'*, but even the experts seem to disagree over which was the correct spelling). And then Henry went to dine with the Lord Admiral John Dudley, Viscount Lisle – later Duke of Northumberland – and his officers on board the flagship *Greate Henry*. During this meal the French fleet was sighted, and the king gave orders for his fleet to sail. Contemporary manuscripts then give this description of what happened next:

And first he hath secret talks with the Lord Admiral, and then he hath the like with Sir George Carewe, and at his departure from him, took his chain from his neck, with a great wistle of gold pendant to the same, and did put it about the neck of the said Sir George Carewe, giving him also therewith many good and comfortable words.

The King then took his boat, and rowed to the land, and every other captain went to his ship appointed unto him. Sir George Carewe being entered into his ship commanded every man to take his place, and the sails to be hoysted; but the same was no sooner done, but that the Mary Rose began to heel, that is, to lean on the one side.

Sir Gawen Carewe being then in his own ship, and seeing the same called for the master of his ship and told him thereof, and asked him what it meant, who answered, that if she did heel, she was like to be cast away. Then the said Sir Gawen, passing by the Mary Rose, called out to Sir George Carewe, asking him how he did? who answered, that he had a sort of knaves, whom he could not rule.

And it was not long after, but that the said Mary Rose, thus heeling more and more, was drowned, with 700 men which were in her; whereof very few escaped. It chanced unto this gentleman, as the common proverb is 'the more cooks, the worst potage'. He had in his ship a hundred mariners, the worst of them being able to be a master in the best ship within the realm, and these so maligned and disdained one the other, that refusing to do that which they should do, were careless to that that they ought to do; and so contending in envy, perished in frowardness.

The King this meanwhile stood on the land, and saw this tragedy, as also the lady the wife to Sir George Carewe, who with that sight fell into a swooning. The King being oppressed with sorrow of every side, comforted her, and thanked God for the other, hoping that of a hard beginning there would follow a better ending. And notwithstanding this loss, the service appointed went forward, as soon as wind and weather would serve; and the residue of the fleet, being about the number of one hundred and five sails, took the seas. The Frenchmen perceiving the same, like as a sort of sheep running into the fold, they shifted away, and got them into their harbours; thinking it better to lie there in a safe skin, than to encounter with them of whom they should little win.

Though the *Mary Rose* had scarce left harbour when she sank, the French were to claim later that it was their cannon-fire which sank her. In fact there is no record of any engagement at all and a contemporary painting shows the *Mary Rose* sinking before the fleets had met, if indeed they did. A copy of the painting can be seen in the offices of the Corporation of Portsmouth.

The loss of the *Mary Rose* was obviously a heavy one. She had been laid down in 1509, and was a reliable as well as a large ship. In addition to the great loss to the navy of the skilled men on board, the sinking of the ship herself could not be just forgotten. So within days of her sinking there were great plans to raise her. On 1 August 1545 the Duke of Suffolk wrote to Sir William Paget a letter which was to say the least optimistic. 'I trust', he wrote, 'by Monday or Tuesday at the farthest the Marye Rose shall be weighed up and saved.' What gave rise to this statement we shall never know. Mary Rose was on the bottom about fifty feet down and getting her up would involve a major salvage operation using two ships – one on either side. Perhaps they had miscalculated the amount of mud and water that had poured into her, but *Mary Rose* was not raised, and in 1552 Viscount Lisle wrote a letter to Sir William making it clear that there was great doubt about how much of worth could be stripped from her by divers in the position in which she now lay.

The *Mary Rose* was then forgotten – until the 1840s. Then, so the story goes, divers of the Royal Engineers who were working on the wreck of the *Royal George* misread their bearings and got themselves dropped by accident on the nearby wreck of the *Mary Rose*. That is the story, but what is now certain is that the Engineer divers under the command of Colonel Pasley did not light on the *Mary Rose*. But some other divers did – and they brought up five brass or bronze cannon, all dating back to the 1530s, and twenty others of iron, from the area. The iron cannon were breech-loaders. This is of particular interest, as breech-loading was not generally adopted again until Victorian times.

The *Mary Rose* was however not only important because of her armament. Alexander McKee first became actively interested in sunken ships in the Solent in 1965. He quickly realized that there is an enormous gap in our knowledge of the history of ship-building, and that the only significant evidence we have of the striking developments that took place between 1066 and 1628 lies in the wreck of the *Mary Rose*.

This last statement is not exactly true, but it is as near as makes no difference, for though the wreck of Henry v's *Grace Dieu* lies in the River Hamble, three-quarters of a mile above Bursledon Bridge, so far little has been learned from her timbers. She was built in 1418 and was laid up in the Hamble, but was accidentally burnt in 1439.

And then Alex McKee had yet another thought. If the ship itself was so important, surely the gear and equipment of the many hundreds of officers and crew, from vice-admiral to cabin boy, would be important too. In other words, a cross-section of Tudor military and naval society had gone down with the *Mary Rose*. Now, if they had been preserved . . . The thought that the *Mary Rose* could be there, perhaps lying under protective mud (as the *Vasa* of Sweden had been since her sinking in 1628), spurred McKee on.

The *Vasa* had been one of the ships built for the King of Sweden to beat off the threat from the Hapsburg Empire. In the summer of 1628 she was to make her maiden voyage – and on 10 August 1628 she set sail from Stockholm Harbour, heeled to the wind and, as her open gun-ports took in water, capsized and sank to the bottom, with all flags flying and all sails set. The comparison with the sinking of the *Mary Rose* is obvious. Protected by the mud, the *Vasa* remained in her watery grave until diver-archaeologist Anders Franzen found her and she was finally raised on 4 May 1961. She was towed to dry-dock, and can be seen today in a special museum.

Could the *Mary Rose* be Britain's *Vasa*? That was McKee's thought. A thought only, for he had yet to find the sunken ship. But instead of going all out to discover the grave of the *Mary Rose*, McKee realized at this point that he did not know enough about underwater archaeology to be sure that he would know what to do with the *Mary Rose* if indeed he were fortunate enough to find her. The case of the *Mary Rose*, McKee decided, was going to be a long one.

So in 1965 he launched 'Project Solent Ships'. His plan, with the help and support of Southsea branch of the B S-A C, was to investigate some of the dozen or so historic wrecks which lie off Portsmouth. 'Project Solent Ships' got under way with the wreck of the *Royal George*. The *Royal George* was important for two reasons. First there was the story that Colonel Pasley's Royal Engineer divers had dived on the wreck of the *Mary Rose* by accident, and that it was near to the wreck of the *Royal George*. And secondly McKee felt that, as the Royal Engineer divers had blown up the wreck of the *Royal George*, at least 'Project Solent Ships' divers could do no more damage.

The *Royal George* was the flagship of Rear-Admiral Kempenfelt. She capsized at Spithead on 29 August 1782 and nearly nine hundred lives were lost. That ghastly death toll included women and children. The reason for this was that the *Royal George*, a battleship of 108 guns, was about to sail from Portsmouth with the rest of a British fleet to relieve Gibraltar, which was being besieged by the French. It was a time for fond farewells, and she sank as the last stores were being loaded and many wives, children, relatives and friends were on board to say goodbye.

McKee worked out where the *Royal George* was by transferring old positions on to modern charts and landed right on the site – or at least on a mount of shingle that could well be the *Royal George*. He found a thirty-two-pounder cannon-ball and a small pottery jar which was almost buried. This was subsequently dated to the late eighteenth century, the time of the sinking of the *Royal George*.

In the meantime McKee carried on his land detection work, and came across accounts by the divers who had actually found the *Mary Rose* and the cannon – not Pasley's men, but the inventors of the first really usable diving helmet. These were the Deane brothers. McKee found a report that one of the brothers, John Deane, had been working on the wreck of the *Royal George* in 1836, when he had been asked by some Gosport fishermen for help in clearing their nets from some obstruction. Deane dived and found the *Mary Rose* – a ship that was by then almost completely covered by sand, mud and clay. Bits of timber still showed, and so did one gun, according to the old report. But McKee suspected that the Deanes, out of consideration for the fishermen, would have cleared any surface obstruction left.

As a result of these clues and of his diving McKee concluded that not only would there be nothing left of the *Mary Rose* above the surface, but also that the wreck must lie much nearer to Spit Sand to the north-east of the *Royal George*. And there at the end of 1965 the diving had to finish.

But McKee worked on throughout the winter. Then came his first breakthrough. Together with another well-known local diver, John Towse, Alex McKee visited the Hydrographic Department of the Admiralty. There they found a large-scale Admiralty chart which showed the positions not only of HMS *Edgar* (a ship of seventy guns which blew up at Spithead on 15 October 1711, killing all on board) and the *Royal George*, but also that of the *Mary Rose*. And the *Mary Rose* was marked as half a mile north-east of the *Royal George*, near Spit Sand!

So far so good. Alex McKee now went to the Public Record Office in Chancery Lane, where he found a bulky file containing the correspondence between John Deane and the Board of Ordnance about the guns he had raised from the *Mary Rose* in 1836 and 1840, together with a report of a committee set up by the board in 1836 to identify the wreck as that of the *Mary Rose*. And in addition to all that, just to prove McKee's theory completely, there was Deane's request for thirteen-inch bomb-shells with which to remove the surface traces of the wreck in 1840!

In the summer of 1966 Alexander McKee dived with Margot Varese, a diver-archaeologist from London University, on the site that they suspected was the grave of the *Mary Rose*. They made two underwater sweeps of the area and found a distinct mound-and-depression appearance of the sea-bed. The mound pointed south-east, which McKee noted joyfully was the last known heading of the *Mary Rose* at the time that she sank. But they could find no timbers on the surface of the mound, nor could they feel anything solid when they probed under the soft surface.

By the year's end McKee was a frustrated underwater detective. He was sure that he knew the exact spot where the *Mary Rose* lay, but could he prove it? More important, how was he going to prove it? At this moment, just when McKee needed something that would penetrate the mud above what he was sure was the *Mary Rose*, Joan du Plat Taylor introduced him to John Mills of EG and G International, who were planning a four-day period of trials and demonstrations to potential customers of their latest sonar instruments.

The demonstration was of two instruments operated together.

One is side-scan sonar, which shows the patterns and contours of the surface of the sea-bed; the other is a pinger probe, which penetrates the sediments of the sea-bed to show their composition. This means that as you move over the surface you have a five-hundred-foot view of the sea-bed either side of the ship on one instrument and a deep penetration of the sea-bed, perhaps to hundreds of feet, directly below your keel on the other. McKee, because of weather and of demonstration demands, was not to get his chance until the last few moments after the demonstrations were over. Then he was allowed 'one or two quick runs' over the site of the *Mary Rose*. Says McKee:

On board were the Home Office, police, oil companies, and representatives of a Dutch geological institute. With such an audience I felt a trace of 'first night nerves'. Being used only to conning motor boats over the area, I did not allow sufficiently for the larger turning circle of the steamer.

So on the first run we passed in front of the bows of the *Mary Rose* instead of directly over her. This proved to be fortunate, because at a range of two hundred feet the sidescanner picked up the wound in the sea-bed of the wreck's entry, to the astonishment of all concerned, not least myself. Another run, and this time both side-scanner and pinger picked up the wreck – showing that it was twenty feet under the sea-bed.

So the diving started and continued. But by the start of the 1970 season the only equipment the divers possessed were their bare hands and a number of spades. Even so they set to work to try to expose some of the contacts they had already probed. The two they chose were some ten feet from the south-western end of the trench they had already dug and seven to eight feet below sea-bed level. As this only meant digging down another three to four feet below the trench-bottom they concentrated their efforts on these contacts.

The main contact turned out to be a plank ten feet in length and riddled with the borings of teredo worm. It was about a foot wide and about four inches thick. It had been fastened with wooden treenails, and had been broken at one end. In the mass of concretions on it was a large metal hook. It was tempting to link the hook and the break in the plank with Deane's removal of timber in 1840, but they would never be able to prove it. Maurice Young, who is a shipwright as well as a very experienced diver on the site, thought the plank probably came from the main hull, fairly high up near the bulwarks. Mr W. O. B. Majer, who is a student of ancient shipbuilding, thought it came from even higher, just possibly from the castling. Both agreed that the plank came from above the waterline. McKee was happy anyway, as it fitted perfectly with the deductions he had made on his site map of where they were digging.

More woodwork emerged from other shafts. One was identified as a 'fashion piece' – a kind of curved capping to smarten up the sides of either the stern or forecastle. The other was a 'staghorn', or large wooden cleat associated with the ropes controlling the yards on the foremast.

More equipment was now available, and with it more ambitious ideas. They decided to try to go down the full distance to the port side. A shaft was therefore dug directly over the mound that marked the estimated position of the port side of the ship. This westward shaft went down much faster than the one from the east, and it was soon twelve feet below sea-bed level.

Working conditions in these shafts were appalling. The walls of this westward shaft for example were higher than the walls of the rooms in an average house. Once the divers had finned down to the sea-bed fifty feet below their boats, they were confronted with a black hole. Had anyone been working in it with airjet, airlift or even just bare hands, the visibility would have been almost nil. The diver had now to sink down into the darkness of the shaft, pass through a layer of weed that was collecting deeper and deeper in the shaft day by day, and finally grope for the bottom of it all in order to start work.

In such conditions it is not surprising that when a gun was found in the westward shaft neither Maurice Young, nor Percy Ackland nor Alex McKee could at first be sure that it was a gun at all. 'But', says McKee, 'I felt it was – the first and only time that I have had a hunch – and even this was based on the bumps made by the reinforcing rings and prior knowledge of the kind of guns raised from the *Mary Rose* by the Deanes.'

The discovery raised another problem – how to handle such a large, heavy object without risk. Theoretically a built-up gun is much weaker than a cast piece. But the Ministry of Public Building and Works provided a ship with a crane, then a dockyard crane to lift the gun (suitably splinted) over another ship and on to a lorry. The time which elapsed between the gun breaking surface at Spithead and its arrival in the Conservation Laboratory at Southsea Castle Museum was just over three hours.

When the gun was first lowered on to the deck of the lifting ship, the divers saw that a few inches of one of the rings was clear of concretion and, for about ten minutes before it rusted over, this was ordinary grey metal – just as it must have appeared in July 1545, before the ship sank. Though it was nearly eight feet long, the 'gun' turned out to be just the barrel of a wrought-iron breech-loader. It looked like the kind which was made from bars of metal held into barrel shape by hoops or rings of iron. The bore was about three-and-three-quarter inches, and the barrel was slightly bent. The muzzle end was blocked with eighteen inches of blue clay, which had to be removed with a chisel, it was so hard. The other end was blocked by a three-and-a-half-inch shot still in the breech.

McKee had expected that the shot would have been of stone, as this is what Deane had reportedly found, but this was pig-iron and in mint condition. It was as it had been loaded some 425 years ago. The oakum wadding was still in place, and that too was in good condition. The gun appeared to be a companion piece to the one raised by Deane in 1840, which has been in Southsea Castle for several years and is badly damaged.

The importance of the armament of the *Mary Rose* lies in both the guns themselves and the way they were used. The loss of the ship was certainly due to water pouring in through her open gun-ports as she heeled. Another contemporary document makes this point very clearly: 'A goodly ship of England called the Mary Rose was by to much foly drowned in the midst of the haven, for she was laden with muche ordinaunce and the portes left open, which they were ferie low and the great ordinaunce unbreeched. So that when the ship should turne the water entered and sodainly she sank.'

The use of gun-ports was then in its infancy. We know that the *Greate Henry*, the same ship on which Henry VIII entertained his captains before the loss of the *Mary Rose*, had two rows of opening ports after her rebuilding between 1536 and 1539, but we do not know if she had those ports when first built. Really heavy guns could not be used by ships to fire broadsides until the invention of opening gun-ports, as great guns had to be fitted low down in the ship for the sake of stability.

We are talking about really heavy guns when we are looking at the armament of the *Mary Rose*. Some of the brass muzzle-loaders recovered by Deane from the *Mary Rose* were bigger than almost identically shaped and designed guns used at the Battle of Trafalgar, almost 260 years later. Both the structure of the ship and her armament, which set the style for naval guns right up to Nelson's time and beyond, are therefore vitally important to our knowledge of history.

Upon examining the gun raised by McKee, Mr K. Barton, the curator of the Portsmouth City Museum, was immediately convinced that the gun came from the crater made by Deane in the course of his work on the wreck. He thought this because of the corrosion. This indicated that the gun had been subjected to a slight deterioration over a long period, followed by a much more rapid deterioration over a shorter period. The slight bending of the barrel was, the experts thought, consistent with a gunpowder explosion and this would fit in with Deane's request for 'bomb shells' to remove surface traces of the wreck in 1840.

But McKee and his fellow-detectives were to have one more surprise that season. Portsmouth Dockyard X-rayed the gun from outside the barrel. The Tudor gunsmiths had rolled a wrought-iron sheet into a cylinder and welded it, then added reinforcing rings. It revealed to the world a previously unsuspected method of construction of those great guns of long ago.

At the start of the 1971 season McKee and his team made another discovery. They found sections of the forecastle intact and in good condition under the mud. 'The only marks are those made by the tools of Tudor shipwrights,' said McKee, adding that this discovery had accomplished in one day something he had thought would take the entire season.

It is a most odd fact that though people will pour money into some comparatively obscure land archaeological excavation, they hesitate to do so for a much more important underwater site. The *Mary Rose* operation has been dogged by financial problems. At one stage it was only a donation by Prince Philip that kept the operation moving.

It is time too to introduce here Mrs Margaret Rule, the *Mary Rose* archaeologist who has worked so closely with Alexander McKee since she joined the team in 1967. Mrs Rule, the curator of the excavated Roman palace at Fishbourne, near Chichester,

Sussex, decided at the age of forty that she wanted to see what was going on down there and took diving lessons with the aqualung. (It is interesting to note here that so important is the work that both Alexander McKee and Margaret Rule have done for the cause of underwater archaeology in Britain that first Alex and then Margaret Rule were awarded Britain's 'Diver of the Year' trophy.) Mrs Rule now dives regularly with the *Mary Rose* team, who must claim the record for the longest running underwater archaeology operation in this country.

So the work went on, but 1972 was the worst year for weather since McKee had started operations in 1965. On only thirty-eight days could the amateur divers, under the direction of Alex McKee and Margaret Rule, dive on the site and even on the days that they could get down underwater visibility was often almost impossible. By the end of the season, even so, it was clear that the collapsed forecastle lay intact on the starboard stern-quarter of the ship. Tantalizing indications as to what may lie inside the hull of the ship were found during this work. Fragments of a small wooden keg were discovered as well as two combs, a thimble, thread spools and wooden knife and awl handles. Just the sort of thing you would expect to find in a seaman's 'diddy box' or a soldier's 'housewife'. Then two wooden handles of kidney daggers were found. These all-purpose knives, not fighting weapons, are the ones that you see hanging from the waists of gentlemen in ancient pictures or brasses. They found stone and lead shot and a stone mould for casting 1lb lead shot. But the most spectacular discovery of all was a pewter flagon with a lid, the earliest known piece of mediaeval domestic pewter to survive in Britain! (see plate 4).

The next year *Mary Rose* scored another first – she was the first ship designated as a historic wreck under the 1973 act (see appendix III). In 1974 a start was made on digging round the stern to see just how well preserved the ship was under the mud and clay. In 1975 the divers uncovered the sternpost of the hull and realized that the ship was heeled over at sixty degrees. And there was the rudder!

Prince Charles had earlier expressed his interest in seeing the wreck of the *Mary Rose* for himself. He shared the naval interest of his father Prince Philip and his uncle Lord Mountbatten in the *Mary Rose* and the possibility of her becoming Britain's *Vasa*.

Prince Charles, during his naval service, had become a trained diver. In addition to that, like his father before him, he was the president of the B S-A C. So, as soon as his royal duties allowed, he was standing on the catamaran diving platform over the site. This was 30 July 1975. What happened then is described by Prince Charles in an article he wrote for *Triton*, the magazine of the B S- A C. In the article he first described his dive under the ice in the Arctic in Resolute Bay, Canada, where the water was so cold that unprotected exposure would have killed him in five minutes, and then wrote:

The final sub-aqua experience of 1975 was a dive I made at the end of July on the wreck of King Henry VIII's great battleship The *Mary Rose*. No-one recorded my ancestor's remarks when the pride of his navy capsized and sank before his eyes as she sailed out of Portsmouth harbour in 1545 to drive off the maurauding French in the Solent. Whatever he said, I have no doubt it was something suitably rich and choice!

I was extremely lucky to have chosen a glorious hot day in July for my visit to the wreck with Mr. Alexander McKee and his merry band of divers. The dive took place with the ebb tide in calm conditions and after their ship-borne hoover had cleared the site of mud and debris I followed Mr. McKee down the guide rope to the seabed. The visibility was the best they had had the whole year – certainly 10 feet if not 15 – and I could clearly distinguish the outline of the timber frames of the port side of the ship. The ship appears to be lying on her starboard side at an angle of about 60°, but part of the transom has been excavated to a depth of about five or six feet and it was possible to see clearly the massive Tudor timbers which appeared to be in excellent condition. Nearby lay a gun port which had been broken off when the ship struck the bottom.

I was so fascinated by the whole exploration that I went down a second time to have another look. It was extraordinary to think that under all that mud lay a complete piece of Tudor naval history, encapsulated and frozen intact in 1545. Mr. MeKee and his colleagues are dedicated sub-aqua archaeologists, determined somehow to succeed in raising the Mary Rose, and I feel sure they will succeed eventually. As President of the B S-A C I am more than proud of what they are doing for scientific diving in this country and for the benefit of naval and British history.

I had dived the *Mary Rose* as chairman of the B S-A C just month before Prince Charles's historic dive. Even if you have a great deal of experience of diving wrecks this dive is still a real eye-opener. The problem which the *Mary Rose* team face is making sure that the hull is sound enough to be raised and put on exhibition for all to see. I can only describe my feelings of what I saw by referring to the words I wrote in Margaret Rule's log within minutes of surfacing from the wreck. Prince Charles had better visibility than I did – obviously a Command performance! – but, even in the five to eight feet that I experienced, I knew that the *Mary Rose* would someday rise from the deep. In Margaret's log I put it like this:

I was not prepared for what I saw. I had thought I would see various isolated planks. Silly, but that's what I expected. The amazing thing about seeing her in fact, and touching her, is that you *know* there is a whole ship there. And you know it before you have completed the 13-minute special tour for aged divers! Most impressive – and now I know why each stage takes so long. And my admiration for those who work in such conditions day after day is trebled!

When Prince Charles first dived with Alexander McKee he did not take what I called the thirteen-minute tour for aged divers. In fact on his first dive he was down for twenty-six minutes. Margaret Rule, who had shown Prince Charles around Fishbourne Roman palace when he was an undergraduate at Cambridge reading archaeology, was delighted with his delight and eager questions about the timbers he had seen. In fact he went down again, this time for thirty minutes and, from talking to the team who were there on that day, I am sure that he was deeply concerned that their dream of a Tudor ship museum in Portsmouth should come true.

To the credit of the City of Portsmouth, who have had the imagination to support the project through thick and thin and have now launched a Lord Mayor's Support Committee (target £15,000), they have had the vision to see that the *Mary Rose*, raised and on display near HMS *Victory* can only be a sensational attraction. Latest diving on the ship shows that most of the timbers are sound – so sound that planing will produce shavings, and sawing, real sawdust. All that the project needs is finance and those who have funds in this country should hang their heads in shame that they are not supporting the raising of the *Mary Rose* to the limit of their ability. During the summer of 1977, the *Mary Rose* team were diving in two shifts so that work goes on for over fourteen hours a day!

FOUR

'In the flagship there is no water, but what they brought out of Spain, which stinketh marvellously'

Lost at sea	On land
1588 Armada ships:	*Elizabeth I reigns*
Santa Maria de la Rosa	*Defeat of Armada celebrated*
La Rata Santa Maria	*'Sea-dogs' plunder the Spanish*
Encoronada	*Main*
Duquesa Santa Ana	
Girona	
Florencia	

The credit for reawakening interest in the Spanish Armada not only among archaeologists but also the general public in recent years must go to one man. He devoted years of his life to the search for knowledge of those long-lost Armada ships. He dived for and found one. He missed a fortune from another by a hair's breadth and dismissed it as just the luck of the game. But he was without doubt the first man to find a sunken Armada galleon using modern diving methods.

That man is Sydney Wignall of Old Colwyn, Denbighshire. Syd Wignall's interest in the possibility of finding Armada wrecks off the coast of Ireland began in 1961, but before that he was a mountaineer of international standing, had led an expedition into the Himalayas and had even been captured by the Red Chinese on a charge of trespass and spying. Mountaineering and diving attract the same kind of people. The risk factor – though any diver will tell you that it is greater for mountaineers – seems to be the common link, but the two sports do have the affinity of adventure.

Certainly Syd Wignall felt the pull of diving, and soon he was acting as cameraman for a RAF diving-club expedition to a sunken Roman wreck off Filucudi, one of the Lipari Islands near Sicily. This gave him the taste for diving – but more important it gave him the thrill of delving into the past history of man. Soon he was reading avidly – and researching deeply – into the history of lost ships. The Armada and its shipwrecks quickly became an obsession.

The primary object of the Armada has never been in doubt, and at least that is one thing upon which historians do agree. Philip of Spain's problem was exactly the same as that, many years later, of Adolf Hitler. Philip wanted to rule England – therefore he had to cross the channel and attack London. Like Hitler he had a vast army on the Continent, in the Low Countries, and needed to invade across the channel. To do this he employed Alexander Farnese, the Duke of Parma. Parma's task was to assemble the army and the invasion barges. The only drawback was that the Royal Navy – or the Elizabethan equivalent – commanded the channel. And that is where the Armada came in. This vast fleet was to cover the operation and prevent the English from attacking the soft underbelly of the invasion, the barges containing troops.

The plan of course went wrong. Though no fully decisive battle was fought in the Channel, the weather played up and the Armada, harried by the English ships, was driven away from any likely crossing point. The Armada ships were loaded with everything that an invasion of England would require – men, shot, cannons, horses, wagon wheels – but this loading was really a disadvantage when the gales started. Already badly hurt by English attacks off Gravelines, where Drake, Hawkins, Howard, Frobisher, all the great names, gave a good account of themselves – the Armada ran before a south-west wind. Then the storms came and the wind drove the ships away to the north.

The voyage of the Armada became a painful mockery of the comparatively easy victory the crews had been led to expect. North and still farther north they went, until they had gone so far that the Duke of Medina Sidonia, on board his flagship *San Martin de Portugal* and in command of what was left of the Armada, could take his ships westward avoiding the shores of the Orkneys and the Shetlands and out into the North Atlantic to begin the long last leg home. The duke led his ships – those that were still with him – westward towards Rockall before he turned south. He was convinced that no quarter would be given to the crew of any ship unfortunate enough to be forced to land in Ireland.

It was a ghastly wallow of ships that travelled down the west coast of Ireland, and nothing like the proud Armada that had sailed so confidently on 28 May 1588. It was now August, and the shot-holes in the Spanish ships, added to the storm damage, meant that even the Duke of Medina Sidonia's flagship the *San Martin* was leaking like a sieve. Stores had gone mouldy or drained away from badly made casks, and there was no water to spare for the horses and mules, which were flung overboard on the duke's orders. His further orders about the daily rations give some idea of the state that the Armada ships were in. Each man was entitled to eight ounces of biscuit, a pint of water and half a pint of wine – and no more.

One of the ships in convoy with the Duke of Medina Sidonia was the *Santa Maria de la Rosa*, officially described as the vice-flagship of the squadron of Guipuzcao. She had been badly mauled in the running fight with the British ships, and had at least four cannon-balls still lodged in her wooden hull. Her rigging and sails were in tatters. She was taking water. To add to the misery, her crew were down to half-strength, owing to disease and a food and water shortage. What water they had was green and scummy, and had to be strained through their teeth to prevent them swallowing foreign objects that had found their way into or grown in the water butts. What food there was was stinking. And then came the gales from the south-west.

It is not surprising that the Armada had such a hard time in its voyage down the west coast of Ireland. Recent research has shown that the north-west section of the Irish coastline gets an average of 40.5 gales per year, with 12 of those rated as severe. And the south-west is not far behind, with 36.1 as the average annual number of gales – and seven of those are rated as severe.

The *Santa Maria* decided to take the line of least resistance and head for the land to seek shelter there. On or about 29 September 1588 the ship was close to the western tip of Kerry. If those on board realized they were too close to the land for safety, there was really nothing much they could do about it, but hope that some sheltered bay would suddenly open up before them. Abreast of

Dunquin the land seemed to be closing in all round them. Ahead and to port there was Dunmore Head, and to starboard the little island of Beginish merged into the background of Great Blasket Island. But the bay hardly provided the sort of anchorage that the eyes of those on board ached to see. The water in the bay was driven by the onshore wind and parts of it almost boiled.

A shout from the forepeak and a pointing finger dragged all eyes to starboard, and there was what to those tired sailors must have seemed a miracle. Tucked in the shelter between the Great Blasket and Beginish were two great Spanish vessels – other survivors of the rout of the Armada. Here it must have seemed to the captain of the *Santa Maria de la Rosa*, Martin de Villafranca, was the aid he desperately needed. He ordered a gun to be fired to signal to his comrades in their safely anchored ships that he needed their help. But there was no sign of any assistance from the anchored ships as he moved towards them, so another gun was fired.

Still nothing happened, and so Villafranca gave the order to cut away their last anchor from its ready position, catted at the bow. Where the *Santa Maria* had lost her other anchors we shall never know, but when two sailors with axes cut away the restraining ropes the anchor plunged to the bottom and an easing of the movement of the ship was immediately noticeable. This, even though the ship still pitched and tossed in the waves racing in before the wind, was a great relief and the men on the *Santa Maria* began to have more hope of survival. Surely when the weather eased the men from the other galleons would come across to them in boats and help them out with food and water? Some even thought that all their troubles were now over. The date was 21 September 1588, the time 12 noon.

The *Santa Maria* was now only 'two cables lengths' from the other ships, but they were not to know that the two Spanish ships already anchored there – the *San Juan de Portugal*, under the command of the Armada's vice-admiral Juan Martinez de Recalde, and the *San Juan* of the Castille squadron, commanded by Marcos de Aramburu, one of the fleet's paymasters – were in no better state than their own. The two galleons had between them only one good boat that could have reached the *Santa Maria*, and in the condition of the sea at that time between the ships it would have been madness to try to get that boat across.

The commanders had heard Villafranca's signals, but they could do nothing but watch and hope the weather eased. Aramburu's account of what happened that day still survives, and, probably because he was a paymaster, he made a careful note of everything that occurred, even before he and Recalde saw the *Santa Maria* come in:

The 18th, 19th and 20th [of September] we remained in the same port without being able to get out. Juan Martinez went on taking water; and I, having no long-boat or other boat, could do nothing; and he but little, and that with much labour.

On the morning of the 21st the wind began to blow from the west with terrible violence. Clear, with but little rain. The ship of Juan Martinez drifted down on ours.

In fact this accident nearly sank both ships. Martinez's ship smashed into the stern of that of Aramburu, broke the grip of both their anchors and nearly took them out into the storm-whipped waters of the sound. But, writes Aramburu; '[Recalde] dropped anchor with another cable and, having smashed our lantern and the tackle on our mizzen-mast, brought the ship to.'

This incident was obviously nearly a disaster, but nothing, it seems, would put off Aramburu from recording every detail. He goes on:

At midday the ship *Santa Maria de la Rosa*, of Martin de Villafranca, came in by another entrance nearer the land, towards the north-west, and on coming in fired a gun, as if seeking help, and another when further in. She had all her sails torn to ribbons, except the foresail. She anchored with a single anchor, as she had no more. And as the tide, which was coming in from the south-east, beat against her, she held on till two o'clock, when it began to ebb, and at the turn she commenced drifting, about two splices of cable from us, and we with her; and in an instant we saw she was going to the bottom while trying to hoist the foresail, and immediately she went down with the whole crew, not a soul escaping – a most extraordinary and terrible occurrence.

In fact Aramburu's ship had a lucky escape, for the stricken *Santa Maria* could so easily have dragged them to the bottom, as their anchor cables were obviously entangled. The disappearance of the *Santa Maria* – almost before Villafranca's crew had time to move to obey his screamed command to hoist the foresail – could only mean that she had struck some submerged rock.

But Aramburu was wrong about not a soul escaping. One sailor 'naked upon a board' did reach shore alive. He was the son of the pilot on board the *Santa Maria* and his name was Giovanni de Monana, a Genoese who had been taken into service with his father at Lisbon. Now he was taken to Dingle to be examined by James Trant, the local agent of Sir Edward Denny. Trant had already examined a boatload of Spaniards who had been captured by English soldiers when they came ashore from Recalde's galleon in search of fresh water and food several days earlier. From this interrogation Trant already had a good idea of conditions out there near 'The Ferriters Great Island', as Blasket was called. He had reported: 'In the flagship there is left but twenty five pipes of wine and but very little bread, and no water but what they brought out of Spain, which stinketh marvellously, and the flesh meat they cannot eat, the drouth is so great.'

Trant, it is fair to comment, was like most Englishmen of the time gloating happily over the Spaniards' plight. Now another stood before him. Poor Giovanni, described as 'marryner' did his best to answer all the questions, but, as he spoke Italian and a little Spanish and his answers were written in English by an Irish clerk, some of the written report of the examination must be regarded as suspect.

He is quoted as saying that the Prince of Ascoli, bastard son of the King of Spain, had been among those lost. In fact he even described the man and the colour of his clothes. But we know that the prince had been put ashore in France and was unable to join the ship again when it sailed. This sort of error is probably due to the language difficulty, with the interrogator not understanding that the prisoner was using the past tense about the prince having been on board. The local Irish had no doubts at all about the story however and one of the places where bodies from the wreck were buried – Dunquin – is still known to this day as the Grave of the Son of the King of Spain.

What was of much greater interest to the interrogator of Giovanni was his tale of how much gold and silver had been left in the ship when it sank, and also his reports of how much armament the ship carried. He said, or is noted as saying, that she carried '50 great pieces, all cannons of the field: 25 pieces of brass and cast iron belonging to the ship; there were also in her 50 tuns of sack.' His estimate of the cash on board amounted to some fifty thousand golden ducats, fifty thousand silver ducats and the plate of gold and silver owned by the rich persons on board at the time.

The answers sounded grand and interesting. The *Santa Maria* was a ship of some 950 tons, and had started the campaign with about three hundred soldiers and sailors on board. It is important to stress here that if the interrogator and the clerk got the presence of the Prince of Ascoli wrong, they were obviously quite capable of getting their tenses mixed up over the cannon. The reason for emphasizing this will become clear later on.

The information was duly passed on to London, but there was nothing that the salvors of those days could do about the wreck of the *Santa Maria de la Rosa*. She was to all intents and purposes outside their reach – largely because of her position. So there the *Santa Maria* lay. Aramburu and Recalde both got back to Spain, but Recalde died soon afterwards. And soon the actual resting-place of the *Santa Maria* was forgotten. The legend of a great treasure ship sunk somewhere in Blasket Sound lived on, but the weather and the tides put off any serious search for her remains. The nearest we know that anyone actually did get to her was the case of a fisherman in the 1830s who found a small brass cannon in his nets. It is said that it had a coat of arms on it bearing a device of an uprooted tree and that it was taken to Clonskeagh Castle, Dublin. Do not look for it there. It disappeared during the Troubles, and of course some blame the Black and Tans for melting it down for scrap.

One of the great authorities on Armada wrecks was William Spotswood Green, and in May 1906 the *Geographical Journal* printed a very complete account by him of the Spanish losses around the coasts of Ireland. He was also the author of 'Armada Ships on the Kerry Coast' (an article in the *Proceedings of the Irish Academy*, February 1909, volume xxvii, section c, n12), but his work should be treated with caution. Green placed the site of the wreck of the *Santa Maria* as Stromboli Rock.

Stromboli Rock is submerged on the mainland side of the Sound opposite to An Gob, the easterly headland of the Great Blasket. It is shown on Admiralty charts as having two-and-a-half fathoms (fifteen feet) over the rock at low water, but Green considers that the rock may well have been awash in 1588 and says that it seems to have been smashed when HMS *Stromboli* ran into it in about 1850.

There were few serious expeditions to the site until July 1963, when Syd Wignall arrived on the scene with Joe Casey and other members of St Helens Underwater Club. They spent two weeks searching Blasket Sound for the Armada ship and, though Syd Wignall now likes to describe the expedition as 'a light recce', the divers did get a very good idea of conditions and developed a healthy respect for the underwater conditions in the area.

Other expeditions were launched with other divers, but the poor conditions and strong tides beat them too. And in June 1963 James Hewitt, a diver on holiday from Newcastle-upon-Tyne, failed to surface while diving in Blasket Sound and was later found dead in ninety feet of water.

Syd Wignall had learnt from his previous expedition what sort of conditions he could expect to find in the area where the *Santa Maria* had sunk. He knew too that unless some reliable and comprehensive search method could be evolved the chances of finding the Armada ship would really depend on luck.

But he had not given up. More time went into research, and he started negotiations with the Spanish government, whom he believed still to be the rightful owners of the wreck. In 1965 he was awarded an exclusive five-year salvage licence from the Ministry of Marine Affairs in Madrid. (This licence was extended for a further seven years from 1969.) Now he planned a bigger and better expedition, but the problem of finding the wreck still loomed large in his thoughts.

Then in October 1965 Syd Wignall met the man who had the answer. The meeting took place in Malta, and the man was Lieutenant-Commander John Grattan, OBE, RN. Grattan had just assumed command of the Mediterranean Fleet clearance diving team. He was afterwards promoted to commander. Wignall and Grattan found out almost immediately that they had similar interests in the field of marine archaeology. And Syd Wignall conveyed to Grattan his fears about the prospects of being able to locate the *Santa Maria*.

Grattan had the answer – the swim-line underwater search system. It was used by some of the Royal Navy's clearance diving teams, but was not in general use in the navy. John Grattan offered to adapt the technique to suit Syd Wignall's needs in

Blasket Sound. What is more, he agreed to lead the diving operations there for two-and-a-half years, this would not be until
1968, but Syd was prepared to wait. They talked for hours about
the problem. Commander Grattan had been able to rely on teams
of well-trained and disciplined Royal Navy clearance divers –
would he be able to do the same sort of search using volunteer
amateurs?

Finally the time came to find out. John Grattan was in charge of
the diving and archaeologist Colin Martin took over the wreck
survey. First of all of course came the searches by the swim-line
methods. This had worked before in the past: in 33 minutes'
diving 35 Royal Navy divers had searched 1,400,000 square yards
of Mediterranean harbour floor to locate some lost equipment –
that is, an area of some 290 acres. It sounds impossible. But
basically all the method involves is a number of divers strung
along a line on the bottom, all moving forward together and all
responding to control and guidance from the surface. All! In fact
it needs highly skilled diving and more important highly skilled
control from the surface. John Grattan provided the skill and the
amateur divers did the rest.

In fact the area searched by this method in Blasket Sound
exceeded fifteen million square yards, or over three thousand
acres. The credit for this, says Syd Wignall, must go entirely to
the efforts of John Grattan, who had trained the divers in the use
of this search technique. Syd Wignall describes the swim line as
an underwater visual vacuum-cleaner: 'It beats as it sweeps as it
sees. We even picked up chicken bones. Believe me, we missed
nothing in Blasket Sound.' They did in fact find seven Armada
anchors, which had come from the ships of Recalde and Aramburu and one which must have come from the *Santa Maria*. All
were broken in some way, which gives point to the sixteenth-
century saying that something was 'as rotten as a Spanish
anchor'.

The swim line found something else of vital importance. One
of the searchers suddenly found a rock that was not on the charts
– a rock that came so close to the surface that when he stood on it
his hands were out of the water. This explained a great deal. It
explained how it was that the *Santa Maria*, which drew only
fifteen feet, could have struck Stromboli Rock at high tide when
there is twenty-six feet of water over it. The simple answer is that

she did not. She struck this uncharted rock. If you look on an up-to-date Admiralty chart of the area today you will see John Grattan's correction putting that rock into the charts.

Then the searchers found a pile of stones on the bottom. Diver Mike Edmonds sat on them and idly chipped away at one with his diving knife. Almost at once a great cloud of black drifted from the 'stone'. It was in fact an iron cannon-ball. So on 4 July 1968, after they had searched 3,200 acres of Irish seabed, Sydney Wignall and his team got their reward – they found the *Santa Maria*.

Perhaps, to be more accurate, they had found a great heap of ballast stones and cannon-balls, but strangely enough there were was no sign of the twenty-five cannon mentioned by the one survivor. In fact there was no sign of any cannon at all. They had without doubt found a wreck site that seemed to fit in with all the other details, but they could not yet say that this was without doubt the *Santa Maria de la Rosa*. There were iron and stone shot there as well as lead ingots with Spanish markings, but this was not enough.

So Syd Wignall returned with twenty divers to explore the site more fully, and, though they did not need it, got confirmation that Blasket Sound was no place for novice divers or novice boat-handlers. Three times inflatable boats were capsized by the seas, and on one occasion Wignall and six others were thrown right out of their sixteen-foot boat by a thirty-foot wave! However they went on with their survey of the wreck site and hit the jackpot when Jeremy Green of Oxford University's Laboratory for Archaeology carried out a search with a metal-detector. He located a large pewter plate under the ballast mound.

Positive identification of the wreck was made when the pewter plate was found to have an inscription on the rim. Not much; just one word – 'Matute'. Several days later the research was completed, and there could no longer be any doubt that the *Santa Maria* was found.

To understand why we have to go back to our sole survivor. Among all the things he said, and which were noted down at his interrogation, was one vital sentence. Giovanni de Manona had said, 'Matute was the Captain of the Infantry of that ship.' Syd Wignall spotted it and went back to his research papers, and there in the muster of Spanish officers taken at Corunna before the Armada sailed was the same name – Captain Francisco Ruiz Matute of the Regiment of Sicily.

The whole of the rest of the 1969 season was spent on surveying the site, airlifting shingle surrounding the wreck and removing ballast stones to uncover the ship's timbers. The divers were working at between 100 and 115 feet, and they found that below the turn of the bilge the entire structure of the ship seemed to be in a fine state of preservation. They found lead ingots, then a study of the mast stepping-box seemed to provide confirmation also that the *Santa Maria* had broken her back and lost her mainmast as she sank. In the galley area at the foot of the mainmast the divers found broken pottery, a flint for lighting fires, brushwood, a broken pewter goblet, a brass balance pan and even a whole Brazil nut!

Of the guns there was still no sign. Syd Wignall subscribes to the theory that the *Santa Maria's* crew jettisoned the guns in bad weather farther north up the coast of Ireland and kept only a small bronze swivel gun for signalling. This theory, if correct, also tells us a great deal about the condition of the Armada ships by this time, for it means that the crew had abandoned any idea of defence or attack and were only concerned with running for home as quickly as they could. We know that the *Santa Maria* did fire two shots on entering Blasket Sound to indicate her distress, and it does look as though that gun – if that was all she had left – was the one hauled up by that fisherman in 1839.

As for treasure, so far the divers have located one silver and one gold coin. For the record, the two coins found were a gold double escudo of Philip II and a silver four-real piece. But it is where they were found that is so interesting. They were in the remains of a cloth purse still attached to the ribs of a skeleton located at the rear of the wreck. And on the chest of that skeleton was a large pewter plate engraved with the initials 'A.H.'. Two known Spaniards with these intials took part in the Armada. One was the poet and writer Antonio de Herrera, who survived, and Augustin de Herrera, who died. Even so, positive identification of the owner of the plate is not yet established.

Sydney Wignall received recognition of his work on the *Santa Maria*. As a tribute to the team-work of the forty-three divers who took part in the expedition, the Duke of Edinburgh's Prize of the BS-AC was awarded to him. The Duke of Edinburgh was president of the club from 1961 to 1964. When he resigned from the presidency in 1964 Prince Philip proposed that he should mark his association with the club by awarding an annual prize. The Duke of Edinburgh's Prize is awarded annually to the member, or group of members of the BS-AC, who are adjudged to have undertaken, published or completed an important project in the underwater field during the year under review. Prince Philip himself makes the final selection from the best three entries.

The *Santa Maria* was not the only great Spanish ship to seek the shelter of the land. Of the same mind was the carrack *La Rata Santa Maria Encoronada*. Carracks were really armed merchant ships, but *La Rata* was more than that. She had towering over-hanging bows and a great sterncastle, and all the guns crammed into her made her much more than an armed merchantman. She was a ship of war. But you would not know it now.

The *Rata*, under the command of Don Alonso Martinez de Leiva, Captain-General of the Milan cavalry, had been the first Spanish ship to fire on the English off the Lizard many weeks before. But the various encounters – in which she had always been in the van – and the storms had left her wallowing, shot-battered and with her sails in tatters.

It was not the way the Spanish nobility had visualized the ship of de Leiva. He was a national hero, one of the greatest knights in Spain, and the favourite of Philip II. The nobility had competed to serve under him in the Armada – and if they were too old themselves had sent their sons to join him. For they were certain that de Leiva would be at the head of the victorious parade through London when the Armada had done its work. De Leiva had earned his reputation in other battles, and the fact that he headed for land – he needed fresh water and shelter for repairs – showed just how badly he was in trouble. De Leiva was not the sort of man to give up easily. If he was forced into land – against orders – then his ship was about to sink.

High waves drove *La Rata* on towards the coast of Ireland and she entered Blacksod Bay, in County Mayo. But even there the winds were so strong that there was nothing the crew could do to prevent her stranding off Ballycroy. But de Leiva was not beaten yet. He landed all his men and all their possessions and then fired what was left of his ship. He knew that there could be no escape by sea, and at first he prepared for a land battle against whoever came. Whether he thought the enemy would be the English or the Irish we shall never know. His first move was to take over the castle at Ballycroy, but after a short while he seemed unhappy about the castle as a defensive spot and moved everything to the Mullet Peninsula.

There he was joined by another ship's company that had come ashore at Inver, in Broadhaven. They waited for an attack that never came. But from out of the driving winds behind them came another ship into Blacksod Bay. This was the *Duquesa Santa Ana* – and as far as de Leiva was concerned she was the answer to his prayers. The *Santa Ana* looked like a ticket home to Spain. So he embarked all the men into the *Santa Ana* and set sail once again. This time his plan was to sail north to the Scottish islands, where he was sure he would find sympathizers. Once there he would reorganize his men and the ship for the final voyage back to Spain.

But by now his presence in Ireland was known, and a letter from the Lord Deputy to the Privy Council tells how a search for him got under way. The search could hardly have started before de Leiva was off in the *Santa Ana*. De Leiva however again found himself on board a ship that was in desperate need of repairs, and should really not have sailed without them. Soon they were bucking hard against storm winds, and he knew that they would not get much farther. In fact before she had sailed seventy miles they were forced on shore again. This time the stranding was more serious and the *Santa Ana* was completely wrecked in Loughros Bay, in County Donegal. De Leiva was badly injured during the salvage work.

Some idea of the number of Spanish ships being smashed against the Irish coast at that time comes in a letter to the English Privy Council from an eye-witness:

As I passed from Sligo, having then gone 120 miles, I held on towards Bundrowes (in the county of Leitrim) and so to Ballyshannon, the uttermost part of Connaught that way, as some say, but denied so to be by O'Donnell and his followers, and riding still along the sea coast, I went to see the bay, where some of those ships wrecked, and where, as I heard, lay not long before 1200 or 1300 of the dead bodies.

I rode upon that strand near two miles (but left behind me a long mile and more), and then turned off from that shore leaving before me a mile and better's riding, in both which places they said that have seen it, there lay as great store of the timber of wrecked ships as was in that place which myself had viewed, being in mine opinion (having small skill or judgment therein) more than would have built five of the greatest ships that I ever saw, besides mighty great boats, cables and other cordage answerable thereunto, and some such masts for bigness and length, as in mine own judgment I never saw any two could make the like.

So ships were coming in all over the place. At this time de Leiva received information that three Spanish ships were safe in Killybegs Harbour, nineteen miles away. He had himself carried there on a litter, but his information was a little wrong. Three Spanish ships had indeed headed for the harbour of Killybegs. One of them did not quite make it and was wrecked outside the harbour. The second it seems got in, but was smashed to pieces on the shore. The third, a galleass called the *Girona*, though badly damaged was safely at anchor.

De Leiva must have been quite a man, for on arrival in Killybegs on his litter he set the survivors from the two Killybegs wrecks, the crew of the *Girona* and the crews of the ships he had brought with him, to work to repair the ship. They used timber from the ship which had been wrecked inside Killybegs to do this, and then de Leiva loaded all the men – about five crews in all, probably over one thousand men – all the plate, the money, the jewels and all the weapons to hand into yet another ship. He was carried aboard and the *Girona* sailed again on 16 October 1588. De Leiva was still sticking to his plan to sail north for the Isles of Scotland. But he did not get very far.

A letter from Mr Henry Dulse dated 26 October 1588 tells the Privy Council the news he had received from a man he sent to spy on the Spaniards at Killybegs:

The 16th of this instant October the said gally departed from the said harbour with as many Spaniards as she could carry, and sailing along the coast towards the Out Isles of Scotland, wither they were then bound, struck against the rock of Bunboyes (near Dunluce), where both ship and men perished, save only five who hardly got to shore; three of which five men came the next day, being the 17th, in company with Sorley Boy M'Donnell unto O'Neill's house at Strabane, where they certified of their late shipwreck. Sorley Boy's coming to Strabane at this time was to get O'Neill's daughter to wife. This rock of Bunboyes is hard by Sorley Boy's house (of Dunluce).

De Leiva had gone down with the ship. So had all the plate, jewels and other treasures, as well as the men he had tried so hard to save.

There matters rested until Syd Wignall came on the scene in 1963. He dived under the walls of Dunluce Castle, found nothing and wrote in his diving log:

Local legend says that the wreck of the *Girona* is connected with the little bay or Port (or Point) na-Spagna. This was worth investigating. We were surprised to find a steep-sided cove with cliffs about 300 feet high, vertical and in places overhanging. The only foot access is via a frighteningly narrow sheep track. No place to carry up cannon by hand.

One important factor, however, was that the little cove, although almost inaccessible, was covered with a multitude of flotsam and jetsam, everything from spars, buoys, cans, rope, deadwood, all piled up on the shingle. No other beach within an area of miles had such a collection. As we looked we could even see new debris being carried in shore by the current.

Is the origin of the name Point-na-Spagna due to the fact that the *Girona* sank elsewhere, but that most of the bodies were carried in here by the freak currents? It looked to me as though anything floating in the sea in the Bushmills area might end up in Point-na-Spagna.

Syd Wignall was closer at that moment to the wreck that he knew, but he turned his attention away to the *Santa Maria de la Rosa*, with the results that I have detailed earlier.

In my book *The Wreck Hunters* I wrote the story of Syd Wignall's short visit to the area. What I did not know then was that Robert Stenuit in Belgium was keeping a file of wrecks. In 1958 he became interested in the wreck of the *Girona* and gave it a three-star marking for its archaeological interest and its treasure. He read my account and added it to his file. In June of 1967 he went to North Antrim, after spending what he now calculates were six or seven hundred hours in the libraries of five countries researching into the loss of the *Girona*.

Stenuit weighed all the evidence he had collected, and dismissed the official reports on the grounds that the English spies had been told lies to conceal the recovery of some of the treasure. He found there was a Spaniard Rock, a Spaniard Cave and of course Port-na-Spagna. So Stenuit preferred to rely on local tradition, dived near Port-na-Spagna, and within an hour had found the *Girona*.

Telling a BS-AC conference at Brighton about this, Stenuit said:

The bottom when we dived first was extremely difficult to see because we arrived there in late April – visibility was very poor – kelp was covering everything and made it very difficult to see even such large objects as cannons or anchors. Large piles of boulders covered every-thing that might have been seen.

The first object I saw, was a large whitish 'pig' of lead. I turned it over and I saw stamped on it five crosses of Jerusalem. I knew then that I had found the *Girona*. Then I found a few grey pebbles which on closer inspection turned out to be pieces of eight. Right there – just lying there among the rocks – waiting for someone to pick them up.

Then Stenuit and his team of divers started really to find things on that tumbled bottom. They found an anchor, then in a cave, in which objects seem to have been piled up by storm surge, came the first of the real treasures, a gold chain and jewellery. During that first expedition in 1967 – it only lasted two weeks – Stenuit discovered enough to show that he had made one of the major archaeological finds around the coasts of Britain. Enough to show too that the site of the sinking of the *Girona* had all the signs of becoming one of the great treasure finds around our coasts.

After two weeks of diving Stenuit returned to Belgium and kept his secret well. In April 1968 he returned with another expedition, this time fully equipped to cope with the conditions that existed on the site. Now the expedition was working from two large inflatable boats, and had four highly competent divers and support equipment including compressors. They started diving at the end of April and conditions were very bad. Stenuit remembers the hailstones, being frozen before diving, and being so cold in the water that they could only work for three-quarters of an hour each day.

The first task was to make an accurate map of the bottom. This they did, and then each artefact they found was carefully plotted on to it. They found and raised the anchor by means of inflatable bags, and towed it to shore. Some parts of the rocky bottom contained large pockets of sand. These had to be sifted through. Slowly, as the season progressed, the water grew warmer, until towards the end of that season's expediton they were working five or six hours a day. The water was shallow, which helped – some twenty to thirty feet only.

Much of the *Girona's* treasures were encrusted in a sort of black concretion. This was chipped away in lumps and raised, to be broken apart very carefully. From this black concretion came some cannon-balls, gold coins, jewels, lead shot and copper rods. Where there was no concretion the divers used a water pump powered by an engine in one of the boats to wash away the sediments.

They started finding silver and more gold coins. Then up came a gold salamander with rubies down its back. Ducats, pieces of eight . . . and then the pace hotted up. From finding gold coins one at a time, they discovered twenty or so together in one pocket of sand. Pestles, mortars, religious medals and forks (forty-eight of them – though before Stenuit's discovery they were not thought to have been in such general use) were found; and dolphins in the shape of supports for a silver clock, or in the form of a tooth-and-ear pick.

Many objects were badly damaged, and Stenuit knew this was because gale after gale over the centuries had moved the items around over the sea-bed. There were silver candlesticks, seals and twelve gold rings, most of them in excellent shape. One of the rings had two diamonds left in the setting. There was a touching inscription on another ring which displayed a heart held by a hand, and the words *No tengo mas que darte* (I have nothing more to give you). A silver crucifix . . . the divers worked on, but at the end of September the weather broke.

Stenuit and his divers returned to Belgium, but Stenuit was still too full of his ship to rest. He spent the winter deep in research on the arms on some of the jewellery he had recovered, matching them to the coats of arms of the knights who were known to have sailed with the Armada. Stenuit studied the background to the two small bronze guns they had raised in the summer. When the breech blocks were carefully opened at the Ulster Museum in Belfast, both guns were found to be loaded! He also thought that one of the other guns, a *medio sacre* (a large long-range cannon) was one of three taken by the Duke of Medina Sidonia from his own land artillery to equip the galleasses of the Armada. This was because the gun had a levelling device only used in land artillery. Stenuit believes that the fact they found so few cannon is accounted for by the fact that a great deal of the armament was jettisoned to make way for all those extra people.

Two astrolabes were also discovered – there are only abou*

twenty left in the world. Stenuit had also found a number of gold Spanish waistcoat buttons and compared them with those worn by Sir Francis Drake in a contemporary engraving. They were identical! 'So', he said, 'guess where Sir Francis got them from!'

Research kept Stenuit busy all winter, but he and his divers returned to the site in the spring of 1969. With bigger lifting bags, they were now able to move boulders weighing as much as nine tons. And it was worth it. Day by day they began to build up a gold chain – at the rate of two links a day. The links were scattered far and wide, and some indication of the care that Stenuit's divers took to recover the tiniest objects can be judged by the fact that at the end of that expedition they had a chain a yard-and-a-half long. Then they found another, complete this time – three yards long – and another. In the end they had eight of them. These chains were worn as a display of wealth, and also as a sort of instant cheque book. To pay a bill you merely twisted off the right number of links and handed them over.

They found pewter plate, more rings, gold jewellery in the shape of a book (see plate 6), 115 copper coins, silver coins, 756 of them in denominations of two reales, four reales and eight reales (pieces of eight); ducats . . . and then 405 gold coins, all of which were in excellent condition. Some of the silver coins had suffered badly – escudos, and one coin from Naples so rare that Stenuit could not find it in any of the special publications he studied.

Some further indication of the way the divers were cleaning the sea-bed of even the tiniest artefacts comes when you know that in the first year of Stenuit's work on the *Girona* they found six gold frames, some complete with their lapis lazuli cameos, and then went on in the second year to find another five. Stenuit suspects the cameos were a set of twelve, and sounds vaguely surprised that his intense search of the sea-bed failed to reveal the twelfth! The cameos are of Byzantine emperors.

I have only given an indication here of the importance of Stenuit's discoveries – and the thousands of items they found. After all his hard work Stenuit was naturally anxious that the items from the *Girona* should not be split up and sold with some artefacts ending up isolated in various collections all over the world.

He said: 'I am trying very hard to see that the Ulster Museum will be able to purchase and keep the whole collection in a special room which is waiting for them. I think it would be a fitting place for the collection to stay for ever.' Fortunately Ulster did just that. The Ulster Museum has now been able to buy the *Girona* Collection, and to keep all the items together for display to the general public.

They paid £132,000 for the *Girona* material to the Department of Trade and Industry. The reason for this is that, since no owner could be produced for the material, the Department of Trade and Industry, to whom the Receiver of Wreck is responsible, became custodians of the finds for the Crown. Out of the £132,000 the Ulster Museum deducted their expenses for conservation of much of the material and Robert Stenuit and his team were then paid their entitlement as salvors for over six thousand hours of diving and ten thousand items recovered.

If you think that is a lot of money to pay for treasures like this from the sea, then you will not be upset when similar priceless collections are broken up into lots as small as one single coin and auctioned to the highest bidder. You will not be upset either that the impact of the whole array of recovered objects from a single wreck is completely lost and dispersed to the four corners of the earth never to be brought together again. If you are not upset . . . then you should be!

No record of the Armada would be complete without some reference to the mystery of the Tobermory galleon, so called because there is no doubt that under the mud of the bay on the Isle of Mull, Scotland, lies a ship which was blown up and sank in 1588. But what ship was she? Up from the wreck over the centuries have come bronze cannon, nearly a dozen, some of French make, breech blocks, cannon-balls, pewter plate and gold coins. Beating all the divers and salvors was the Tobermory mud. Her name has variously been given as the *Florencia* or the *Duque de Florencia*, which sets quite a puzzle because the *Florencia* is listed as returning safely to Spain.

Latest diver to work the wreck is ex-navy Commander John Grattan, who organized the swim-line search for the *Santa Maria de la Rosa* about which you have read earlier in this chapter. He has a contract with the Duke of Argyll to search for and salvage the wreck and has had great success compared with the attempts of many previous salvors in that he has actually relocated the wreck.

The bottom of the bay is pitted and cratered with the attempts of those earlier treasure hunters – for the Tobermory galleon is said to have carried fantastic wealth – and practically nil visibility does not help much when you tackle Tobermory mud. John Grattan however had the idea of using a special anti-mud weapon which he calls 'The Nudger', possibly because not only does it nudge the mud away like mad, but it will do the same to any diver foolish enough to get in the way of the 1,400 gallons a minute which pour out of the 2-inch venturi tube snout of his underwater water pump at a pressure of 250 pounds per square inch. Using the Nudger he cut through the 22 feet of mud – 60 feet down – that covered the area he wished to search, but then found to his horror that the Tombermory mud will allow penetration into it until the walls of the hole are 17 feet high vertically – and then collapse! After blasting away the mud the divers used steel probes until they found what they were looking for and then finally dug down carefully until they exposed a small area of what was without doubt ancient decking.

At the time of writing, there the matter rests. John Grattan dives on.

Postscript: I hesitate to put into the Armada the discoveries of the RAF Sub-Aqua Association, (largely made up of RAF branches of the B S-A C), off Frenchman's Rock on the Isle of Islay, Scotland, for the simple reason that it is at the moment impossible to prove this site to be that of an Armada shipwreck. The RAF divers, who come from Hendon, Northolt, and West Drayton, have found iron cannon, swivel guns, and heaps of grape and bar shot. The site is shallow, difficult and dangerous, and as I write, there is no conclusive dating evidence.

FIVE

'Hang Them from the Yard-Arm'

Lost at sea	On land
1588 Armada ships:	*Elizabeth I reigns*
El Gran Grifon	*Shakespeare in London*
La Trinidad Valencera	*Execution of Mary Stuart*
San Pedro el Mayor	*Defeat of Armada celebrated*

Francis Drake saw his opportunity and seized it. As the Armada hulk *El Gran Grifon* straggled through the small swell behind the tip of the Spanish fleet's crescent formation, Drake swooped with all sails bent to take advantage of the light wind. The *Gran Grifon* saw the danger and struggled to rejoin the Spanish line. She was too late. Drake put *Revenge* on broadside course, gave her every gun, came about and gave her the other broadside. Then raked her again as he ran at 'half musket shot' distance across her stern. More English ships joined in, but though the *Gran Grifon*'s decks were now slippery with blood (some reports say that seventy were killed or wounded) and she had taken at least seventy balls in her hull, she finally managed to regain the main force.

The date was Wednesday, 3 August 1588. *El Gran Grifon* was never to see Spain again. This action near Portland Bill was only the beginning of her miseries. She fought again, after repairs, at Gravelines and then joined the fleeing Armada through the North Sea and up to the tip of Scotland.

On 20 August the Armada passed between Ronaldsay and Fair Isle and the *Gran Grifon* was no longer with them. On the night of the seventeenth they had run into squally weather and in the dawn the *Gran Grifon* had gone. In fact she was still in company with three other Spanish ships, the *Barca de Amburgo* and the *Castille Negro*, two other hulks and the big Venetian *La Trinidad*

Valencera whose adventures we will follow later. For a fortnight the four ships struggled on against headwinds. On 1 September the *Amburgo* signalled she was sinking and her crew was transferred into the *Gran Grifon* and the *Valencera*, with the last named taking the majority of her company of 250 men.

On 5 September at dawn the *Gran Grifon* found herself alone. The *Castille Negro* had disappeared – we do not know what happened to her – and the *Valencera* was heading for shelter. The *Gran Grifon* beat south-west into the Atlantic and on 7 September ran into a great storm.

It is interesting to note here when talking about the terrible weather that the Armada encountered that it was not until the North Sea oil industry became really established that the London Weather Centre issued wave-height warnings. The oil men had scoffed at Mr Laurie Draper of the Institute of Oceanography's predictions that extreme waves could occur even in the comparatively sheltered (from the North Atlantic, that is) waters of the North Sea. Mr Draper said that over a fifty-year period the waves in the North Sea might on occasions reach a height of ninety or a hundred feet. Now that sixty-five-foot waves have already been experienced, they are not scoffing any more. A chart of predicted possible heights produced by Mr Draper in 1971 shows clearly that the course the Armada took down from the Shetlands to southern Ireland could be subject to waves of 110 feet. That sort of wave height does put a new complexion on discussions of the fantastic storms that the Armada undoubtedly met.

The great storm which the *Gran Grifon* encountered early that September must have been a monster. Her seams already weakened by battle damage opened up so much that you could insert your hand into the gaps. In his excellent book *Full Fathom Five* about the wrecks of the Spanish Armada (published by Chatto and Windus), archaeologist Colin Martin quotes from the diary of a survivor among the *Gran Grifon*'s complement. The *Gran Grifon* ran out to St Kilda, then down to Galway Bay but then the wind switched and blew them right back to Scotland. Wrote the survivor: 'We were fit only to die, for the wind was so strong and the sea so wild that the waves mounted to the skies, knocking the ship about so that the men were all exhausted, and yet unable to keep down the water that leaked through our gaping seams.'

The wind was now astern and the *Gran Grifon* ran before it. This gave them an opportunity to patch the holes with ox-hides and planks. So they ran until 23 September. Then the wind switched again and they decided to try to reach Scotland. Finally an island loomed up and they determined to land at all costs. On the twenty-seventh of the month the end, thought the diarist, was near.

In fear of the heavy sea we tried to get near the island again, but after trying for four hours we found it impossible. The sea kept giving us such dreadful blows, that truly our one thought was that our lives were ended, and each one of us reconciled himself to God as well as he could, and prepared for the long, long journey that seemed inevitable. As to force the hulk any more would only have ended it and our lives the sooner, we determined to cease our efforts.

The poor soldiers too, lost all spirit to work at the pumps. The two companies – 230 men in all, and 40 we had taken from the other ship had pumped incessantly and worked with buckets, but the water still increased, till there were thirteen spans over the carlings and all efforts failed to reduce it an inch. So we gave way to despair, and each one of us called upon the Virgin Mary to be our intermediary in so bitter a pass; and we looked towards the land with full eyes and hearts as the reader may imagine. And God send that he may be able to imagine the smallest part of what it was like, for after all there is a great difference between those who suffer and those who look upon suffering from afar off.

That is, I think, one of the finest descriptions of despair at sea that I have ever read. And what insight into human nature is revealed in that one sentence about what it is like to suffer and what it is like to read about it!

Colin Martin thinks the diarist may have been Juan Gomez de Medina, whose flagship *El Gran Grifon* was. From it he had commanded all the *urcas* or hulks. Whoever he was, he wrote with great authority about all the troubles that befell the ship:

At last – when we thought all hope was gone, except through God and his holy Mother, who never fails those who call upon him – at two o'clock in the afternoon we sighted an island ahead of us. This was Fair Isle, where we arrived at sunset, much consoled, though we saw we should still have to suffer. But anything was better than drinking salt water. We anchored in a sheltered spot we found, this day of our great peril, 27th September 1588.

For what happened to the ship then, we have to rely on local legend, which says the ship reached Stroms Hellier Cove and that most of the crew escaped to safety when she foundered by climbing from masts and rigging on to the cliffs. They were repatriated to Spain after nearly starving on the island for six weeks during which time some fifty Spaniards are said to have died.

Then Colin Martin and Syd Wignall decided to look for the wreck. On Colin's third dive he found a bronze cannon. Then he and Syd Wignall found more guns, iron this time. And then lead ingots, ingots just like the six that they had found on the *Santa Maria de la Rosa* and just like those Robert Stenuit had found on the *Girona*. Alan Bax arrived and he and Colin Martin surveyed the site. Expedition followed expedition. They found broken pieces of guns, breech blocks from swivel guns, cannon-balls, bar shot, over four thousand musket balls, a leaden seal bearing the arms of Philip II, a rudder pintle and a solitary four-real silver coin, close to a tempered steel blade, which may well have come from Castile.

And then they made a very significant discovery – while they were cataloguing the finds in the County Museum at Lerwick, where curator Tom Henderson was conserving the material. As they counted out the great pile of lead musket shot, they found about a dozen which had been splayed out and flattened on one side. Anyone who has recovered bullets even in modern wars will know what that means – the shot had been fired. Such marking could only have come from the balls hitting a solid object. Beyond doubt these bullets must have been English and probably fired from Drake's *Revenge* in that pass across the stern at 'half musket shot' in August 1588. They had penetrated deeply into the *Gran Grifon*'s timbers only to fall out when the ship disintegrated as she sank on Fair Isle.

Some sort of myth seems to have grown up around the story of the Armada that it was the sea that beat them, not the English ships. In fact the Duke of Medina Sidonia had lost seven of his best ships before he even escaped into the North Sea. All the great ships of Spain had been battered by the English ships – some have even been described as having blood running out of their scuppers, so great were the casualties on board. The duke himself had a wound in the thigh, and men had been killed all around him.

Some idea of conditions on board the Armada ships can be gained by reading that on the morning of 9 August more than half the fleet had ignored the signal to face the enemy once again. And the duke had held a court-martial on board and sentenced twenty captains to be hanged. Only one was in fact hanged and paraded through the fleet at the yard-arm of a pinnace *pour encourager les autres*; the others were removed from their ships and given into custody of the Judge Advocate General.

Such tactics of course did nothing to raise morale and, when the final tests came for many of the ships as they turned down the west coast of Ireland and ran straight into gales, it is not surprising that some ignored orders to give Ireland a wide berth and headed for what shelter they could find.

So it was with *La Trinidad Valencera*, an armed merchantman of eleven hundred tons. She had kept company with *El Gran Grifon*, but now it was all too much. She was leaking badly, her storerooms were already flooded and, as there seemed no likelihood of stopping the flow of water into her, her commander Don Alonso de Luzon ordered her master Don Beltran de Salto to find what shelter he could in Irish waters. On 14 September 1588 *La Trinidad Valencera* sailed into Inishtrahull Sound and ran up along the coast of Inishowen still driven on by a westerly gale. Her search for shelter finally ended in the haven of Glenagivney Bay where, with much thanks, her anchors were dropped. But even at anchor her pumps were needed to keep her afloat.

The ship was originally a Venetian merchantman and had belonged to the Grand Duke of Tuscany. Her name then was the *Balanzara*. She was in Lisbon with a full cargo of merchandise when she was commandeered under the Duke of Medina Sidonia's orders, renamed *La Trinidad Valencera* and made part of the Armada. As a warship she carried 360 men and was heavily armed with forty-two cannon. But by the time she dropped anchor in Glenagivney Bay she had far more than that aboard. Off the north coast of Donegal you will remember she had picked up most of the crew of another Armada ship, which was foundering, the transport *La Barca de Amburgo*. In fact on board her by the time she reached shelter were nearly six hundred men.

It is understandable that the first action after reaching the anchorage was to start ferrying some of the men ashore. At first all they had with which to ferry themselves ashore were two small boats, but as time passed local boats joined in and the shuttle service went back and forth for almost two whole days. As the number of people on board got smaller, so did the efforts on the pumps. Finally pumping stopped altogether. When it did so, the water gurgled steadily into the holds and then, with a sudden lurch – which probably caught the rest on board by surprise – the *Trinidad* settled down to the sea-bed. Despite this gentle end to the ship, some reports say that forty men were drowned when she sank.

The same reports put the number of those brought to shore safely at 540. These men under the command of Don Alonso were directed by the local people to the house of the Catholic Bishop of Derry Dr Reamonn O'Gallagher, who was known to be active in helping Armada survivors. But they never got there. On their march they came up against some of the Queen's forces, about six hundred men under the command of Richard and Henry Hovenden, who were the Earl of Tyrone's foster-brothers. After a small skirmish and a great deal of parleying, the Spaniards, under promise of fair treatment, laid down their arms and were then robbed of anything they had of value.

The next day the Spanish officers, including Don Alonso, were taken aside and the rest of the Spaniards lined up in a field. At a signal the troops set upon the defenceless men and massacred them – one description says that the infantry were on one side of the field and the cavalry on the other; between them the slaughter took place. Three hundred were killed on the spot, but about 150 escaped by running through a bog where the troops dared not follow. The survivors were brought by local people to the bishop, who sent some on to Mac Sweeney at Doe Castle and the others to Sorley Boy (who figures in the *Girona* story – see chapter 4). About forty-five officers were taken to Drogheda. Some died on the way or in prison. The rest, Don Alonso still among them, were taken to England and were later ransomed. And the wreck of *La Trinidad Valencera* settled deeper into the sandy sea-bed to which she had sunk. . . .

On 11 January 1971 there was nothing unusual about the training night of the City of Derry s-a c at the local baths which they used for getting beginners accustomed to the aqualung. These baths nights are the usual thing with any sub-aqua club. Though they are used most importantly for training beginners, they are also a meeting-place for all the club's trained divers. If they are not training others, they gossip among themselves. And in this gossip details of dives, wrecks and other underwater information are passed back and forth among the members. Now the Londonderry divers have always been interested in wrecks in their area, just like any other group of divers all over Britain and for that matter the world.

They had always known about the *Valencera*. They knew too that her wreckage should be in Glenagivney Bay. All their research showed this – as did many hours of discussion with the local fishermen of the area. The Londonderry divers found it difficult to decide whether the stories the locals told were indeed folklore handed down from generation to generation or whether they were based on information sown in the locals' minds by other researchers who had visited the bay over the years in search of the wreck. However two years ago the club decided to start serious searchwork in the bay to try to find the *Valencera*. All their searches failed. Many a dive came to nothing, and they began to wonder if there really was anything left to find.

But that January night at the baths was different. (Not that the divers knew it at the time.) Their diving officer 'Charlie' Perkinson pinned up, as he had many times before, a list of dives for those training to qualify for 'club diver' standard. On 20 February 1971 thirteen divers turned up for the training dive. Paddy Stewart was one; Archie Jack was another. They were swimming along quite normally when suddenly they came face to face with the muzzle of a cannon sticking out of a rock crevice. 'Ready for firing' was their description when they surfaced. Both men saw it at the same time, and almost swallowed their mouthpieces with surprise. Though this dive had been scheduled as a search for the *Valencera*, no one seriously believed they would find it – after all there had been many dives before in the same area which had produced nothing.

Jack and Stewart called the other divers over to witness the cannon. Careful bearings were taken from the surface. The moment the team was ashore 'Charlie' Perkinson held an impromptu meeting at which it was decided that the find should be kept a secret between the thirteen of them until the legal aspects of the wreck could be sorted out. It says much for these thirteen men that the secret was kept for two weeks until the legal problems were sorted out, though each one was bursting to tell his diving friends the news. Finally on 2 March all the club's members were told and a press release was issued on 4 March.

From that moment on their find was public knowledge. But the Londonderry divers had organized themselves well. Their sixty members included many men with professional qualifications ideally suited to the task of carrying out a proper archaeological survey of the remains of the Armada ship. Right from the start the club had realized the historical importance of their find and established their claim to be 'salvor in possession' by buoying the wreck. Negotiations had begun with the Spanish government to acquire the rights to the wreck. They stressed to the Press, who descended on them, that their work was not a treasure hunt – pointing out the fact that the survivors had two days to get off the wreck, and it was hardly likely that they would have left any portable treasure such as coins or jewels aboard.

The thirteen divers who had been on the initial dive – C. H. Perkinson, Dr J. Whellan, G. Heatley, D. O'Donnell, J. Sculltock, C. Villa, J. Kydd, Father Michael Keavney, P. Stewart, A. Jack, B. Mooney, A. Ashworth, E. Green (and seven-year-old Ross Perkinson, who had also gone on the trip) – had played their part by keeping the secret, but now they took an active role in the work of surveying the site.

The site is sheltered, facing due east with a slight diagonal current due to the tides. The depth is thirty feet to the sandy bed. The area is extremely well sheltered from the frequent west and north-west gales by cliffs. The east wind is a hazard in the bay, but it is less frequent and less severe. The divers had two ways of getting to the site. A sandy strand, served by a steep cliff road, was only four hundred yards from the site. The other route is by boat, and the nearest harbour is the fishing harbour six miles away at Glengad.

From the moment that the first cannon was found, it was clear to the Londonderry divers that there were many other artefacts present in the sand. Most seemed confined to an area of about two hundred square feet. Along the east side of the site are two ridges of rock with a gully some ten to twelve feet deep between them. Many objects were concentrated in this gully. Visibility is normally at least twenty feet.

The sand seemed to be the preservative on this site. In fact articles appeared and reappeared as the sand patterns shifted over the next few weeks. Even so objects were heavily covered with concretion, and one of the first finds was so thickly covered that the divers were convinced that they had found a swivel gun. They humped this piece of concretion from TV studio to TV studio, telling all Ireland that this was, so they thought, an Armada swivel gun. Later, when the concretion was gently tapped to remove the covering of the centuries, they had a swivel gun all right, but part of the shape also concealed a very well-preserved pair of navigational dividers. These were in such good condition that the original toolmaker's markings could be clearly seen.

Apart from the cannon the first finds were iron and stone cannon-balls, a pewter vase, a small piece of a pottery jar and various lumps of concretion, which remained to be broken open to find out the contents. But it was the cannon that were the real glory of the site. Though the *Valencera* was reported to be carrying forty-two cannon, other reports that came to light in the club's research suggested that a more correct figure would be thirty-two. And of these a good proportion were likely to be made of bronze.

The largest cannon made at that time would have been the 'whole cannon', which fired a 50-lb iron shot from a bore of $7\frac{1}{4}$ inches, was 12 feet long and weighed 4 tons. The *Valencera* was said to have carried four of these. The Londonderry divers in those first few weeks of exploring the site found one beauty – a whole cannon of bronze with a coat of arms – and what looked extremely like the breech of a second poking out of the sand. Several other bronze cannon were also just visible in the sand swells.

It is not surprising that the Derry divers lived, talked and dreamed nothing but Armada cannon. It is not given to many divers to make such a discovery in their diving lifetime, and naturally enough the divers revelled in it. They hoped that their discovery would contribute to research on the actual firepower of the Armada. But more was to come.

Though the City of Derry divers knew by now that they had made a major discovery of great archaeological importance, they really did not know how great until the arrival on the scene of one of the leading experts in the world of nautical archaeology to give them his opinion of their find.

The two men who know most about Armada wrecks in this country are Syd Wignall and Colin Martin. Both wrote to the committee set up by the Derry divers to handle their discovery. Both stressed the importance of raising the surface items only after they had been plotted in position on the initial survey. Two weeks before Easter 1971 the Derry divers had completed their survey work, locating buoying and plotting all visible items. Then they had a major problem – how were they to raise cannon weighing three-and-a-half tons and get them ashore where they could be properly handled?

Finally this was solved when the chairman of the salvage committee, Andy Robinson, found a trawler skipper who could make the lift. Len Forbes, the skipper, was not the sort of man to be beaten by any Spanish cannon. At his home port of Portstewart in Northern Ireland, about twenty miles from Glenagivney Bay, he got a derrick from a scrap-yard. With this and a hand-winch he rigged up a lifting system, which proved very successful. So successful in fact that on the Tuesday before Easter a bronze culverin weighing one-and-a-half tons was raised with no trouble.

The trawler then sailed into the little port of Moville, and the first cannon to see the light of day since the sinking of *La Trinidad Valencera* was hoisted ashore by the local coal crane. The next day the first whole cannon was swung ashore. On the third day of the big lift the third cannon – another whole cannon – came ashore under the watchful camera eye of Colin Martin, who had now dropped all his earlier work to help with the survey of the site. On the Saturday the fourth cannon was brought safely in. This one was a beautiful culverin of Venetian origin.

Colin Martin's appreciation of the historical significance of the find submitted to the Committee for Nautical Archaeology after his visit to the site is of great importance. Here is an expert reporting on the value of what the Derry divers found:

Four bronze guns have now been raised. Two are a matching pair of $7\frac{3}{4}$ in. bore whole-cannons, with lifting and breech dolphins, both dated 1556 and bearing the full arms of Philip II encircled with the insignia of the Order of the Golden Fleece. The escutcheon is of particular interest in that it quarters the lions of England – an honour to which Philip was entitled for, at that date, he was married to Mary Tudor. The breech inscription, identical on each gun, reads:

IOANES MANRICVS A LARA FIERI CVRAVIT OPVS REGIMY DE HALVT
ANNO 1556

[Freely translated, this means: Juan Manrique de Lara [who was Captain General of the Spanish Artillery] had the cannon made by Remigy de Halut [a famous cannon-founder with workshops at Malines near Antwerp].]

One of these guns is in near perfect condition, having been totally buried in sand; the other, which had been exposed directly to seawater, is somewhat defaced by surface corrosion.

It is premature to attempt to identify the other two guns with any certainty, but both are long small-bore 'culverin' types, and appear to be Italian in character. It may not be over fanciful to suggest that these might be guns from the ship's own armament, while the whole-cannons are more likely to be part of the ship's increment of ten added at Lisbon. Don Alonso de Luzon, in his interrogation, states that the ship carried 32 pieces of brass and iron (evidently he is here recalling the figure of her original armament, if the patently more reliable figure of the Lisbon muster is accepted) 'whereof 4 were cannons of brass; but what kinds the rest were how many of brass, or how many of iron, he knoweth not, neither whether the same will be saved or not'.

Don Alonso seems remarkably ignorant of the technicalities of his ship's armament on this reckoning, but then he was a soldier, and may have held things nautical in some contempt; then again, he may have wished to impart to the English no more information of this kind than he had to. Whatever type and number of guns the ship actually carried, it is extremely probable that most or all of them lie today in the vicinity of the wreck.

The City of Derry Sub-Aqua Club does not intend to begin a systematic programme of excavation and recovery until a full survey has been carried out and adequate conservation facilities arranged. None the less, recoveries already made in the course of this survey indicate the character and condition of what is to be found on the site. Roundshot – stone and iron – is numerous, and traces have been noted of musket and arquebus barrels. Pottery has survived well, and it is probable that whole vessels will lie buried in the sand. The greater part of a copper kettle has been found, crushed but restorable to its original shape. An almost complete pewter vessel has been recovered. Most startling of all is a pair of brass navigational dividers, found within the matrix of an iron concretion, which has survived in quite perfect working order for almost four centuries. It seems certain that all manner of artefacts – domestic, personal, military and maritime – lie in the sand, in an often remarkable state of preservation. It is, moreover, the more deeply buried and hence at present invisible objects which will have survived in the best condition of all.

In addition, traces have been noted of the ship and its fittings, and it will be surprising if sections of the lower hull do not remain, buried under sand and ballast. Already some large baulks of timber have been found, apparently jointed in some kind of structural sequence. At least one anchor has been discovered, together with iron components evidently from a capstan.

Without question this find is one of quite outstanding interest to maritime historians, archaeologists, and the public generally. The site can be expected to throw much light on the armament of the Spanish Armada, particulary with regard to the heavier battery pieces. A study of the structural remains will probably add technical detail to the knowledge of large sailing-ships at this critical period of their development. The fact that the ship is a Venetian one is particularly opportune, since much knowledge of contemporary Venetian shipwrightry has already been gleaned from documentary sources. The discovery of machinery – evidenced by the postulated capstan parts – may illuminate or even add to the knowledge of 16th century nautical technology.

From the social and military viewpoint, the site seems certain to contain a great quantity of well-preserved objects which can be expected to form a collection on a par, for example, with recoveries from the Roman frontier fort at Newstead in Scotland or the sunken 17th century city of Port Royal in Jamaica – a collection, that is, representing an entire community and its way of life. The museum possibilities of this are too obvious to stress. The story of this wreck, moreover, is so well documented in contemporary sources, and so many named individuals can be associated with her, that some of the discoveries are likely to bear direct links with events and people. . . .

Colin Martin was obviously impressed. But they still needed to know how much the sand concealed. The man who could answer this was the next to arrive on the scene. Jeremy Green is the expert in the use of complicated instruments that will tell you what is concealed in just such a site as the Derry divers had found. He is the expert in this country on metal-detection on marine archaeological sites. He spent six days on the *Trinidad* site and his survey revealed that in an area of two hundred square feet was the biggest collection of Armada objects ever discovered. Such richness is perhaps best illustrated by the fact that after the divers had raised one of the whole cannon, they found in the sand where she had been lying a brass latch-cover which was designed to keep the touchhole dry – and it fitted back perfectly!

In the very beginning as soon as I heard of the discovery I was able to interest my friends, the late Paul Johnstone and Ray Sutcliffe of the BBC's superb *Chronicle* programme in the work of the Derry divers and to everyone's delight the BBC produced a splendid television film showing how amateur divers could be entrusted with such important archaeological work. That film is now a classic and the name of the Derry divers, their restraint and their care, is without peer in archaeological circles. They did more for the cause of amateur diving in the archaeological field than practically any other project so far attempted.

The work went on. But money problems have dogged the work as its importance grew and grew. The B S-A C has given hundreds of pounds to help with conservation work. So have the British Academy, the Irish Society, the City of London and the New University of Ulster. Conservation help came from Magee University College, the National Museum of Antiquities of Scotland and the Ulster Museum. Colin Martin of the St Andrews Institute of Maritime Archaeology has worked without fail to help the conservation of the objects discovered. And Ray Sutcliffe has taken the BBC *Chronicle* team back to the site to film more of the Derry divers' work and so contribute to the cost of the diving.

The *St Andrews Newsletter* of 1976 reports:

A ten week season of this Armada wreck off the coast of Donegal was completed in August by the City of Derry Sub-Aqua Club working under the guidance and direction of the Institute. Excavations revealed a number of widely scattered ship's timbers, though no signs of any coherent structure. All the frames and planks examined had been iron bolted and not treenailed, which may explain the apparent total disintegration of the hull. It is known that the late 16th century Venetian merchant ships, such as this one was, were built for intensive service over a relatively short working life, and it is probable that within such a policy iron fastenings would have offered substantial advantages over wooden ones. Various fittings from standing and running rigging, some with associated cordage, were also found in good condition. Two of the ship's anchors have been studied *in situ*, and 3 metres of 40 cm hemp cable associated with one of them has been raised for further investigation.

Preliminary work on X-raying concretions preparatory to extricating their contents was carried out with the generous co-operation of the Radiology Department at Altnagelvin Hospital, Londonderry. Initial results are promising, although most concretions are being left *in situ* until more satisfactory facilities are available for dealing with them.

A considerable quantity of pottery was found, adding much of interest to an already substantial collection. In addition to a large variety of predominantly Iberian coarse wares pieces of Italian majolica and Chinese porcelain have been noted. Pewter plates, beakers, a flagon, a spoon, a candlestick and a small chalice have also been found. Copper utensils include a variety of handles and lids, and a complete bucket into which had been packed a steel helmet and a pewter plate. Among the small finds are two religious medals, two copper coins, a glass bead and a bottle neck, a brass key, and various brass fittings from arms and clothing.

Although known organic deposits were deliberately avoided, two small pockets were encountered. Among the objects recovered from them were several leather water bottles, two wooden spoons, and the well preserved fingerboard of a cittern.

But all this does not solve the huge financial problems of properly excavating the site. It seems sad that it may be that some of the artefacts will have to be sold to pay for the conservation of the rest.

The *San Pedro el Mayor* was a hospital ship of medium size, about 550 tons burden. She had left Spain with the rest of the Armada with thirty sailors and one hundred soldiers on board – and some fifty others whose task was to tend the sick and organize the hospital. She was an *urca*, or hulk, a cargo-carrier which had been pressed into service, and was one of a squadron which had fourteen ships in it. They were slow compared to the galleons and galleasses, but were needed for the supplies they carried.

We know that the *San Pedro* was off Plymouth on 21 July 1588 during the first skirmishes – and three months later she was back again. But she was no longer the ship she had been. In that dreadful journey round the British Isles, with the wounded and dying who had been transferred to her during the battles and afterwards, her captain and crew abandoned all hope.

This despair is the only thing that can account for the fact that after leaving Ireland she turned east in search of any port, English or French – anywhere in fact where she could seek shelter and help. With the south-westerlies still behind her, she was blown into the Channel. There were fewer and fewer left on board with the strength to control her. Finally there were not enough even to cope with the sails and tackle. Hither and thither she was blown, until she was heading straight for the nest of her enemies, Plymouth. Then the wind shifted a little and she came into Bigbury Bay and then, with no control at all, into Hope Cove. And there on the Shippen Rock her voyage ended. Soon she was a complete wreck, and the dead and dying went down with her. Out of the original 180 men, only forty survived. What about all the sick and wounded who were taken aboard her during the battles? That alone gives you some idea of the state the *San Pedro* was in before she hit in Hope Cove.

The 'search' of the survivors on first landing would account for the coins that have been found on the beach at Hope from time to time – they may have been trampled into the ground in the struggle for loot. Alternatively of course they could have come from the wreckage of the ship. There seems to be no positive evidence that parts of the ship did not sink intact to the bottom. In fact we have some evidence that large parts did find their way to the sea-bed. A diver, George Tessyman of Dartmouth, once found the frames or ribs of some ancient vessel there buried in the sand, but when he returned to the spot two weeks later to make a proper investigation a storm had shifted the sea-bed and, search as he might, he could not find the shipwreck again.

Much more recently John Humphreys, who runs the diving service Nautech from premises at Green Street Green, in Kent, and is a former diving officer of Bromley branch of the B S-A C, had a strange tale to tell of a dive in Hope Cove. He dived in the Cove without knowing the story of the *San Pedro*. He swam from Outer Hope towards the bay and around the Shippen Rock. He found that the rock and shale bottom finished in a line with the seaward end of the harbour wall and there the sand began. He reports:

At this spot, which was only about ten feet deep, there was a shelf – I thought it was rock at first – covered with kelp, and to the best of my memory about twenty yards long.

I particularly remember the scour on the beach side, which was filled with dead spider crabs which the local fishermen had rejected from their catch. Later that year I read an account of the wreck and like many other divers I decided that the next time I returned to Hope I would have a closer look. The next opportunity to do this was some time later and I found the same shale and rock bottom around the Shippen, but the ledge near the end of the wall had disappeared! Obviously the sand had shifted and covered it. As the only place a wreck can hide there is under the sand – and the sand in Hope Cove does shift about – it seems logical to me that she is down there almost within wading distance of the quay.

SIX

'Barres of silver have latelie bin found'

Lost at sea	On land
1617 The Great Silver Wreck near Kynance Cove in Cornwall	James I reigns
	Thirty Years War starts
	Charles I reigns
1667 Santo Christo De Castello near Mullion, Cornwall	Civil War
	Charles I executed
	Oliver Cromwell, Lord Protector
1675 Royal Yacht Mary on passage from Dublin to Chester, on the Anglesey Skerries	Charles II reigns
	Fire of London
	Milton writes Paradise Lost
	Bunyan writes Pilgrim's Progress

Treasure! That is what every wreck diver is expected to discover under the sea. The plain truth is that most divers will spend their entire underwater lifetime on the sea-bed without finding, or expecting to find, any such thing. The discovery of a treasure wreck is something that happens to someone else, but never to you. That is most divers' experience.

Some are happy to have found a wreck that no one else has found before. Many others dive on wrecks that are well known and find their thrill, not in cascades of pieces of eight, but in merely seeing a sunken ship under water. Yet others spend hours of their precious airtime under water in surveying and measuring a wreck which though historic is known not to have been carrying anything of great value. All have found their treasure in their own separate ways.

Yet there are some divers who experience that once-in-a-thousand lifetimes thrill of actually handling a coin, or even better a silver or gold bar, under water. Such a one is Richard Larn, known more simply to divers throughout the country as Dick. He runs a professional diving school – Pro-Dive in St Austell, Cornwall. He is an ex-Royal Navy petty officer and diver, but more importantly for this book he is one of the best-known archaeological wreck divers in this country. Add to that qualification that he is a prolific author of books about wrecks, and that his wreck files are very good indeed, and you have something of the measure of the man. He seems to specialize in discovering or working on wrecks of the sixteenth or seventeenth century, but though at first I found this puzzling it is now clear that he is based in an area of this country which probably has more wrecks than any other part of Britain and so he has more chance of discovering wrecks of that period.

If Cornwall is Dick Larn's home, it is also the home of more legends, stories and gossip about treasure (remember the Scillies count as Cornwall!) than any other county in England, though Devon and the Shetlands run it pretty close. Mounts Bay, at the extreme south-western corner of the Cornish peninsula, is accredited with at least four major treasure ships, one of which is reported to have carried silver coin weighing as much as nineteen tons! Legends about Gunwalloe Cove for example abound and I have seen coins found on the beach. If you go there you can see the remains of tunnelling out under the sea to reach what was described as a treasure ship with so much aboard that the coins fell into the tunnel in a shower. Unfortunately the sea poured in at the same time so we have only the words of the miners who barely escaped with their lives to take for it! Gunwalloe is a good treasure spot. The Duke of Cumberland's prize ship, sent home from the Azores in 1589 with cargo then valued at £100,000, is somewhere on the sea-bed in the area.

Read then what Dick Larn has to say about the area and the discovery of a real treasure ship:

The Lizard, the most southerly point of the British mainland, is a rocky headland which has been a hazard to shipping for as long as men have sailed the sea. In 1570 Sir John Killigrew petitioned Queen Elizabeth I for permission to erect a lighthouse there. His infamous reputation for piracy and smuggling cast doubts on his motives, which were undoubtedly more mercenary than humanitarian, and his application was refused. Forty-eight years later, another Sir John, son and heir to the estate, renewed the appeal, quoting several shipwrecks which he maintained could have been averted had his father been allowed to proceed with his beacon. Although strongly opposed by the Trinity Brethren, the project received royal consent, and the fire was lit in 1618. Even before that first winter was over, the proprietor was complaining to Lord Dudley Carleton of the cost, and in a particular letter dated 17 February 1619, stated that the beacon consumed '10 shillings in a stormie night'. It had been the intention to levy $\frac{1}{2}$d a ton on every vessel that passed the Lizard and hence benefited by its beacon, but unless ships were stopped and boarded in the channel, there was no practical method whereby light dues could be collected.

In desperation, Killigrew again petitioned Lord Carleton, now English ambassador to the United Provinces of Holland, seeking funds, claiming that it was they, the Dutch, who lost the most ships, and who therefore should contribute the most to help reduce the losses. Such suggestions were nothing new, the same argument having been employed when the Killigrews wanted to build a beacon on the Goodwin Sands as well, some years previously, a petition which also evoked no response. By March 1619, with the Lizard beacon consuming vast quantities of coal, and still no income, more correspondence passed between Falmouth and Holland, attempting to substantiate the many claims made as to the frequency of shipwrecks. Killigrew wrote: 'According to yor comand I have sent such testimonies as at present I can gett, nether is yt possibell to gett parfitt notice of whence and what the ships are that yearly do suffer on and neer the Lizard, for yt is sildom that anie man scapes and the ships split in small peeces, I assure yor Lo'ship that most of the houses neer the Lizard are built with the ruins of ships.'

In a letter dated 17 February 1619, concerning Dutch shipping losses, Killigrew asserted: 'Amsterdam affirms that no knowen loss hath happened, I well know that within this ten yeare that nation hath lost neer that place £100,000.'

No actual details of individual ships are given, except for one, which was of exceptional value and importance, said to have been either Dutch or Spanish, en route to the Dutch States, and described by Killigrew as 'that which came from St Lucas, with barrs of silver and a quantity of reals of eight'. This was the vessel which was recorded in Cornwall's history as the 'great silver wreck', variously reported as having sunk on 'the Lizard'; on Bumble Rock; Polpeor Cove, and elsewhere, so that by the twentieth century there was no clear picture as to its true resting place, and whether or not it really was a treasure ship.

Three hundred and fifty-one years later, during the summer of 1968, the Lizard claimed another victim, the last to date, a relatively small trawler named *Kerris Reed*, which sank almost on top of the silver ship of

1617, although some time was to elapse before this fact was appreciated. When she broke away from her tow in the night, the *Kerris Reed* drifted past the outlying reefs of the Lizard, and into Kynance Cove, where she foundered under the high cliffs, near the Rill. No one saw her go down, and it was pure chance that a Cadgwith fisherman spotted the wreckage beneath the surface whilst 'shooting' crab-pots. By the time a group, consisting of Roy Davis, Brian Smith, Ted Nicklin and myself had dived on the site, which lay in less than thirty feet, the trawler was already smashed to pieces, and of little interest. Twelve months later, the wreck was found to be completely engulfed in sand, and the incident was forgotten.

Five more years passed, without a thought for the *Kerris Reed*, until the partners of the Lizard Diving Centre, Mike Hall and Ken Simpson, asked for its location. Their visit to the site coincided with a timely, if not providential sea-bed movement of sand, so that where there had been a flat sandy bottom, they found a steep, boulder-strewn slope. Reduced by the sea to small fragments, the trawler wreck was of no value or interest, so Ken Simpson turned away, and swam over the slope towards the Rill. As he passed slowly along the bottom, the exhaust bubbles from his aqualung clearly marked his progress on the surface. When less than a hundred feet from the *Kerris Reed*, Mike Hall, in the boat, noticed the divers' progress had stopped, and that for some time a great 'splurge' of bubbles indicated hard physical effort – or sheer excitement, then Ken surfaced. He passed into the boat a great handful of flat black pebbles, or what at first glance appeared to be pebbles, until closer inspection showed them to be silver coins, Mexican 'cobs' or 'wedges', better known as 'pieces of eight'. With a calmness born of experience the diver announced, 'there's a cannon site alongside the *Kerris Reed* and there are coins concreted the length of one gun, and others – lots of others, loose in the sand and shingle'. In fact, that first day they recovered over two hundred such coins, and returned to the beach at Cadgwith elated, and somewhat stunned by what they had found.

The partners involvement with a sport diving centre, plus other commitments, and the constant worry that someone else might notice their activities, and stumble on the site after they had left, made them decide to make only random, infrequent return visits. It was quickly evident that whatever weather condition had removed the sand was in reverse, and that deep sand was already encroaching. Within only a matter of weeks the entire site was once again buried to a depth of several feet, but the total number of coins salvaged was now close to seven hundred. Uncertain as to the best course of action, Ken and Mike sought the advice and help of Roy Davis and myself. Within a relatively short period of time, an application was made and approved, for the site to be designated as an historic shipwreck, by the Secretary of State, so that now the wreck had both the protection of law, and some six feet of sand!

Identification of the wreck was now of paramount importance. The only significant clues came from the coins themselves, the dates of which ranged from 1598 to 1614, with mint marks of Mexico, Potosi, Seville, Granada and Toledo. Fortunately, the team had the benefit of an extensive card index system and notes, made when one member wrote a history of local shipwreck, and hence some ground work had already been completed. Slowly, there emerged from the archives, both in London and Truro, an incredible mass of correspondence for the only wreck which fitted the clues, the 'great silver ship'.

The earliest correspondence relating to the wreck is dated March 1618, so that reference to the salvage of silver bars must be to work carried out the previous summer. Thirteen months later, another letter mentions that 'barres of silver have latelie bin found, and divers other barres are supposed to lie as yet undiscovered in the same place', and suggests continuing efforts at recovery. Despite the remote nature of the site, there was strict control over salvage work, as is made clear when James I commanded Sir Francis Vivian, 'in the meantime you are to be carefull that noe other person or persons whatsoever be permitted to grabble or make search for the same.' Three bars recovered during 1620, weighed a total of 104 pounds, and were valued at £700, and as his one fourteenth share, William Robinson, who with his brother was sole salvor for a time, received £50. Other bars weighed as much as sixty pounds each, and it was one of these that some local men stole and smuggled over to Amsterdam, where Tristram Lord sold it for £200, of which £45 was his share – but unfortunately he was caught!

Slowly there unfolded an incredible story of intrigue, corruption, greed and collusion, involving two English kings, and many men in high places. Jacob Johnson, the famous seventeenth-century Dutch diver, attempted to use his skill at the Lizard, but despite his Admiralty warrant, which included a special clause to cover the great 'silver-wreck', the local inhabitants denied him access. It is interesting to note that Jacob, the diver, proceeded directly to Dartmouth from Cornwall, and there, 'in the sea without the Castle, dived and weyed five peeces of ordinaunce', which so upset the local council and mayor, they refused him permission to work there again. It would appear that his success was his undoing.

There is still much work to be done, both under water and on land in the archives. Only one cannon has been raised so far, this being an early, typical sixteenth century 'banded' gun. Other finds include lead sounding weights, lead bottle seals, buttons, shot, and a number of unidentified, brass artefacts. Until such time as the sea once again releases its hold on the 'great silver shop', the divers must be patient, and be satisfied with what they have achieved to date. But what happened at the Lizard is a pattern that must be repeated elsewhere, many times over, provided the enterprising diver can be there, when the sea-bed uncovers its secrets.

The movement of sand accounts for a number of the sudden discoveries of long lost wrecks. Dick Larn has been studying this over a long period and says that this is a particular feature of the entire coastline of Mounts Bay, Cornwall, from the Lizard to Lamorna Cove.

'Immense quantities, certainly in the order of millions of tons are either stripped from off the foreshore, or else deposited almost overnight, in a pattern which defies prediction,' he says. The sand appears generally to move in the opposite direction to the wind. A south-east gale will reduce the sand, but a south-west gale seems to bring in sand from deeper water.

Dick is using as his 'guinea-pig' wreck the small iron steamship *Grip* which was sunk in Gunwalloe Church Cove in February 1897. During Dick's study over the past twelve years the wreck has only been uncovered completely twice and then for a few weeks only. Then it vanishes again under fifteen to twenty feet of sand. During the time the *Grip* appeared so did three other cannon sites in the area and they were completely covered again before they could be surveyed.

Of course if this vast movement of sand could be predicted many more lost ships could be investigated by divers. In the case of the silver wreck of 1617 all the divers can do is to wait for another clearance of sand from the site as the labour involved in digging a hole some fifty feet in diameter and fifteen feet deep to survey a single square metre at the bottom is just not worth it. And it does not help either that even in calm weather a hole of this size is half filled in again overnight!

The diver's fingers were shaking with cold. He had been under water for two hours in the cold May sea off Cornwall. He fumbled inside the neoprene of the left wrist of his wet-suit and finally extracted the cause of his excitement. A silver disc slid down into the palm of his hand. As the two divers in the boat looked at the disc, the small boat lifted and fell in gentle swell under the Angrouse Cliffs of the Lizard peninsula. The diver with the silver disc in his hand was Dick Larn. The other, Peter McBride. Fumbly cold fingers rubbed at the muck on the face of the disc. Shapes became letters, letters joined into words and they could finally read the inscription: 'Ferdinand IV. Xung et Boh. Rex. Coren. in. Regem. Romanorvm. XYIII.IV.NY. MDCLIII', which, roughly translated, means, 'Ferdinand IV, crowned King of Bohemia and the Romans, 1653'.

'Christ,' said Dick Larn, 'that's old!' It was a statement of the obvious but he could not help it. It was not a coin. It was a coronation medallion, but it indicated that the divers had found another very old wreck indeed. It was not until their next visit, two days later, that they realized how fortunate they had been. A sewer outfall discharged directly over the site. 'By some freak combination of wind, sea, tide and the "inactivity" of the inhabitants of Mullion,' says Dick Larn, 'we had chosen the one day when conditions were perfect. Over the next two years, by which time we had a cumulative total of more than four hundred dives on the site, we never once encountered such visibility again!'

There were cannon on the site, but they were odd in that the majority had been worn down by the scouring action of shingle, so that only half of the barrels remained. The bore of each gun appeared as an open trough, in the breech end of which sat a cannon-ball, which oddly enough appeared to have suffered no erosion whatsoever. Another interesting feature of the cannon was the bed of solid 'concretion', ten or twelve inches thick, on which each gun was perched, and from which brass and copper artefacts protruded in abundance. In general the sea-bed was shingle. It was obvious that this was very deep in places and constantly on the move.

From Dick Larn's first brief period on the site, it appeared to him that the vessel had hit the cliffs beam-on and had sunk intact into this steepsided gully, and that a great deal of material probably lay covered by the shingle. The variety and quantity of the items found under the shingle was quite remarkable, considering the age of the wreck. For example Peter McBride located a bronze breech block from a cannon, two huge ingots of lead, each weighing some three hundred pounds, copper cakes and hundreds of pins. These were followed by Roy Davis, the third member of the team, uncovering several brass candlesticks, an iron knife, carpenter's chisel and gouge blades, and a variety of shot and musket-balls. Says Dick Larn:

By the spring of 1970 we had collected a great mass of information, but it was quite obvious that unless we had a major breakthrough in our work, we would never identify this wreck. For the period in question there is so little recorded information available, and with vessels being wrecked in Mounts Bay at regular intervals, no one bothered to make any special mention of this or any other particular loss.

We then made two finds which we felt sure would assist in the wreck's identification, but again we were to be disappointed. The first was a beautiful brass miniature saint with clasped hands, perfect in every detail, standing only two and a half inches tall; whilst the second was an intact pewter plate.

The plate was found beneath a large rock, buried deep in the only hole we had fully excavated until then. It was completely black with age, and folded in half, and the prospects of bending it out flat without causing it to crack were remote. There was a faint mark on the underside of the plate, but nothing visible on the upper surface – at least not on the part we could inspect.

Dick retained the plate in that condition for over a week, wanting to open it out, but afraid of the damage he might cause. Several silversmiths and antique-dealers were consulted, but none of them was prepared to attempt the task. In desperation he read up the details of pewter and decided that, if this was as old as he suspected, then it was good quality and would withstand some rough treatment. It took two days of gentle heating and bending, a fraction at a time, until he got it opened out, and then beaten flat so that the crease hardly showed. Not a crack appeared, and he was rewarded by the sight of a perfect minature crest on the rim. It depicted a Tudor rose, surmounted by a crown, within which were the initials HB. The maker's mark on the underside of the plate, an angel with outstretched wings, included the letters JB, and the divers felt sure that here was the vital clue they so badly needed. It was not to be. There are probably as many pewterers' marks recorded as there are hallmarks of silversmiths, if not more, yet among the thousands they consulted, none of them were identical with the one on the plate.

A number of small brass buttons were found too, all bearing the same Tudor rose as the crest, while the bowls of clay pipes marked EB were the work of one Edward Battle of Bristol in 1660, which suggests that the ship called either at Bristol to load, or at least in one of the West Country ports – perhaps Penzance or

Fowey. And everywhere on the wreck site they found brass pins. Thousands of them. So many that they called her 'the pin-wreck'.

It is quite remarkable that they had so many seemingly useful clues, yet were quite unable to establish the name, date or nationality of the vessel. But, after two years' continued research and work on the site, they discovered a possibility regarding her identity. This was a reference of 1669 to a ship described variously as a 'Dane', a 'Hamburger' and a 'Dutch ship of 500 tons, laden with masts, deals and provisions for the French Kings fleet.'

The last clue was to prove the most important. It is now eight years since the Mullion pin-wreck was first discovered, during which methodical salvage work by Peter McBride, who found the site, assisted by Dick Larn and Roy Davis, has continued. There is no doubt now that the 'pin-wreck' is that of the *Santo Christo de Castello*, which struck the high cliffs near Polurrian Cove on 7 October 1667, to become a total loss. Her captain, Giovanni Lorenzo Viviano, and most of the crew reached land safely in their own boats, but twenty-five men and women were drowned, which suggests she carried some passengers.

Work on the site has been a slow, painstaking process of locating the isolated pockets of rock hard concretion beneath the shingle. These are then released using small explosive charges, before being raised to the surface for examination. The majority of the artefacts recovered have direct Dutch connections, with no descrepancies in the identification of the vessel. The most attractive item is a bronze figure of a negro boy, some nine inches in height, carrying a roll of tobacco on the right shoulder, with the left hand holding a very long 'church-warden' type pipe. This was undoubtedly a trade sign, the sort of thing which would be found on a shop counter, in those early days of the tobacco habit.

Perhaps the most conclusive find was that of a single brass weight of four Amsterdam pounds, which bears a whole series of stamped 'check' dates. Possibly this was some sort of 'standard', which was submitted for testing to some official or department on an annual basis. The base of the weight is clearly marked 1652, 1654, 1655, 1659, 1662 and 1664. Why some years have been omitted is open to speculation; perhaps these were periods when the weight was in use on board ship, away from Amsterdam, or else lying unused in a company warehouse?

In 1975 the salvors of the *Santo Christo de Castello* were informed

by the Department of Trade and Industry that they could anti-
cipate a 95 per cent salvage award, and consequently they were
able to purchase the entire collection for £968, receiving most of
the money back in due course. Since then the entire collection has
been on show in the Royal Institute of Cornwall at Truro, and this
is one of the first occasions in the British Isles that amateur salvors
have purchased all their own material from a wreck, and then
placed it on long-term public display, a refreshing change from
the more usual practice of a collection going to auction, and being
spread all over the world.

Was she a young lady of noble birth? Or was she a prostitute
smuggled aboard to relieve the tedium of long, sea voyages? We
shall probably never know the answer, but we are sure she was
aboard on the last journey of the Royal Yacht *Mary* when she sank
on passage back from Ireland on 25 March 1675. Because divers
have found her bones. . . .

When Charles II returned to this country after eleven years in
exile he arrived back in England aboard a Dutch-built yacht of less
than a hundred tons. For reasons best known to himself, Charles
was so impressed by this particular vessel that he remarked that
he would have an identical one built for his own personal use. As
a diplomatic gesture, the magnificent yacht, built for the Prince of
Orange, was presented to the king in 1660 as a gift. Along with
the yacht went two ornamental bronze cannon, specially cast in
Amsterdam that year, but, since a king's ship justified more than
two guns, a matching set of eight smaller cannon were commanded of Sir William Compton, Master General of the Tower of
London. In due course these were cast and finished, then placed
aboard in late 1661.

Charles II chose the name Mary after his sister, the Princess
Royal, widow of William II of Orange, as a compliment to the
Dutch, and took possession, ensuring that every taste and luxury
was catered for aboard. The yacht, a 'smak', of 92 tons, measuring 67 feet overall, with an $18\frac{1}{2}$ foot beam, initially carried only the
ten bronze cannon, the Dutch guns measuring 5 feet 11 inches
long with a $3\frac{1}{2}$-inch bore, and the English guns 5 feet $0\frac{1}{2}$ inches
with a 3-inch bore, but in later years the vessel carried up to
twenty guns. She served the king for only about a year, after
which she passed into the hands of the navy, which used her as a

yacht on ceremonial occasions and a stores- or passenger-carrier between times, mostly between Ireland and Holyhead. It is therefore doubtful if either Nell Gwynne or Louise de Keroualle, Duchess of Portsmouth, ever had the pleasure of being entertained aboard!

In 1674, when she was still only fourteen years old, it was proposed that she be scrapped, but she was still in service on 25 March 1675 when she struck a rock and sank off the south side of the Anglesey Skerries, close to Holyhead, while returning from Ireland, drowning the Earl of Meath and thirty-four passengers and crew; the captain, twenty-three marines and two sailors were saved.

The site of the wreck was well known at the time, and in the Domestic State Papers at the Public Record Office there are many references, including one that states, 'a Welsh vessel saw the Mary underwater', but it would now appear certain that no salvage whatsoever was carried out until the present day. Bronze cannon have always been valuable, and would have been the first items recovered.

For the next 296 years the wreck lay undisturbed. Then in mid-July 1971 it was accidentally discovered by divers. Who found it first is in question, but certainly the Merseyside branch of the B s-A C consulted Dr Peter Davies of Liverpool University, the area representative for the Committee for Nautical Archaeology, and asked his advice. Dr Davies was able to get hold of eight cannon, and commence preservative treatment. Some of the guns are badly eroded or corroded and may well be beyond treatment.

A point worth noting at this stage is the fact that no one locally knew the name of the wreck. Newspaper accounts suggested she was a seventeenth-century privateer, but others shrewdly suggested a royal ship, and were not far wrong. Syd Wignall assisted in raising four of the cannon and then, in conjunction with Dr Davies, set about identifying the ship. Both Peter McBride and Dick Larn were approached, and within a few minutes simultaneously turned up the same name from their wreck files. This information, with details of the vessel's armament and construction, copies of her drawings and paintings of her at sea under sail, were all made available to Dr Davies, who decided to form a research group and pool everyone's know ledge. A great deal of the diving since then has been done by Chorley branch of the B S-A C. The site lies in thirty feet of water, and 211 silver coins of Elizabeth and Charles I, bar and round shot, musket-balls, lead ingots and pewter utensils have been recovered.

A great mound of ballast which was found was composed not only of lead blocks but of old iron shot, of a much larger calibre than the guns she carried. This was presumably because the necessary weight could not be achieved by using conventional shingle or stone. As already mentioned, a reference exists to the *Mary* carrying twenty guns, and this theory may be supported by the fact that the muzzle of at least one iron cannon protruded from the ballast heap. Nine bronze cannon have been raised.

There can be no argument that the *Mary* – since it was the first royal yacht – is of great historical interest. There are few wrecks so well documented, and every conceivable detail can be unearthed quite readily. Even conceivable detail that is except the identity of the young woman whose skull and bones were found in a concretion of iron cannon-balls, which probably protected the bones both chemically and physically.

The Department of Anatomy at the University of Liverpool has assembled enough of the bones recovered by divers to say that she was young, nineteen or twenty, and that she was indeed a woman, but apart from that neither the divers, nor the researchers nor the archaeologists can say anything more. The yacht was bound for the port of Chester from Dublin and it could be that the girl was just hitching a lift. Who knows?

Certainly the work on the *Mary* has gone extremely well, so well in fact that Dr Davies told me that he thinks it will only take another one or two seasons to complete and then the wreck site can be descheduled and open to all divers to explore. Mind you, if the archaeological divers have done their work as well as I suspect they have, there will be nothing left for other divers to find.

Do not think either that the hard work done by the *Mary* divers brought them any financial success. In fact, despite the fine collection of items recovered from the wreck, the divers tell me that they have not even recovered their out-of-pocket expenses from some of the items sold to the Merseyside County Museum. But, they add, they would not have missed taking part for the world!

SEVEN

'None of ye men saved butt five and a boy'

Lost at sea	On land
1672 Royal James *at Battle of Solebay*	*Charles II reigns*
1690 Anne *after Battle of Beachy Head*	*Penn founds Pennsylvania*
Dartmouth *in Scotland*	*James II becomes king*
1691 Harwich *in Plymouth Sound*	*William of Orange lands at Torbay*
Coronation *on Penlee Point, Cornwall*	*William and Mary become king and queen*
	Battle of Killiecrankie
	Massacre of Glencoe

The *Anne*, a seventy-gun, thousand-ton ship of the line, was badly hurt. When the smoke of battle cleared for a moment she was seen to be so badly damaged that she had to be towed into the middle of the combined Anglo-Dutch fleet to save her from capture by the French.

The Battle of Beachy Head on 30 June 1690 had started badly, had gone badly and finished so badly that London gossips said that 'the Dutch had the honour, the French the advantage, and the English the shame.' Two ships in that battle are of particular interest to wreck divers. One is the *Anne*; the other the *Coronation* in which Sir Ralph Delavall, Vice-Admiral of the Blue (or rear squadron), had hoisted his flag and from which he would command the squadron. Captain of the *Coronation* was Charles Skelton. The whole English fleet was commanded by Arthur Herbert, Earl of Torrington.

Torrington was not to be envied his command as the battle began. He was outnumbered by the French with nearly eighty ships.

against his fifty-six. The French admiral, the Comte de Tourville, worked his way up the Channel with the intention of blockading the Thames. Torrington had to give ground, but on 29 June he could go on skirmishing no longer. Orders from Queen Mary and the council ordered him to fight. At 8 am on the 30th, Beachy Head only four leagues to the north-west, the battle began. The Dutch ships were in the lead and were in action within the hour. They fought well but were caught between the fire of the main French fleet and other French ships which had doubled round behind them. Then, as the French were in a crescent moon formation, the Blue squadron were heavily engaged, but Torrington and his squadron in the middle of the line could only fire at long range. Both the *Anne* and the *Coronation* were in the Blue squadron and Sir Ralph used them both very hard, closing to musket-shot distance before opening fire.

The wind enabled the French to keep edging away from really close quarter battle, but around 2 pm the wind dropped and the real slugging match began. It went on for an hour. The great ships closed one another until one captain in the Blue squadron reported that the enemy shot was going right through his ship. By 4 pm the action had ceased. The *Coronation* had been hit, but Captain Skelton had handled her bravely and well. And Sir Ralph Delavall, who had fought his squadron hard, came out of the affair with honour. So did the rest of the Blue squadron, but they had suffered heavy damage. None however was as badly damaged as the *Anne*. Her commander Captain John Tyrrell could not move her himself and this was when he had to be towed back into the shelter of the English line.

On 1 July at Torrington's council of war it was decided to abandon any ships that were too disabled to keep up in the Allies' retreat. However the French showed curious reluctance to follow up their victory and, rather than abandon the *Anne*, Captain Tyrrell wallowed along behind the main fleet. The captains of the *York* and the *Swallow*, both of whom were his friends, gave him a tow at great risk to their own ships, but finally they had to abandon the towlines and hope that the *Anne* could stay close enough to the fleet to avoid capture. By 3 July the *Anne* was dropping back further and further and Captain Tyrrell took no comfort from the sight of four badly damaged Dutch ships being scuttled or fired near Hastings. The Dutch ships were the 64-gun

Wapen von Utrecht, the 72-gun *Maagd von Enkhuizen*, the 60-gun *Tholen* and the 50-gun *Elswout*. The fact that de Tourville did not close in for the kill at this point is made even more amazing by the fact that in the whole battle he had lost no ships at all.

The next day the *Anne* was wallowing hopelessly. Captain Tyrrell fired a gun to attract attention to her plight and Torrington sent his yacht back to find out what the gun meant. Tyrrell sent a message to the admiral that his ship was in danger of capture unless she could be protected, but Torrington replied that no help could be given. The *Anne*, her captain and crew needed no translation of this message – they were on their own. They struggled on, but now they were heading in for the shore to beach her.

David Lyon of the National Maritime Museum at Greenwich, who together with archaeologist Peter Marsden has written a splendid report on the *Anne* in the *International Journal of Nautical Archaeology*, has unearthed a contemporary pamphlet which describes the end of the *Anne* as follows: 'Saturday 5th July. . . . This afternoon the Anne Frigat was set on fire, we not being able to help her any longer after the French came up with her. She was ashore the day before in Rye Bay, and we have saved most of her trade, except her guns which will be taken up again.' Those of her crew who survived the action escaped safely after the beaching. Torrington was court-martialled, acquitted but never given a command again.

There the tale of the *Anne* rested for the next two, nearly three centuries. Not of course that she was forgotten in local stories and memories. Locally she was known to be on the beach at Pett Level and to be exposed partly at low springs, but she really did not come to the attention of today's archaeologists until 1974.

Then stories about divers' finds on the site and other reports of the use of mechanical excavators alerted archaeologists to the potential of the ship. Now the *Anne* is a protected wreck under the 1973 act and is being systematically examined by Peter Marsden. Sand movements make such a survey not only difficult but dangerous. Iron cannon-balls, grenades, musket-balls, clay pipes, spoons and a pewter plate have all been found. The grenades are particularly interesting, with a drilled wooden fuse hammered into the body of the grenade, and they seem to have only a four-second fuse (if modern gunpowder burns at the same rate as the variety used in those grenades). This would seem to make these grenades a very close quarter weapon indeed!

The Battle of Beachy Head was to be the last battle for the *Coronation* too. And for her commander Captain Charles Skelton. Not that the *Coronation* was badly damaged, because she was not and neither was Charles Skelton injured. Nor was he condemned for his part in the battle – on the contrary he was highly praised. So when Edward Russell was made commander in chief of the fleet, after Torrington, just before Christmas in 1690, he was happy to ask Skelton to remain in command of *Coronation* under him.

During the spring and summer of the following year Russell tried hard to bring the French fleet to battle. The fleet, of which *Coronation* was part, consisted of fifty-seven English ships and seventeen Dutch, but the French were not to be drawn. Plans were made to attack the French in their ports, but they came to nothing, and not one of the attacks was made. A bad spring was followed by a worse summer. It was windy and rough, and to these difficulties of the fleet was added the endless, actionless patrolling of the Channel.

The log of the *Royal Oak* (now in the Public Record Office) shows that the fleet was anchored in Torbay on 23 August 1691. It is almost certain to have included the *Coronation*; the *Harwich* and the *Northumberland* were there for sure. On Sunday, 30 August the *Royal Oak*'s log showed them out on another channel patrol. Great swirling copperplate writing – to fill up the big space left for the first entry on a page under 'Remarkable Observation and Accidents' – says: 'All Continuing faire and Pleasant Weather. At 8 of ye Clock this morning the West End of ye Lizard Bore NWBW 6 Leagues.'

And it is here, as we examine the last hours of both Captain Skelton and the *Coronation*, that a most extraordinary incident seems to have taken place. Before *Coronation* reached the Lizard she must have come into Falmouth Bay, hove to and lowered one of her longboats. On board that longboat was Mr William Passinger, first lieutenant of the *Coronation*. And Mr Passinger's orders from Captain Skelton were quite specific. He was to collect fresh water and provisions in Falmouth.

Why the *Coronation* needed fresh water and provisions within less than a week of sailing from the Torbay anchorage is difficult to understand. Perhaps the provisions were especially for the captain's table; certainly it was unlikely that such an old hand as Skelton would have failed to refill all his water-barrels while at anchor in Torbay between patrols. But we know that the incident did take place, and what was more extraordinary, that the mission was never completed because, while Lieutenant Passinger was on shore, *Coronation* sailed without him.

The attempts to lure the French fleet into action were still going on. At noon on Monday, 31 August the log-keeper of the *Royal Oak* noted: 'Still continuing faire weather and Easy Gailes. At Noon Ushant SSE 10 Leagues.' But on the next day, Tuesday, 1 September, the *Royal Oak* was only five leagues off Ushant and the weather had changed to 'squally weather blowing verry fresh'; on the second, 'still continuing squally freshening weather' with Ushant at eight leagues.

The fleet turned back for Plymouth in the early hours of the morning. The weather was obviously going from bad to worse and the log of the *Royal Oak* records 'verry Squally Stormy weather' as the great ships of the Channel Fleet raced for Plymouth and shelter. The wind that drove them on their way from Ushant to Plymouth was first of all coming from the south, then it swung to the south-west and rushed them on their way, but finally settled in the south-south-east and freshened even more, until it was blowing a full gale. This was the fleet's undoing. A friendly wind blowing them home had now turned into a killer. A south-south-east gale was blowing almost at right angles across the entrance to Plymouth Harbour.

The *Northumberland* made it – only to go aground in the Hamoaze, that four-mile-long part of the estuary of the Tamar which has been the principal ship anchorage of Plymouth Harbour for generations of Royal Navy ships. The *Northumberland* was lucky. The *Harwich* was next in, but she did not even make the Hamoaze. Captain Robinson of the *Harwich* realized his danger as the full strength of the wind hit him inside the Sound itself. He let go his anchors, but the strength of the wind and the ebb-tide setting on shore made his wrecking certain. He was not helped in his attempts to keep off shore by the ships all around him, which were doing their best to avoid the same fate. Despite all Captain Robinson's efforts, he was soon in only ten feet of water at his stern and thirty feet at the bow. Pumping and bailing had little effect, and she was quickly a wreck on the rocky shore. A wreck, but not a total loss. In that position a great deal of the ship could be salvaged.

If the *Harwich* was lost going into the Hamoaze, the *Royal Oak* at first seemed in even greater trouble. She would, it seemed, not get as far in as the *Harwich* and looked like being a total loss. But luck was on her captain's side, and he finally ran fairly gently aground 'under Mount Edgecumbe House' (and after being aground until 9 September was able to lift out her guns and be taken into the Hamoaze for repairs).

The greatest tragedy was reserved for the last. Skelton brought his *Coronation* in towards the entrance to Plymouth Sound, but as he did so it seems likely that the wind increased and a gust caught her. She looked as though she was going to capsize, and the battering that she took from the huge seas that were now running had started a leak below decks. The *Coronation* was seen to take on a savage list. Skelton realized his danger – later they were to say that his gun-ports were not properly caulked or lined to keep out rough seas – and acted swiftly.

With the amount of water that he had below, his masts were now the danger, accentuating the list until *Coronation* felt as though she was about to turn over under his feet. His orders were trumpeted into the teeth of a full gale, and the ship's carpenters sprang to their task. Within moments the great masts toppled down; they did not need cutting right through before they snapped under their own weight.

Skelton may not yet have realized that he was lost. He was taking in water below decks. His masts had gone, probably his anchors had been dropped and nothing it seemed could hold him off the savage rocks of Penlee Point, the most easterly point of Cornwall. The gale now whipped the white spume off the wave-tops and *Coronation* was going even before she grounded on the sea-bed below Penlee Point. When she hit she rolled, for a moment she was seen with her only ensign staff standing and then she was gone. And gone with her was Skelton and a great part of his crew.

The loss of *Coronation* and probably over three hundred men ranks as one of the greatest losses of life in any one shipwreck in the history of the Royal Navy of those times. It shocked the town of Plymouth, and when it became known it shocked the country too. It even shocked Henry Greenhill, the port agent of Plymouth for the commissioners of the Admiralty. But Henry Greenhill, being a pompous, miserable, mean man, did not start off with the loss of the *Coronation* in the letter he wrote to the commissioners on 4 September 1691:

May it Please Your Honours, I have received yours of the 1st instant and shall furnish Captain Evans with what Stores shall be needful for his Ship, if they are in Stores or can be procured and am glad that you are satisfied of the injustice of his late complaints. I have written Mss. Lowes of Bideford whom I employed to hire the vessel for Kinsale to send me a Certificate of the Agreement, which shall be transmitted to you in Order to you making out a Bill for the same.

Yesterday our Fleete was forced into this Harbour by a Violent Storme of wind att S:S:East, the Coronation was unfortunately lost between the Rame Head and Pen Lee Point having first cut all her Masts by ye Board, most of the third rate made the Hammoze where about Three or Four of them went ashore and the Harwich oversett, but the rest are or will all gett off Shore with little damage.

The Admiral hath directed me to supply such Ships as have received Damage with what is of absolute necessity for enabling them to go up this River, which we are now about and shall use the best husbandry possible and be as spareing as we can, though I fear this unhappy disaster will draw from Us a considerable quantity of Stores.

It is now reported that the Sovereign and the Dutchesse are come into the Sound, who before were missing, and several other English and most of the Dutch Ships have as yett no notice of, and suppose they did not beare away with the Fleete, but there is a rumour of their being in Torbay, God grant itt may prove true.

I beg your pardon for not giving you this Account by Express sent Last night to the Admiralty, having been on board the Elizabeth and other Ships all ye afternoone in wind and raine till late att night and greatly fatigued.

Your honoured and most humble Servant

Henry Greenhill

Plymouth ye 4th September
1691

There was about 22 of ye Seamen belonging to ye Coronation saved in their longboat and drove ashore upon some of ye Wreck, the Capn and Coll. Laston both drownd.

P.S. Since writeing the foregoing I understand that ye James Gally and

Portsmouth are come in and have brought with them a privateer of 14 Gunns they afterwards fell with 4 French Greenland men, Very Strong who engaged them in which engagement Captain Bridges lost his right Arme. I have not yet spoken with the Commanders and therefore cannot give you a more particular Account.

Greenhill is one of the few sources for investigating the last moments of the *Coronation*. The loss of the crew has generally been accepted in later years as being in the region of three hundred men, but there seems to be no evidence to support this figure. If in fact there was a full complement aboard *Coronation*, the loss would seem to have been much higher than three hundred. Greenhill himself seems only to know of twenty-two men saved in one longboat. And the court-martial into the wreck seems to throw little more light on these losses. It was held on board the *Dutchess* in the river Medway on Thursday, 22 October 1691.

President of the court-martial was Sir John Ashby, Vice-Admiral of the Red. His fellow-judges in the great stern cabin of the *Dutchess* were Captains Jones, Nevill, Lestock, Bokenham, Gother, Hoskins, Edwards, Waters and Baker. And in careful copperplate the clerk recorded that 'all [were] duly sworn persuant to a Late Act of Parliament instituted an Act concerning the Commissioners of ye Admiralty'.

The first matter to be dealt with was the loss of the *Harwich* and after hearing the facts the court 'did discharge and acquit Captain Henry Robinson and all the rest of ye Officers belonging to ye same'. Then came the case of Skelton and the *Coronation*. The clerk's pen squeaked steadily on:

Also enquiry was made concerning the losse of their Majesties late ship ye Coronation, which was oversett off ye Ramhead on ye Coast of Cornwall. Resolved, that the opinion of ye Court is, that by a Butt-head starting, or some Planke giving way Shee sprung a Leake, and thereby was lost. And doe not find that there was any Neglect or failure of Duty in Captain Skelton, Late Commander of ye sd Ship ye Coronation, or any of the officers belonging to ye same.

Allso itt appears to ye Court that Mr. William Passinger Lately 1st Lieutenant of ye Coronation, was absent from ye sd Ship by his Captain's Order, being sent to Falmouth for water and fresh provisions, and therefore the Court does discharge and acquit the sd Mr. Passinger, as to what relates to ye losse of ye Ship Coronation.

There, it seems, the court finished with the *Coronation* and went on to another pressing subject:

James Delgarn Gunner of their Majesties Fireship ye Vultur, was accus'd of Imbezling and taking away some their Majesties Stores belonging to ye sd Ship, viz. two Barrels of Gun-powder, one coyle of Rope, and three bundles of Marline, which matter plainly appearing to ye Court by evidence upon Oath, and allso by his own Confession, Resolved that he is Guilty of ye Charge Laid against him, and that he falls under the Eigth Article, and accordingly does passe sentence that the sd James Delgarn shall bee hang'd by the neck till he is Dead; on Board such ship as the Right Honorable Commissioners of Ye Admiralty shall direct.

Under this sentence of death all the captains have appended their signatures, and though one wonders how long Delgarn had to wait for death, there seems to be no way of finding out.

Nor does there seem to be any other contemporary written record of the loss of *Coronation*. Certainly, even with the help of the vast knowledge of the late Mr A. J. Norris at the Public Record Office, I was unable to find anything more. Perhaps there was nothing more written. The commissioners of the Admiralty soon had other things to occupy their minds – on 12 September the seventy-gun *Exeter* was accidentally blown up in Plymouth Harbour, and the French had still to be beaten at sea (at the Battle of La Hogue). So the *Coronation* rested, or what was left of her rested, on the sea-bed off Penlee Point. She was not to be found again – though some salvage may have been done shortly after the wreck – for another 275 years.

In 1967 some Plymouth aqualung divers were working over the sea-bed in the region of Penlee Point. The divers, Terry Harrison, Alan Down and George Sandford, suddenly spotted some cannon-balls, and then some more. Few wreck detectives are lucky enough to find such an obvious trail, but it led them close in to the rocky coast until they were about half a mile from Rame Head, and there, near Penlee Point, in twenty to thirty feet of water, were cannon. The Plymouth divers kept the position of the cannon a closely guarded secret until they made contact with Lieutenant Commander Alan Bax, RN, and then showed him where the cannon were.

Alan Bax was then still in the Royal Navy, but was already showing signs of becoming one of Britain's leading underwater archaeologists – a position that he occupies with merit today. If you think it is surprising that the Plymouth divers should suddenly reveal their secret to another diver, then it is unlikely that you have met Alan Bax. He is without doubt the essence of honesty and integrity. When others abandoned British waters for the easier kudos of underwater archaeology in the Mediterranean Alan Bax, now retired from the Navy, travelled all over Britain encouraging amateur divers to record their finds in a proper scientific manner.

A leading member of the Committee for Nautical Archaeology, he now runs the School for Nautical Archaeology at Plymouth. SNAP is part of a larger project, Britain's leading underwater centre at Fort Bovisand, Plymouth. Fort Bovisand is one of twenty-three forts built in the 1860s to defend Plymouth against possible invasion by Napoleon III, and many of the casemates which housed ten-ton muzzle-loaders have now been converted into diving stores, accommodation and classrooms.

From this centre are run courses in all aspects of diving, navigation, underwater photography, seamanship, catering in fact for everyone, from complete novice to experienced diver, and of course it is heavily occupied with underwater archaeology. Underwater archaeology in the West Country means the School for Nautical Archaeology, which was first put on its feet by a grant of £100 from the B S-A C. At weekend courses at the school throughout the year hundreds of amateur diver students have learned their first lessons in the underwater arts of recording and mapping the sites of the lost ships of long ago.

And so in telling Alan Bax of their find of cannon on the sea-bed off Penlee Point the Plymouth divers had found exactly the right man. Bax had the knowledge, and among the students who attended his courses he had the manpower, to map the site. He realized almost at once that the only ship large enough to have carried the sort of cannon that lay there on the sea-bed to have been lost in the area was the *Coronation*. But first he had to satisfy himself by diving to see exactly what had in fact been found.

On 10 April 1968 Terry Harrison led Alan Bax to the site, and Bax was amazed by what he saw. Conditions were not ideal. The log of the dive reads:

Date: 10th April, 1968.
Divers: Harrison, Bax, Clarke, Swinfield, Fletcher, Mitchell.

Time: 0950–1200
Low water: 1030
Wind: East Force 3
Sea: 3 to 4 ft. swell from S.E.
Air Temp: 48 deg. F.
Water temp: 47 deg. F.
Seabed: Granite rocks and gullies covered with kelp two to three feet
long. Sandy patches in the small clear spaces between boulders offshore.
Pebbles and larger stones inshore.
Depth over cannon: 40 to 50 feet.
Current: Nil
Underwater visibility: 15 to 20 feet.
Weather: Hazy overall.
Diving vessel: 60 ft. steel Admiralty M.F.V.

With his rough sketch-map of the area, Alan Bax included this
conclusion: 'From the above and the Plymouth divers' reports that
there are other cannon in the area, I would suggest that this is the
wreck of an ancient Man of War/Merchant ship well worthy of
investigation and protection.'

Alan Bax's comment may now seem somewhat naive. But he
was not to know that future exploration of the site would reveal
some 40 cannon and other fascinating items.

I should make it clear that Alan Bax has never claimed that the
wreck is that of *Coronation*. But later discoveries leave little doubt.

I have dived the site with my wife, Penny, and son, Kevin, and
it is, we all agree, the wreck diver's dream come true. The depth
at low tide is only some 30 feet and it is like a Hollywood film
producer's idea of the site of an ancient wreck. Only the eerie
music is missing and the hiss and bubble of demand valves
almost supply that!

You glide through gullies bottomed with silver sand and
shingle. The gullies are roofed over with great fronds of swaying
kelp as you follow archaeological survey lines. Each time you part
the kelp the maw of cannon muzzle looms menacingly out at you.
You can swim the length of cannon and hold the cascabels last
touched by some ill-fated gunner like James Delgarn. Beside
most cannon lie their ammunition – cannon-balls swollen by
exposure to sea salts so that they will no longer fit into muzzle
bore.

Exploration of the site goes on year by year and groups of

amateur divers painstakingly survey the site and raise lumps of concretion for further examination. Is it *Coronation*? Some said it couldn't be – despite the strong evidence recently raised of splendid bronze pulley wheels, which are the right period for the wreck. What's more some of those wheels bear the Navy's broad arrow mark plain for all to see.

Even with this evidence there was doubt. But . . .

In the summer of 1977, Peter McBride, who is featured elsewhere in this book, carried out a magnetometer search in the area and got a very strong reading only half-a-mile from the Penlee site in 65 feet of water. Diving on the spot produced some 14 iron cannon and, most important of all, a pewter plate, which bore the arms of the Skelton family. McBride had found the wreck of the *Coronation* or rather part of it. There is now little doubt that *Coronation* broke in half – or drifted on from where she oversett depositing 40 cannon on Alan Bax's site before settling down on the place where Peter McBride found his plate.

Before he died Captain Skelton would have known of the loss of another ship which would have brought back memories to him of a battle of nearly a score of years ago. In 1672 the Third Dutch War had hardly started when the Dutch Admiral de Ruyter surprised the English and French fleets, which were ten ships stronger than the Dutch, at anchor and revictualling in Southwold Bay, Suffolk. The date was 28 May 1672 and the battle is known as Solebay. It was a fierce fight with heavy casualties on both sides and Lieutenant Charles Skelton (as he was then) was in the thick of it in the *Rupert*.

The Suffolk shore was crowded with spectators and the guns could be heard miles away. The Dutch strike gave them their revenge for the unprovoked attack by the English on a Dutch fleet as it sailed peacefully from Smyrna up the channel only two months before. After the Battle of Solebay the English fleet was not ready for sea again for over a month and plans to invade Holland were ruined.

From the deck of the *Rupert*, Skelton saw during the battle the huge hundred-gun flagship of the Earl of Sandwich, the *Royal James*, attacked by two Dutch fireships and then about noon by a third which set her ablaze. The Dutch led the world in fireship tactics – you could call them the 'torpedoes' of their day. The earl

finally abandoned his ship but the boat which carried him became so overcrowded that it turned turtle; all were drowned.

At that time Skelton saw an act of heroism that might well have
taken another ship to the bottom with the *Royal James*. From out of
the smoke came another ship. It was the *Dartmouth* which closed
with the blazing flagship and picked up what survivors she
could. It was of course an extremely risky business to go so close
to a blazing ship at any time. The *Royal James* finally sank when
ravaged by fire almost to the waterline. Even so, she would still
be a superb find for wreck divers today. She carried many
matched pairs of fine bronze guns.

The *Dartmouth*, a thirty-two-gun frigate, was launched in 1655
and took part in many actions. In 1666, the year of the Fire of
London, with the help of two other English ships she captured
three Dutch merchantmen. In May 1689 she took part in the
Battle of Bantry Bay. She survived through the reigns of Charles
II and James II and saw William III on the throne before she met
her end.

Though there were probably many mourners in England for
over a hundred men, including her captain, who died when she
sank on 9 October 1690, there were few in Scotland. For the truth
is that *Dartmouth* was at the time of her sinking engaged in a
highly debatable form of warfare, debatable that is in the minds of
the Scottish clansmen: that autumn she was being used to put
down the Scottish clans.

Major-General Hugh Mackay was sure that the way to settle
the matter of the clansmen who still supported King James was to
invade the Highlands and let the clans see the might of King
William's sword. Finally William agreed and Mackay planned an
advance up the central Highlands with a naval diversion up the
west coast. This is where the *Dartmouth* came in. Captain Pottinger, who included the sloop *Lamb* under his command, was
ordered to take on board his ships six hundred foot soldiers of the
Cameronians.

In his famous book *Glencoe* (now in a Penguin edition), John
Prebble tells how Pottinger was ordered to set sail for Inverlochy.
On his way he was to alarm the rebels' coasts, cut their com-
munications, take away and burn all their boats. Though they
were not to make landings without certainty of success, they
could help the Argyll Campbells in their assault on the Macleans

of Mull. They were to take the surrender of any rebels who submitted and give them the full protection of King William and Queen Mary. They were also to make sure that the soldiers 'were kept under exact discipline both as soldiers and Christians, to hinder cursing and swearing, and all other unchristian and disorderly customs'. It sounds an impossible task, but certainly Pottinger and Major James Ferguson, who was in command of the soldiers, went to work with a will. They burned all the boats they could find around Mull. Cruising off the Isle of Skye, they opened fire on the home of the MacDonald of Sleat.

'Passing his house', reported Pottinger, 'I complimented the same with thirty or forty shots, sending the guards to the hills.' He then ordered the *Lamb* further in towards the shore and manoeuvred her until she could bring her broadside into action. Both ships then 'playing smartly upon the same with our best guns. Major Ferguson landed his men under the protection of my guns, burned both houses to the ground in the Highlanders' view, the whistling nine-pounders sending them scampering to the hills to overlook what they could not prevent.'

That was in July 1690. And for the next two months Pottinger and Ferguson went happily on with their work of harassing the clans wherever they could find them. On 9 October the *Dartmouth* was at anchor in Scallastle Bay, just two bays up the Sound of Mull from the rebel stronghold of Duart Castle. What the *Dartmouth* was planning at that time we do not know, but at 6 pm a violent storm swept up the coast of Scotland and any plans of Captain Pottinger's came to an equally violent end.

At the time the captain must have thought he was safe. In the Sound of Mull he was anchored in the shelter of the two thousand-foot-high Beinn Mheadhon, but the wind ricocheted down the sound, tore the 265-ton *Dartmouth* from her anchors and then drove her out into the open water. At one stage it looked as though the ship would make it into the more open water of Loch Linnhe, but then she was dismasted and after three miles she crashed stern first on to the rocky islet of Eilean Rudha on Ridire, where she 'immediattly splitt to peeces; none of ye men saved butt five and a boy'. Which means that about 124 men died that night.

It is likely that the rebels managed to get hold of a gun or two from the wreck (two on the ramparts of Duart Castle look suspiciously like recoveries from the *Dartmouth*), but for two centuries, nearly three, she mouldered on the bottom – and would be in the same state today if four amateur divers on the first day of their holiday in August 1973 had not decided that the little island looked a promising place to have a dive. Within seconds those divers, John Adnams, Ray Bishop, Roger Holman and Allan Carr, found themselves staring in amazement at a large bronze ship's bell among the kelp in thirty feet of water – and the bell's open end was firmly encrusted to an iron cannon. You can imagine their excitement, but over the next few days of their holiday despite the temptation they only raised the bell for identification purposes. They counted the cannon (nineteen of them) and anchors (three), and surveyed the site, which included an area of woodwork. The *Dartmouth* had been found again.

Then the Bristol BS-AC divers had to go home. But they called in the experts. Dick Larn travelled up to Oban to help. Colin Martin took over the archaeological direction of the site. Peter McBride, cannon specialist, came along to survey the guns. Expedition followed expedition and the Bristol divers, under the guidance of the experts, made more and more fascinating finds. The wreck is designated under the Protection of Wrecks Act and no diving is allowed except by the archaeologists and the Bristol diving teams working there over a radius of fifty metres around the islet.

The finds over the years of diving have been many and interesting. The ship's kettle has been found, pewter spoons, brass dishes, brass spoons, many broken wine bottles, grenades still filled with gunpowder, iron shot, musket-balls, dividers, a brass protractor, log slates, a shoe under one of the guns with some bones, all in all a slice of life – or rather death – at sea in the seventeenth century.

One discovery was not part of the daily life of the ship. Or at least one would hope it was not! The divers found in the wreckage a lady's ring brooch of Scots design, which was used to fasten the plaid across the breast. A keepsake from a Scottish lady collaborator? Or loot from one of Ferguson's forays against the homes of the rebels? Certainly you could never call the *Dartmouth* a treasure wreck. Captain Pottinger's letters were always complaining about his lack of pay. To back him up the only coins found so far on the *Dartmouth* site are two gold guineas and three worn halfpennies!

All the objects recovered have gone to the National Museum of Antiquities, Edinburgh for conservation and later display. A large section of the keel and lower hull-timbers are undergoing conservation treatment. They too will go on display. Scots who visit the display and learn that the *Dartmouth* was engaged in putting down the clans when she came to grief will no doubt feel that justice has been done!

EIGHT

'This Wreck remains as a Booty for those who can find it'

Lost at sea	On land
The Dutch East Indiamen:	*Reigns of James II, William and*
1686 Princesse Maria *in the*	*Mary, Queen Anne*
Scillies	*Battles of Blenheim, Oudenarde*
1743 Hollandia *in the Scillies*	*and Malplaquet*
1749 Amsterdam *at Hastings,*	*Reigns of George I and George II*
Sussex	*Bonnie Prince Charlie lands in*
	Scotland

'What every wreck diver needs is a Rex Cowan.' This remark was made to me by a tired diver at the end of another fruitless dive for a wreck we were both beginning to suspect did not exist except in some fertile nineteenth-century imagination.

Now the uninitiated might suppose that a 'Rex Cowan' was some piece of equipment rather like a 'Mae West'. In fact Rex Cowan is a very much alive wreck hunter who, though he does not dive himself, is well to the forefront of the investigation of many wrecks around Britain. He finances excavations of sunken ships that would otherwise be impossible for lack of funds and is now a member of the government's Runciman Committee. The Runciman Committee advises on granting licences for the pre-servation and archaeological investigation of historic wrecks (see appendix III).

He is also lucky, which any wreck diver will tell you is as important as any other ability when it comes to the business of finding wrecks. Being lucky ranks only second to determination – and no one could ever accuse Rex Cowan of being short on determination. I think his way into the world of wreck diving is the strangest of all those who figure in this book. Most were divers first, marine archaeologists later. A few, very few, like Margaret Rule, were archaeologists first, divers later.

Rex Cowan was, I think, first enraptured by the adventure and the hunt for riches, but then was himself quickly seduced into the quest for knowledge. Certainly he was a restless man after he came out of the RAF. He started to train as an engineer, gave that up, then qualified as a solicitor and built up a London practice. During that time he went on holiday to the Scillies, liked what he saw and bought a holiday flat there. At thirty-nine – he is now fifty – he gave up being a solicitor and wandered from job to job. He ran a photographic studio, then tried a furniture 'boutique', then ran a firm making scientific instruments. All were personal failures.

The biggest moment of change in his life came when he was asked in 1967 to write an article about the Royal Navy divers who had discovered the wreck of Sir Cloudesley Shovell's ship, *Association*. He says:

The moment I jumped aboard their ship and talked to them, I knew . . . I knew that this was it. This was what I wanted to do. I met Jack Gayton on that day, I met Roy Graham on that day [later both were to lead Cowan's diving teams]. When I get the smell of something that is right, I don't bother to say, 'Let's wait, or let's plan, or is it safe?' I know by that time that it's right. On the minesweeper that day I saw the glimpse of a new world of exploration. I knew that was what I wanted to do.

What he says he wanted to do then was to satisfy his 'infantile curiosity'. And his curiosity at that time took the form of finding the Dutch East Indiaman they called *Hollandia*.

The Dutch have provided for the modern British wreck diver more wrecks in our coastal waters than almost any other country. And I include the Spanish, Armada and all. So I propose to let this book's chronological order slip a little and deal with the wrecks of the Dutch East India Company all together.

At times in our history Britain has been without doubt the greatest naval fighting machine in the western world. But we have never, despite all our proud boasts about our empire and trade, been anything like as big as the Dutch were at the height of the power of their Vereenigde Ostindische Compagnie. The Dutch East India Company (the VOC) was so powerful at one time that it was probably more powerful than Holland itself. It is no exaggeration to say that today's commercial giants – ICI, Shell, Ford, General Motors, BP and any other names you care to think of – were cottage industries compared with VOC at its best.

Certainly the VOC was richer and stronger than many nations of its time. Its empire stretched from the Cape of Good Hope to India, Ceylon, Sumatra, Java, the Celebes and Spice Islands, and the ports of Malaya, China and Japan. Its rise and fall took place in one of the most fascinating periods of the history of the seas. It was not until the Fourth Anglo-Dutch War from 1780 to 1784 that the Dutch grasp on seaborne trade was broken, and it was not until 31 December 1795 that the VOC was formally declared bankrupt and dissolved.

The trouble was really that the VOC had built in it the seeds of its own bankruptcy. Its size and its power bred its own destruction. It ran an army, a navy and a complete colonial administration. Despite all this it was inefficient and did not cost its activities effectively. And on top of that, though the VOC was a public corporation, its employees expected to make private profits. The VOC tried to stamp out this practice. Other East India Companies were more astute: they let this go on and even licensed it, catering for private greed. But the VOC's repression did not work – in fact it is a favourite maxim among wreck divers that, if you find a Dutch East Indiaman, you may well find more on board than official records relate. Corruption flourished and helped the VOC on the way to its final collapse.

But however powerful the VOC was at the height of its power, the one thing it could not control was the weather, which was waiting for its ships whichever way they chose to go on their voyages to Batavia. If they went the long way round – around the top of Britain and down past the Atlantic-battered shores of Ireland, they risked first the Shetlands and then the gales shrieking in from thousands of miles of open sea. If they went down through the North Sea and English Channel, well, if at war, the English or French might well get them; if at peace, the North Sea and the English Channel can be as destructive as any Atlantic blow.

The wrecks off the Shetlands, the *Liefde* and *Kennermerland*, for example, bear witness to the chances of the first course. The wrecks of ships such as the *Amsterdam* are equally evocative of the dangers of the short cut. And if the great ships of their time avoided those two horrors, they could end up defeated by a third. Which brings us back to the *Hollandia* and her wrecking in 1743 in the Scilly Islands.

How the *Hollandia* got into the position in which she was to sink with all aboard will be a secret that Captain Jan Kelder took to his water-choked death with him on 13 July 1743. But his death was not a sudden death. It was a death that he could probably see coming for some minutes, but which like any human being he struggled to avoid to the very last gasp.

In the black of the night he ordered the guns of his big ship, 150 feet long and one of the largest built in Amsterdam in 1742, to be fired again and again. And though the people safely abed in St Agnes in the Scilly Isles heard them, there was nothing they could do. The noise of the cannon came to them borne on the rain-squalls of a westerly wind, but the heavy seas pounding the island effectively stopped any rescue operation being mounted. In such circumstances one can imagine that the boom of the guns was listened to in some houses with despair, in some with fear, but in all with relief that they were not out at sea on a night like that.

The 750-ton *Hollandia*, carried 276 people, including a hundred soldiers, instead of the normal number of well over three hundred men. She sailed out of Texel on 3 July 1743. On board too were thirty passengers. With her were two other voc ships, the *Den Heuvel* and the *Overnes*.

On 9 July, Captain Jan Boot, homeward bound from Bilbao, met the three ships 'in good order' in the Channel. And so far the three captains were carrying out their sailing instructions to the letter: 'Firstly that they shall go down the Channel and, arriving at the Lizard or Land's End, shall set a South-Westerly course to Latitude 43 degrees in order to bypass Cape Finisterre by 60 miles.'

We do know that Captain Jan Kelder must have got his ship as far as the Lizard, even Land's End, but what happened after that is a mystery. From there he should have set sail south-westerly as instructed. But he did not. In those missing days, he apparently turned north, and then he either circumnavigated the Scillies or made an even more hazardous run through one of the two main channels between the islands, via Crow Sound to Broad Sound, or via St Mary's Sound again into Broad Sound. Any one of these three courses could have brought *Hollandia* to her final doom.

Mrs Zelide Cowan, wife of Rex Cowan, has been responsible for the most splendid historical research into the loss of the *Hollandia*. She it was who gave me permission to use her research into the *Hollandia* and other Dutch ships for this book. It is fascinating to see all the reports of the loss which she has collected together.

First to print the news of the shipwreck was the Amsterdam *Dinsdaegse Courant* of 23 July 1743. This report says that on 13 July, the date of the wreck, 'Captain Willem Bakker met two ships two miles South of the Scilly Isles at half-past six in the morning in thick weather and heavy seas, the wind to Westerly.' They told him that one ship was wrecked on the Scilly Isles.

There is among Zelide Cowan's research evidence too that somehow Captain Kelder had got himself to the north of the Scillies, or 'Sorlings' as the Dutch called the islands. This evidence is in a letter from the Governor General of the East Indies, Baron Van Imhoff. His interest in the circumstances of the loss of the *Hollandia* was very much a personal one. The ship was carrying his youngest brother, Hendrik Francois Van Imhoff, Hendrik's wife Mechteld and her sister Anna. To his cousin in Amsterdam the baron wrote on 12 October 1744, 'that when the other ships took the right course (as every seaman knows) namely a South-Westerly one, and that they kept the Channel open, standing well away from the leeshore the obvious course (as every seaman knows) – how in God's name did they find themselves *above* the Sorlings?'

So where did the *Hollandia* sink? There was always a great deal of interest in this question. East Indiamen, outward bound, carried huge sums in coin to finance the East India trade. And the *Hollandia* was no exception. Captain Jan Kelder on that ill-fated voyage was in charge of vast amounts of coin. He signed for twelve chests containing 4,000 pieces of eight of Mexican silver, 8,000 silver ducatoons. These he was to hand over to the Governor of Batavia and their value was nearly 122,000 guilders. In addition to that he had 4,284 guilders to pay the sailors and another 2,922 for the pay of the soldiers on board. And it is possible that he took his own salary and expenses of 300 pieces of eight with him too.

The voc of course did not just abandon all that money without attempting to recover it. In fact by September of that year they had hired a Devon man, John Lethbridge, probably the most famous British diver of his day. Lethbridge used a simple weighted barrel with viewing plate and armholes for his salvage work and was often remarkably successful. But not this time. A contemporary report says: 'A Diver there upon was sent by the Dutch Merchants to discover and Weigh the Plate, of Considerable Value. But the Tide Running strong at Bottom and the Sea appearing thick the Diver could not see distinctly through the Glass of his Engine so returned without success. This wreck remains as a Booty for those who can find it.'

So the voc gave up. And the *Hollandia* was largely forgotten until the spring of 1968 when Rex Cowan started making his plans. At the same time Zelide Cowan stepped up her research in Holland in the records of the voc, helped by Dutch naval officer Jan Verkuyl, and in places in Britain like the Public Records Office (see appendix I). Only two real references to the last position of the *Hollandia* existed. One comes from the book of Captain Robert Heath, published in 1750, called *A Natural and Historical Account of the Isles of Scilly*. Heath had been posted to the Scillies in May 1744 to survey the islands. In his book he writes:

About the year 1743 a Dutch East Indiaman outward bound, was lost off St. Agnes in about 20 or 22 fathoms of water, with all the people.

Their firing of Guns, as a signal of their Distress, was heard in the Night; but none could give them Assistance. Many of their Bodies floated ashore at St. Mary's, and other islands, where they were buried by the Inhabitants. And some were taken up floating upon the Tide, and were buried. A Dutch Lady, with her Children, and Servants, going to her Husband, an East-India Governor, was prevented seeing of him by this unhappy Accident.

Rex Cowan considered this. And concluded that 'off St. Agnes' was a mighty big area to search!

The other reference to the sinking was not a great deal more helpful. It comes from another work about the islands, this time by the Reverend John Troutbeck, *A survey of the ancient and present state of the Scilly Isles*, published in 1794. Troutbeck describes the ship as having 'struck upon the Gunner Rock in Broad Sound off St. Agnes Island and sank down in about 22 fathoms depth of water'.

Now the Reverend John Troutbeck was chaplain to the Scillies in the 1770s, but was not exactly a paragon of Christian virtue. Not only is an old island prayer of doubtful morals sometimes attributed to him: 'We pray thee, O Lord, not that wrecks should happen, but that if they should happen, that thou wilt guide them into the Scillies for the benefit of the poore inhabitants'! But also in 1796 he was forced to resign his post and leave the islands under something of a cloud, having been clearly implicated in a large smuggling operation.

Knowing Troutbeck's background, Rex Cowan was more inclined to believe Heath's version that the *Hollandia* was not wrecked upon Gunner Rock. But on the other hand it could be that Troutbeck was repeating oral tradition. After all some of the islanders who were there at the time of the wreck could have been still alive in Troutbeck's time. Yet why did Heath not mention Gunner Rock?

Broad Sound, which is the south-west channel for getting in and out of the Scillies, is no place to be in rough weather, particularly when the wind howls in from the west. We know that on the night of the wreck the wind was from the west or at least that it was blowing from that direction at 6.30 in the morning when the two other ships which had sailed with the *Hollandia* were sighted. So Rex Cowan worked on the hypothesis that both Heath and Troutbeck were right. That Troutbeck was right when he said the ship had struck Gunner Rock (but wrong if he thought she had sunk right there) and that Heath was right when he said she was lost off St Agnes. Put together, the reports suggested that the *Hollandia* struck the Gunner and drifted eastward with the wind to sink some distance away. But how far?

Rex Cowan guessed at a mile, since priming and firing the ship's cannon would have taken about eight or ten minutes in rough seas. Of course the distance she drifted would depend on tide, wind-strength and above all another factor – how badly the ship had been holed. As she sank lower the tide would have more effect than the wind. Still Rex Cowan could get no closer with his calculations. A mile was his 'guesstimate'. And so a mile it was.

The first dives took place in June 1970 to make sure that the ship did not lie at the foot of Gunner Rock. A search all round out to a hundred yards from the base of the rocks showed no sign of any wreck. Then Cowan used his divers strung out on swim lines.

Five divers in his team covered strips a hundred feet wide. By the end of July they had located absolutely nothing at all and were beginning to appreciate the enormity of the task they had set themselves. Then Rex Cowan called upon science to help, in the form of a marine magnetometer. Now these underwater metal-detecting instruments are all very well, but the secret of their success is in keeping the instrument travelling over the sea-bed at a constant depth and on accurate lanes. In other words what you need is a calm sea and superb navigation conditions. The area they were searching east of the Gunner provided neither. The boats rolled sickeningly in huge swells and the magnetometer rose and fell in sympathy over the sea-bed. August came. No wreck. And the search was temporarily abandoned.

During the autumn and winter of 1970 experiments were carried out with an improved search instrument, the proton magnetometer. Rex Cowan examined his theories time and time again. And Zelide Cowan applied herself to more research. In April 1971, the diving started again. Leader of the divers was Lieutenant Commander Jack Gayton, a very experienced retired Royal Navy diving officer, who is still leading the team today, no small achievement in this area of the diving world!

But now the team had two objectives. During Zelide Cowan's Dutch research she had found documents about another Dutch East Indiaman – wrecked much earlier than the *Hollandia*, but not very far away. This was the *Princesse Maria*, which was sunk in 1686, in among the Western Rocks.

The proton magnetometer was to be used in both searches but the main effort was to be concentrated on the *Princesse Maria*. However for months there was no sign of either ship. By early September the divers were fed up, money to pay for the search was running low, and it looked as though all the team's efforts had been to no avail.

The sixteenth of September started like any other day. The diesel engine of the diving launch thumped her twenty-eight feet through the water with David Stedeford of Bryher at the wheel. The boat was now searching fifty-foot lanes of sea-bed about one-and-a-third miles east of Gunner Rock. Jack Gayton took over the wheel just before noon and in doing so went slightly off course at the turn into the next lane. Suddenly an anomaly, like a distorted 'W', appeared on the magnetometer chart. The spot was carefully marked, but the divers were not able to get into the water until the following day. They found nothing. The visibility under water had closed in, but on 18 September despite this the delighted divers saw through the murk the unmistakable shapes of cannon, anchors and lead ingots.

But what ship was it? Despite the wreck's amazingly close position to Rex Cowan's estimate of where the *Hollandia* had drifted after striking the Gunner, there was no positive proof that this was her. Identification came a big step closer the next day when one of the divers found a bronze cannon bearing the monogram of the Amsterdam chamber of the voc. So now they knew they had a Dutch East Indiaman. But which? The divers worked on a hundred feet down. And then within days they came upon a huge lump of silver coins, fused together by the concretion of over two hundred years under the sea. As the ships of the voc only carried large quantities of money on the outward run, they now knew that she was outward bound too.

So Rex Cowan, who had gone on believing that they would find the ship when almost everyone else had been ready to give up, had his moment of triumph. 'After all,' says Rex, 'if I hadn't believed in my theory – well then the ship could have been anywhere. Anywhere at all.' But she was not just anywhere. She was in fact just a third of a mile outside the area, not only of his estimate of her position, but also of his concession from the Dutch government.

His concession? What had happened was this. When the voc went bankrupt, all its assets, wrecked or not, went to the Dutch Crown. And Rex Cowan before even starting his search had concluded an agreement with the Dutch government. The agreement specified that he and his team should have 75 per cent of all they found on the *Hollandia* and the Dutch government 25 per cent. Fair enough. But the agreement also specified the area within which the ship lay. And she was outside that area. Rex knew that he had to get that area extended. So as soon as the ship was identified, he flew to Holland to renegotiate the area of sea-bed covered. Fortunately for him, within hours he had that extension.

This was not the end of his problems. He knew that once the news of the treasure find was out, then others would want to start diving on her too – agreement or no agreement. Add to that the approach of autumn, and the gales for which the Scillies are renowned would soon make diving impossible.

First step was to record the site as it was before the divers commenced lifting material. This was done in sketch form by one of the divers, ex-navy CPO Nowell Pearce. Then they started lifting the silver coins. Night after night the divers would return to port, looking deliberately downcast – they had no need to simulate tiredness, that came naturally enough from all their hard work on the sea-bed at a hundred feet – and for more than three weeks their deception worked. The secret was kept despite the fact that they were sometimes bringing back over a thousand coins a day. The coins were hidden in a plastic dustbin in the bedroom of the Cowans's Scillies flat. But in October the secret was out.

The excavation of the *Hollandia* site is one of the longest running in British underwater history. At the time of writing it has been going on for six years. It is not easy work. Everything is concreted to the sea-bed. This concretion, though it makes the recovery of some objects extremely difficult, does also protect items from damage. When this concretion is broken off in lumps and brought to the surface some amazingly delicate items can be extracted undamaged from inside it.

On the *Hollandia* site the divers have used crowbars, chisels, shovels and very small explosive charges in some places. Rex Cowan says that this use of explosives is justifiable. 'Parts of the site are so hard that explosives are a less damaging way of cracking the surface of the concretion than any other.' The concretion on the *Hollandia* site has undoubtedly helped to give us some idea of how the ship finally settled on the sea-bed, holding as it does groups of objects together *in situ*. And plans of the site, properly surveyed, together with items recovered have enabled archaeologist Peter Marsden to hazard a theory about what happened to the *Hollandia* on that ghastly night over two hundred years ago when the final sea smashed over the sinking ship and sent her to the bottom.

The *Hollandia* appears to lie with her bow to the north. To the south end of the main wreck debris were found three rudder pintles, and four small bronze breech-loading cannon, which Peter Marsden thinks were almost certainly mounted on the poop deck. It was here too that the divers discovered a low

mound. It contained more than thirty-five thousand silver ducatoons and pieces of eight. Among the coins were found the
bronze and copper fittings of some chests, which had long rotted
away. The handles of the chests were specially shaped so that
you did not crush your hand when lifting such a weight. The
presence of the money all together here is another indication of
the stern of the ship for such treasure would have been kept in the
captain's quarters.

The centre of the ship is indicated in the middle of the site
where lead ballast ingots were found. The twelve-pounder and
six-pounder guns in the area indicate the position of the lower
and upper gun-decks. Parts of two anchors are at the north end of
the site marking the bow. But there is a bit of a mystery here for
another cluster of wreckage lies to the south of the place where
the rudder pintles were found.

Peter Marsden thinks this means that after the ship struck the
rocks, which shattered the forward part of the bottom of the hull,
she was carried on to the east by the wind as the captain ordered
his guns fired as a signal of his distress. The *Hollandia* sank lower
in the water until the pressure of water against the forward part of
her shattered bottom collapsed it completely and it fell away to
form the debris to the south of the main site. No ship could
survive this and the *Hollandia* rapidly filled with water, but was
carried a little further before striking the sea-bed to form the main
and north sites.

A huge range of items have already been recovered from the
wreck of the *Hollandia* and day by day more are being sent to the
finds-processing office which has been established on board HMS
Belfast, the cruiser which has been saved from the breakers' yard,
and is moored opposite the Tower of London as a permanent
floating museum.

These finds all tell of the sad and sudden end of the *Hollandia*:
pieces of muskets belonging to the VOC soldiers on board,
cartridge-belts, musket-balls, military mortars in bronze, which
were not part of the ship's armament but were going to the troops
already in the Indies, navigation instruments, including the
fragments of an early octant invented by James Hadley in 1731, a
green glass wine-bottle still full of wine, brass taps for barrels,
pewterware, buckles of bronze, silver and gold from shoes and
belts, a gold cloak clasp, silver tableware (bearing the coats of

arms of the Bentinck and Imhoff families), a bronze tobacco box, a copper cuff-link . . .

And one of the oddest finds of all – a bronze plaque of a salamander breathing water on to a fire. For a long time this puzzled Rex Cowan. Then research turned up a description of a fire-engine used by the voc, and Rex Cowan knew one more thing about the *Hollandia* – she had a fire-engine on board! Then he knew too what the strange bronze pipe, like an extension tube for a modern vacuum-cleaner, which divers had recovered from under five feet of concretion, really was – the nozzle of that same fire-engine!

Marsden regards the recoveries from the *Hollandia* of great importance. He points out that, of the Dutch East Indiamen wrecks located so far, this is the only one which would appear to have had no salvage work done on her before. Certainly the work on the *Hollandia* has cost a lot of money. Rex Cowan calculates that for each minute he keeps a diver under water his costs are in the region of £3 – this, apart from the cost on the surface of over five hundred drawings, cataloguing, research and preservation. He estimates that the work on the *Hollandia* will take at least ten years from start to finish and that it has cost, and still costs, between £12,000 and £20,000 a year. So the whole excavation will have cost about £200,000 by the time it is finished. To set against that he has the gross value of the artefacts, cannon and coins, which he splits with 25 per cent going to the Dutch government and 75 per cent to Cowan and his team. In the end he expects to break even. Out of his share he has put money into other loss-making expeditions.

So, if he had an earlier dream of great riches, this has faded. What then drives him on? He says,

Even in the beginning of all this I was very excited about people, arma-ment and the every day things of the time. History always excited me. But to be even more honest I think it was this glittering idea of the great unattainable booty. . . . I think of that sentence of Troutbeck's about the wreck, 'This wreck remains as a Booty for those who can find it.' I took that as a tempting dare!

Nowadays I know different. I know the great treasury in ships lies not in silver and gold treasure but in the marvellous satisfaction in all the other things you discover.

The men working with me have seen satisfactions beyond that of finding lovely glittering silver which after a while bores you out of your tinies anyway. And they have seen pieces of people's lives in the past. They have seen how research and investigation can be fun and bring the past to life.

The men with me have learned that a grotty little piece from the sea-bed can turn into an exciting story. I try to tell them that story. Without expertise and discipline that grotty piece is just a grotty piece.

A good example is that medallion of a salamander from a fire-engine on the *Hollandia*. All of a sudden I discovered the story of that grotty little piece. The thing flowers. And I tell them the story. Then they see the things they have recovered in museums valued and treasured for other people to admire. That's the sort of satisfaction I'm talking about.

Most people would be crazy to buy the series of problems that come from an excavation of a wreck for the sort of money that comes out . . . there isn't very much.

Having said that . . . it's the best life in the world. You ask me to devise a perfect life which has in it the whole spectrum of activities – academic work, making films, writing, exploring, adventure, open air, intellectual exercise, practical exercises, scientific exercises . . . you rub shoulders with almost everybody, with museum people, historians, archaeologists, you have travel, movement, excitement – even the selling of the material! . . . The perfect life? This is it!

On top of all this you must apply the same criteria that would be expected in other fields of research. And you must do your best in this very new subject and encourage the best from others, instead of spending your time criticizing the inadequacies and warts in the field of which there are many.

The people who have worked with me have changed – they talk now of pre-disturbance surveys of a site instead of earlier days when they talked only in terms of finding the ship.

People who think of this work only in terms of finding something and going down and digging it up and running their fingers through it are people who have a mistaken idea of what is most satisfying in life. And sooner or later they don't really find it satisfying – they end up in bitter disappointment, they end up in conflict, and they never find a fire-engine on a Dutch East Indiaman!

Though Rex Cowan found his *Hollandia*, it was to take two years longer to locate the *Princesse Maria*. In fact he did not definitely locate the site of the *Princesse* until 1973.

It was customary for the Dutch East Indiaman to sail from Texel bound for Batavia in groups of at least three. And, just as the

Hollandia was to sail with two other ships for company along almost the same course fifty-seven years later, so the *Princesse Maria* set sail with two others from Texel on 9 January 1686. The *Princesse Maria* was a bigger ship than the *Hollandia*, indeed she was one of the biggest ships ever built by the voc. Though she was only ten feet longer than the *Hollandia*, she displaced eleven hundred tons. Four hundred people were crammed into her, soldiers, sailors and merchants, and she carried vast sums of money and trade goods for Batavia. Perhaps the large number of people on board reflected the confidence that the Dutch had in this ship. She had already made the Batavia run more than once and had been used as his flagship by Admiral Marten Pit for two years out in the Indies.

The weather turned vicious only days after the three ships sailed and they took shelter in various ports along the English coast. Twenty days after sailing – on 29 January 1686 – all three ships were sheltering in Plymouth. On either the thirtieth or the thirty-first they sailed on again – straight into more trouble. Gales roared out of the west and for days no more was heard of the Dutch ships. The gales were probably south-westerlies because we know that the *Princesse Maria* was forced on to the Western Rocks of the Scillies early in February when she should have been riding out the storms well out in the open sea on her course for Cape Finisterre.

The exact spot of her striking is not known except that it must have been near the rock known to this day as Silver Carn. In shallow seas she was smashed and battered until she foundered close by. And certainly 398 of the four hundred souls on board died with her. There is some suggestion that two people survived the actual wreck, but died later. Whether they survived the wreck and were killed to make sure that the voc did not retain legal title to the wreck, no one knows. (The ancient laws about what was or was not a wreck contained an open invitation to murder survivors: 'if any man or living thing escape to shore alive, it is no wreck.') What is certain is that the Scilly islanders were on the scene as soon as the weather allowed, looting and fishing up anything and everything that they could reach.

Lieutenant Roy Graham, a retired Royal Navy diving expert, began an extensive search using divers, proton magnetometer and metal-detectors in 1972 and continued this in 1973. At the end of July off the Western Rocks, a straight line of weed on an otherwise empty sandy bottom gave the searchers their first clue to the wreck site. After an airlift had been used to remove the top surface, a large area of decking was revealed. Soon it was clear that the divers were moving over the very broken and very dispersed remains of a large wooden vessel.

At this stage everyone realized that more divers were needed to cover such a large site. In the Scillies at that time were diving teams from a BS-AC special branch no. 439, RAF Coltishall, and Roy Graham asked them to help with a pre-disturbance survey of the site, which by now had cannon showing, and then to help with the excavation of the ship.

Did the Scilly looters of 1686 get everything? The answer is that they did not, for finds to date include some silver coins, pewter bottle-tops, yellow building bricks, navigational instruments, clay pipes and, wonder of wonders, a Bellarmine flagon intact, corked, and full of forty pounds of mercury.

Now mercury has been found in many of the Dutch East Indiamen wrecks – some coins from the *Hollandia* site were found to have a coating of mercuric chloride showing that they had been close to the reaction of mercury with sea-water. The reason for this trade in mercury was the discovery in 1550 that the extraction of silver from medium quality ore by using mercury was commercially viable. Prior to this much of the ore from silver mines was uneconomic to smelt down for silver. This was the reason for the Dutch shipping so much mercury to the Indies – not, as is commonly supposed, that there was so much syphilis out there that all the mercury was needed for its treatment!

The jar of mercury from the *Princesse Maria* is believed to be the only one to have been recovered intact from a Dutch Indiaman wreck. Its survival is all the more surprising because the ship's wreckage is strewn over an area of nearly twenty thousand square yards. Parts of the wreckage are covered by eight to ten feet of sand, though it is in a sheltered position.

Captain Willem Klump, was given command of the 700-ton, 54-gun *Amsterdam*, shortly after she was built in 1748. Like most other East Indiamen she was 150 feet long, had a beam of 35 feet and was intended for the Cape Town–Batavia run.

In fact she was originally part of the Autumn fleet, which se.

sail from Amsterdam in November 1748. (Usually, voyages to the East Indies were made twice a year, the two fleets were termed 'Spring' and 'Autumn'.) On board there were 329 men, one-third of them soldiers en route for duty in Batavia, and three women. In her holds, apart from the usual stores for the colony in East Indies, were 'a great many thousand dozen' bottles of French wine and twenty-eight chests of silver bars.

The *Amsterdam* set sail with the rest of the fleet, and immediately ran into appalling weather. It was too much for this comparatively untried ship, and she had to turn back for repairs and alterations to her rigging which such tests by storm soon showed to be necessary. Then she tried again, only to limp back in after another battering from the high seas. Finally Captain Klump got the *Amsterdam* out of the Zuider Zee for the third and unlucky time on 8 January 1749 – and straight into a south-westerly gale. Twelve days later – twelve days of endless tacking and battering by that same wind – she had still not passed Beachy Head and sought shelter in Pevensey Bay, which in those days was called Pevensey Haven, a well-known spot in which to shelter from south-west winds.

Klump must have thought his ship was cursed, for already he had lost fifty of his crew. Some fatal disease was aboard – some said it was yellow fever brought into the ship by some crewman fresh back from the tropics – and in addition to the fifty dead he had another forty seriously ill below decks. Those of his crew who were not down with the sickness were completely exhausted – nothing was dry in the crew's quarters, and each new storm added more water to the sodden bedding. The endless pitching did little good to the sick, whose conditions were even worse, for they were lying in water most of the time.

As Klump fought his ship to shelter he might have been forgiven for thinking that nothing worse was likely to happen. But it did. Before he was properly into shelter, the ship struck a shoal and her rudder was ripped off. It was too much, and many of those aboard panicked. The ship could not now be steered, and so she drifted with the wind until her anchors finally held off Bexhill.

Some people from Hastings came aboard to assist the crew in getting the ship to Portsmouth as soon as the winds became more favourable. There is no written record of what they thought of conditions on board, but they may well have been shocked at what they saw. There then the *Amsterdam* stayed in apparent safety, if not comfort, until the early hours of Sunday, 26 January, when fate struck a last blow at Captain Klump. Either the anchor cables could not stand the strain any longer, and they parted – or else someone cut them. And *Amsterdam* was adrift again.

What happened then as Klump struggled to control his crew is not clear. It is known however that some of the crew thought that they were doomed and broke into the ship's cargo of wine. Some others must have kept their heads and fired the ship's guns to announce their distress to the shore. Local records at Hastings say that at three in the afternoon when people were at church they heard the guns. As they rushed out of church and as most of the town gathered on the sea-shore, the *Amsterdam* drifted in from the sea. She came on and on, until she finally stopped, well and truly beached.

Among the first of the townspeople on the spot was Sir Charles Eversfield. A letter describing his disgust that 'all the crew were drunk' exists to this day. Very soon a large crowd had gathered on the beach opposite the stranded ship and, when the tide was low enough, those of the crew and soldiers who could still walk got ashore in safety. Then the looting began. Within a few hours hundreds of local people were plundering the wreck. A company of foot soldiers were rushed to the spot and some sort of order was restored. It is not known whether at this moment the people realized that *Amsterdam* was stuck into an area of yielding clay.

The soldiers guarded the silver and got twenty-seven chests ashore – the twenty-eighth had been broken into and only thirty of the fifty bars that should have been inside were recovered. The Mayor of Hastings was glad when the silver left under escort for London, for it meant that most of the soldiers left the town with it. The mayor did not like soldiers. He called them 'the greatest thieves I ever knew. They not only robbed the ship, but their quarters also.' The mayor may have had another reason for disliking the soldiers. Once they had gone, the town was completely out of control, and even the mayor was selling French wine from the ship at a shilling a bottle!

By February 1749 the ship had sunk into the sand as high as her upper deck, and no matter how the salvors tried to get at her main cargo the tides and water and sand beat them. And there reluctantly they had to leave it. You could hardly call the *Amsterdam* a wreck suitable for divers, and though locally it has always been known that the wreck was there – her sides and some beams can be seen at very low spring-tides about three miles west of Hastings town – there were no large-scale salvage attempts during the years that followed.

In fact it was not until July 1969 that modern man had a go. In this case modern man took the form of Mr Kenneth Young, the site agent for William Press and Son, Ltd. Mr Young was in charge of the building of a sewer outfall only about two hundred yards from the wreck site. Mr Young had always been interested in wrecks, and reading about the *Amsterdam* spurred him on to have a look for her – with a mechanical excavator! He dug several deep holes into the wreck position (when the tide would let him) and out came a slice of eighteenth-century life – a pewter tankard, fine horn combs, a lady's ivory fan, wine-glasses, bottles, brass candlesticks, bronze cartridge-cases, leather shoes, bronze smoothing irons, forty green glass bottles still containing red wine, stoneware jugs . . .

And then the most fantastic find of all – five bronze cannon, still wrapped in the sacking which had covered them when they were stored with the rest of the cargo. Each cannon was dated 1748 and bore the insignia voc entwined, with a capital A above it for the Amsterdam branch of the voc.

At this moment Mr Young realized the importance of his find and the firm agreed that the discovery must be reported to the Committee for Nautical Archaeology. Alan Bax of the committee went to the site, and at his request Mr Young dug a deep hole beside the ship. The photographs of that hole astounded the committee. There, in a hole on a British holiday beach, was evidence of a major marine archaeological discovery. Not only was the main mast found to be lying alongside the ship with some of its rigging still intact, but six feet down from the upper deck were a row of gun-ports, still closed by their lids!

The committee, with the help of William Press and Son's equipment – and experts such as historian and diver Bill St John Wilkes – carried out a hurried survey at the end of September 1969, and that survey established that the ship and her contents are of the greatest importance. Of such importance that the *Amsterdam* has been designated as a historic wreck under the 1973

Protection of Wrecks Act. This protects her from all intereference except that of archaeologists appointed to investigate her.

Since then the Dutch government has claimed ownership and this has been established even though the ship is lying in British territory. This must come as something of a relief to British archaeologists, for, much as they would like to preserve her for all time, there is little chance of the money being raised for such a purpose. The *Mary Rose* is likely to be the first ship to become Britain's *Vasa* – funding her raising and preservation will be a mammoth task, but it will be easier than raising a similar sum for a Dutch ship.

Now the Dutch government proposes to tow the wreck and the five thousand tons of sand which cover it in a caisson back to Holland. This operation will mean a national effort but the Dutch government committee studying the problems believe that it will be worth it. Housed in a special museum in Amsterdam, they believe it will give a great boost to Dutch tourism.

Peter Marsden, who is so closely concerned now with under-water archaeology around Britain, is the archaeologist in charge of the site of the *Amsterdam*. He estimates the cost of the operation as up to £5 million, but points out that once the ship is in the special dockside museum site in old Amsterdam that is likely to be earmarked for her, the five hundred thousand visitors that could be expected each year would soon make the venture as self-supporting as that of the *Vasa* in Stockholm. In fact the last voyage of Captain Klump's great ship may well end at last in 1980. A mere 232 years after she first set out!

NINE

'On Stoura Stack she broke her back'

Lost at sea	On land
The East Indiamen going 'north-about':	Reigns of Charles I, Oliver Cromwell, Charles II, James II, William and Mary, Anne, George I and George II
1640 Haan *in the Shetlands*	
1653 Lastdrager *on the Isle of Yell*	
1664 Kennemerland *in Out Skerries*	Battle of Sedgemoor and the Bloody Assizes
1711 De Liefde *in the Shetlands*	The South Sea Bubble
1728 Adelaar *in Outer Hebrides*	War with Austria and Spain
1729 Curacao *on the Isle of Unst*	
1737 Wendela *on Isle of Fetlar*	
1740 Svecia *in the Orkneys*	

More East Indiamen came to grief when they took the longer, but often more practical route around the top of the Shetlands. More practical at times because that way they could completely avoid countries with whom the Dutch might be at odds – particularly of course France or England. It was not necessary for the countries to be at war. Bad feeling and heavily gunned privateers, to whose activities it was politically expedient to turn a blind eye, were enough to turn an East Indiaman's bow to the north, rather than risk running the gauntlet of the English Channel. Some of them turned north to their death. . . .

Sadly, one of these was *De Liefde*. With such a nice name – 'The Love' – she deserved better. A typical East Indiaman, she was built in 1701 and made three successful voyages to Batavia and back. She never completed the fourth. Her master, thirty-nine-year-old Barent Muijkens, was caught in a gale on the night of 7 November 1711 and decided – there was nothing much else he could do – to run before it. In the early hours of Sunday, 8 November, the *Liefde* stopped running. She crashed into the sheer cliffs of the Out Skerries, about fifteen miles north-east of Lerwick, in the Shetlands.

The impact must have been tremendous, for only one man survived it. He was found wandering by the islanders after they came out of church, but all the rest had drowned in the foam at the foot of those steep rocks. As the crew of *Liefde* consisted of at least two hundred seamen and one hundred soldiers, that meant that some three hundred people had drowned in the wreck. Gone with them were trading goods and supplies for the company's staff at the Cape and in Batavia. Gone were all the food-stuffs that were to keep the men alive on the long voyage. And gone too were some chests of very important cargo.

The minutes of the meetings of the 'Gentlemen Seventeen' (as the directors of the voc were called) show that they intended to ship some 1,850,000 guilders from Amsterdam in ten ships that autumn. This means that the *Liefde* – if she carried her share – would have been laden with nearly 200,000 of the silver coins. Records after her sinking say that 227,000 guilders were needed to replace the loss.

The Shetland Islanders undoubtedly recovered from the wreck all they could reach, and two Dutch divers in 1712 said that they could not raise anything (well, that is what they reported!). Then in between 1729 and 1735 a 'London Diver' is recorded as having recovered some two thousand ducatoons and 160 ducats (and we have only his word for that!). (The ducatoon, which features in many bullion recoveries from East Indiamen, was first issued in 1618. It was nicknamed 'the Silver Rider' after 1659 because of the engraving of a mounted warrior on it. It became one of the most popular silver coins in Europe and the East.)

So there what was left of the *Liefde*'s treasure remained for 229 years, until in 1964 HMS *Shoulton* with naval divers on board visited the site and found two silver coins, which were presented to Lerwick Museum. The naval divers also found a cannon, but had no time left to raise it. But another diver did the job – Mr Eric Giles – and presented the cannon to the museum too.

In the spring of 1965 John and Peter Bannon, together with a friend, Michael Harrison, became interested in the wrecks around the Shetlands. They formed a small expedition to search for another Dutch East Indiaman, the *Kennemerland*, sunk in 1664. This ship was also reputed to be a treasure ship, and the Bannons added to their expedition two service divers of experience – Lieutenant Commander Alan Bax, RN and Royal Marines officer, Malcolm Cavan.

Once in the Shetlands they heard the story of the cannon raised by Eric Giles, and decided to search that same area. Bax dived first, and found only a carpet of kelp covering a rocky sea-bed. Despite underwater visibility in excess of fifty feet, he could see nothing remotely resembling a wreck site. Then Malcolm Cavan dived in another spot. Within two minutes he surfaced, waving frantically. First thought was that he was in trouble, but as the others brought the boat closer they could hear what he was saying – 'I've found it, I've found it!' And the proof was in his hand – two silver coins! So they had found an ancient wreck with coins in her cargo. But it was not the *Kennemerland*. It was the *Liefde*, wrecked some fifty years later in the same area.

After that first discovery expedition was to follow expedition to the wreck. In Alan Bax's report on the diving site he says that the granite cliffs which *Liefde* struck rise from fifty feet under the sea to nearly one hundred feet above water. The divers nicknamed the main work area 'Silver Gulley', and it is a jumble of boulders large and small in among a thick layer of kelp standing some three feet above the bottom. Visibility is seldom less than thirty feet, and the water temperature was an average 52 degrees Fahrenheit.

The divers found that all the artefacts including most of the coins were buried in a hard black substance, and this matrix was largely composed of sulphides. It seems almost as though it had been poured all over the site and the coins came out cemented together in lumps. How and why this matrix was formed no one quite knows, especially as in places it is nearly eighteen inches thick. It was this thickness that saved a treasure chest from destruction for some 258 years. The protection given meant that some of the wood of the chest was in almost the same condition as it was when the ship sank centuries ago.

Once all the measurements possible had been taken explosives were used to break up the rocks covering the site. Then everything possible was raised by hand and by airlift to be sifted through in the boat. This use of the explosives was justified because there was no other way of prising out the larger rocks which were solidly jammed in position over vital parts of the site. Every single find was listed day by day, and each item was plotted in properly on site plans. Here for example are the finds for two days taken from the lists of one August's work:

August 12th: 8 Ducatoons, 1 small piece of gold coin, 16 Knife handles, 1 Small piece of bell, 1, Lead stopper, 1 Wrought iron nail (3 inches long), 2 Fruit stones, various pieces pipe stem, glass pottery, Canvas, metal, and brass lock.

August 13th: 19 Ducatoons, half a cannon ball, 1 Piece of string, 1 Musket ball, 1 Small pewter spoon (in half), 2 Small wrought iron nails, 1 Piece of knife handle, 4 Small brass pieces, 1 Small piece of lead, various pieces pottery, wood, metal and bar shot.

Day by day, expedition by expedition, the divers – including such well-known names in the diving world as Jim Gill, Owen Gander, Stephen Halliday and Ian Morrison – worked on. They found more and more evidence of the way the sailors had lived all that time ago, and more and more evidence of the kind of materials carried in a Dutch East Indiaman, but there was one major group of items missing despite all their searching.

Where were the cannon of the *Liefde*? It is true that one cannon had been found on the site – that twelve-pounder raised by Eric Giles and the Shetland Islanders in 1964. But, search as they might the later divers could find no more. And there should have been another thirty-nine of them. The 150-foot-long ship with a beam of 40 feet had displaced about 500 tons, and her armament was listed as: ten iron 12-pounders, two bronze 8-pounders, eighteen iron 8-pounders and ten smaller guns.

Missing too were the eight anchors the ship would have carried – and some would have weighed more than a ton each. The divers found plenty of cannon-balls for all the weights of guns, including bar shot. The divers even found four breeches of her four-pounders consecutively numbered and stamped voc, but still no cannon. The only answer of course must be that some of those early salvors had been very good at their job, and very silent about just how much of her treasure they had recovered.

The work still goes on in the Shetlands. The vast majority of the coins discovered have been silver ducatoons dated between 1632 and 1711. Most have been in good condition, protected by that black matrix. The coins in the chest numbered four thousand, and all were dated 1711, presumably newly minted the year that the *Liefde* sank. Some of the coins recovered have been auctioned in London, and the Dutch government bought some lots at the sale, which realized over £14,000. John Bannon, as managing director of Scientific Survey and Location, the firm formed to deal with the exploration of the ship, has been co-operating directly with the Dutch government as official owners of the ship.

It was, oddly enough, a pleasure dive away from the hard work of the *Liefde* site that led to intensive exploration of the wreckage of the *Kennemerland*, the ship the expedition had set out to find in the first place. Diver Dick Clark took a break and dived near Stoura Stack. There he found a very badly corroded iron cannon. And, though he did not know it then, he had relocated the *Kennemerland* and triggered off other diving expeditions to the site.

The Shetlands have a grim record for wrecks, but it is perhaps not so surprising that so many of them have been Dutch East Indiamen. Bill Forster, of Nottingham branch of the BS-AC, was one of those who took part in the first expedition that followed Dick Clark's discovery of that cannon of the *Kennemerland*. This 1971 expedition was composed mainly of student divers from the sub-aqua club of Aston University, Birmingham, which is another branch of the BS-AC (special branch no. 241). One of the driving forces behind the expedition was Richard Price, but it was Bill Forster who documented the expedition carefully in a booklet, *The Wreck of the Kennemerland*, published by the university in 1974. In that booklet Forster produces a pretty startling roll-call of the Dutch East Indiamen who went astray in Shetland's stormy waters. There was the *Lastdrager* in 1653, discovered by Robert Stenuit of *Girona* fame in 1974. There was the *Kennemerland* in 1664, the *Zeepard* in 1665, the *Tobian Leijdsman* in 1688, the *Pijl-swaard* in 1690, the *Capelle* in 1690, the *Hetland Van Schouwen*, again in 1690, and even a fourth that year, the *Alkmaar*. Then there was *De Liefde* in 1711, the *Rijnenburg* in 1713 and the *Nieuw Vyvervreugd* in 1756.

Not all of these were necessarily wrecked on the Shetlands. We

know of course that some of them were. Others just disappeared
in the Shetlands area. All however were trying the '*Achter om*' –
the north-about passage to the Atlantic. After all navigation was a
very hit-and-miss affair – and this book is of course more concerned with the hits than the misses. (In his splendid book *The
Wreck of the Amsterdam* (published by Hutchinson), Peter
Marsden tells the story of the *Akerendam*, another Dutch East
Indiaman, which set out in 1725 to take the 'safe' route round
Scotland and disappeared. No one knew what had happened to
her. Now we do – she was recently found by divers working off
western Norway!)

If the fact that the East Indiamen went 'north-about' outward
bound did not save them from trouble, the same route inward did
not save them from disaster either. The East Indiamen, by mer-
chantship standards, were heavily gunned, but this did not stop
privateers or hostile fleets from attacking them whichever route
they took.

Bill Forster has pinpointed one classic example of this which
gives a clue to today's wreck divers of another possible site worth
investigating. On 15 June 1640 four Dutch ships, homeward
bound, were at anchor in Bressay Sound near Lerwick in the
Shetlands waiting for another ship to join them and convoy them
home to Holland. Just after dawn ten Spanish frigates sailed in
bent on loot and destruction. In fact these Spanish ships had been
fitted out expressly to capture the homeward-bound ships. It was
ten against four at anchor and though the Dutch fought hard, the
Haan and the *Reiger* sank with guns still firing. The *Jonas* upped
anchor and tried to make the open sea, but finally, trapped by
two faster Spanish ships, ran ashore and blew herself up. Only
one of the four Dutch ships, the *Enkhuizen*, struck her colours –
and that only when she was a shattered hulk beyond repair. The
Spaniards, not pleased, returned home with little to compensate
for all the casualties and damage they had suffered.

All wreck divers will note with interest the following sequel
nearly three hundred years later. In 1922 Lerwick Harbour was
being extended. Divers working on this came upon the wreck of
the *Haan*. Much of her hull was intact but, rather than hold up the
work, many of her timbers and four of her guns were hurriedly
moved out of the way of the foundations of the pier building. The
oak recovered at the time was described as 'hard and sound'. It

seems incredible by today's diving standards that her cargo was not fully investigated – but what of the *Reiger*, which history says sank close by? Well, perhaps we have a clue to her last resting-place too. During World War I a ship in Lerwick was taking on stores when a sling slipped and a side of beef was lost over the side. Beef in the Shetlands was very important and a diver was sent down to recover the carcase. He did that, but also reported the wreck of an ancient ship. That is all that was done. So she is there for the diver who finds her. If she is anything like as well preserved as her sister ship, then her excavation could be sensational.

The *Kennemerland* was built at a cost of 33,000 guilders in 1661 and was named after a district in northern Holland. Her size was as laid down for most other Indiamen (length 150 feet, beam 35 feet, draught 17 feet 6 inches). She was armed, as usual, with twenty-four cast-iron guns, six bronze cannon and two minions. She was a good ship. Her maiden voyage to Batavia started on 17 April 1662 and she returned safely on 25 August 1664.

The VOC were hard drivers of both ships and men. They did not allow much time for a turn-round after a ship returned from a long voyage. So they planned for the *Kennemerland* to sail again at the end of November – just three months for a refit after a two-year voyage. Then a change of plans about the carrying of bullion meant that the *Kennemerland* and the *Rijnland* did not sail from Texel until 14 December 1664. Between the two ships there were 240,000 guilders-worth of coin. We know how much of that was in the *Kennemerland*.

And the reason that we know is because the *Rijnland* was so battered by bad weather that she returned to repair damage. The records of the VOC say that the 119,700 guilders-worth of coin in the *Rijnland* were transferred to another ship for later despatch to Batavia. So the value of the coin on the *Kennemerland* was 120,300 guilders. Not that the coin did her much good. Six days out, running before a gale from the south, the night visibility was so bad that four men were posted in the shrouds to keep a look-out for land. Suddenly the ship was among breakers – the look-outs had no time to warn anyone – and then the ship crashed into the cliffs at the south of Stoura Stack, a rock pinnacle near the entrance to Out Skerries Harbour.

Local tradition says that one of the masts crashed down on to

the top of the rocks and three of the men in the rigging were either
flung or scrambled to safety. One of the men so saved was the
pilot. What he could possibly have been doing in the rigging at
the time does cast some doubt on the truth of the story. Be that as
it may there is still to this day a rhyme in the Shetlands which
goes:

> The Carmelan frae Amsterdam
> Cam on a Maunmas Day,
> On Stoura Stack she broke her back
> And in the Voe she ca'.

The fact that such information was passed on in local tradition
must surely indicate what a big event the wrecking of the *Kennemerland* (Carmelan) was at the time. Maunmas Day was the
feast of St Magnus, the patron saint of the Orkneys, and was
celebrated in the Shetlands as well. And they must have had a
ball. It is said that so many casks of wines and spirits were cast
ashore from the wreck that the whole island was drunk for three
weeks. They say too that it was the islanders' failure to collect
their Christmas booze that led to the news of the wreck spreading
to the mainland of Shetland. This is unlikely. Bill Forster in his
excellent research agrees that the news of the wreck did not reach
the Earl of Morton, who owned the Out Skerries, for twenty-four
days, but attributes this more to bad weather than booze.

The tenth Earl of Morton had held the estates of Orkney and
Shetland since they had been bestowed on the eighth earl in 1643
as a reward for supporting the Royalist cause. He was not slow in
claiming everything and getting the salvage started. One version
says that the stern portion of the ship was washed up on the beach
on the Isle of Bruray. If this is true, it was handing the coin on the
Kennemerland – which would be in the captain's stern cabin – to
the earl on a platter.

Immediately Charles ii heard of the wreck he started to try and
claim the whole of the Orkneys and Shetlands for himself with a
very keen eye on the treasure. He even went to the extent of
ordering a hearing in the Scottish Court of the Exchequer in
Edinburgh in 1667 to claim the *Kennemerland* treasure for the
Crown. He did not get much satisfaction. The court found that
William, Earl of Morton should return to His Majesty twenty-four

bags of gold containing a hundred ducats, pay a fine of £2,000 and also return two brass guns from the wreck. If Morton really got the whole of the *Kennemerland* bullion he must have been laughing all the way to his own private bank! However the king did have his revenge. On 27 December 1669, an act of parliament was passed reclaiming the Orkneys and Shetland from the Morton family (in 1742 another act returned them!).

So the 1971 expedition did not expect to find a sea-bed carpeted with coins. What they did find was underwater visibility in excess of a hundred feet, some cannon (iron and corroded), anchors and a great many of the yellow building bricks which to divers now are a distinctive feature of the wrecks of most East Indiamen. They were often carried as ballast and used for voc buildings in Batavia. (These are the same style of bricks which were found by Rex Cowan in his exploration of the *Princesse Maria*. They were called *Overijsselsde Steen* and were made in the Dutch province of Overijssel.)

They found too three Bellarmine salt-glazed stoneware flagons. These fat-bellied jugs were manufactured in vast quantities in Frenchen on the Rhine. The face in relief on them gives them their name of Bellarmine – because the Protestants of Holland nicknamed them to ridicule Cardinal Robert Bellarmine (1542–1621) who was well known for his influence on Catholic theology.

But as they lifted these jars for preservation by Tom Henderson and display in the Shetland County Museum in Lerwick of which he is curator, a small tragedy took place. Two were safely raised. One is thought to have held gin, one had traces of mercury in it. The third, which bore the arms of the City of Amsterdam and was corked, slipped from the diver's grasp and some forty pounds of mercury shot in glistening quicksilver trails over the sea-bed from the shattered fragments as the jar hit the bottom. A shame, but not a disaster. As you will have read earlier there is one full jar in existence from the wreck of the *Princesse Maria* in the Scillies.

In 1973 Richard Price put two years' planning and research into operation when he led another university expedition to the site. This time the members came from both Aston University and Manchester University diving clubs. Just before setting out – a month in fact from departure date – the expedition still needed an archaeologist. The diving officer of Cambridge University branch of the B S-A C, Keith Muckelroy, volunteered. Keith was then in his final year studying archaeology and has been greatly interested in the site of the *Kennemerland* ever since. He is now archaeological adviser to the B S-A C and has been a full-time diving archaeologist with the St Andrews Institute of Maritime Archaeology at Fife.

The 1973 expedition had four main objectives: firstly to assemble a sample of the goods on board a Dutch East Indiaman of the mid-seventeenth century; secondly to investigate the process of the disintegration of the wreck, and to relate this to folklore on the subject; thirdly to attempt to account for the differences in preservation of objects on the site; and fourthly to develop techniques for dealing with such a site suitable for a team of student divers operating with minimal resources.

So the expedition set to work. They were immediately faced with a problem. The depth over the site varies in the extreme. At the southern end, off Stoura Stack itself, the water is between 100 and 120 feet deep. The bottom is a featureless pebble and rock bed with no great marine life. On the other hand at the northern end, where the depth is less than thirty feet, there is as one would expect an embarrassingly luxuriant growth of weed over gullies and broken rocks.

Richard Price, the expedition leader, felt sure that an investigation at the northern end of the site would pay dividends as it was obviously extremely rich in artefacts. So the team set to work to remove the weed. They cut and hacked the seaweed away and dumped it well out to sea, since anything less than this sort of clearance would merely have left the site choked with dead weed – as some diving archaeologists on other sites have found to their cost!

Some four hundred finds were made during this expedition, including large quantities of lead shot, stoneware flagon fragments, a gold ring, bronze ship dividers, five brass tobacco-boxes shaped like large hen's eggs, a sword scabbard in leather, sounding leads, scent bottles, pins and lace-making instruments, and a lump of concretion which was raised on the last day of the expedition and was later found to contain fifty-nine silver coins.

Was this all that escaped those salvors of ancient times? Or was it the contents of a private chest of one of the crew who planned a little private trading? It was found in what the divers called 'Bellarmine Gulley'. It is interesting that nearby were found dice, thimbles, pendants and chains as well as the tobacco-boxes. To the north of these finds were more rings, pendants and the scent-bottles. It sounds as though one of the crew was a seventeenth-century 'spiv' or 'black marketeer'! Or maybe he had been to Batavia with the ship before and knew exactly what the local ladies wanted!

The 1973 expedition was a great success in all four of its original aims. It took ten weeks of diving. From the particular groupings of the yellow ballast bricks, Keith Muckelroy has worked out a possible explanation of the way the remains of the *Kennemerland* lie now. He reckons that the greater concentration of bricks in the southern part of the site must indicate that not only did the ship 'break her back' on Stoura Stack, but also had her bottom ripped out almost at once. This led to the discharge of much of her ballast. But a substantial part of the ship may well have carried on over the deeper waters to the north of the stack.

So either she broke completely in two with her bow section foundering off the stack while the stern floated northwards, or her upper decks parted from the keel and floated for a short way before sinking independently. Both fit the archaeological evidence (see figure 4). At the northern end of the site the sea-floor rises quite sharply and in a southern gale you can see the surf begin to build up at this point. This is where a second area of bricks was found and the line of cannon and the gullies full of artefacts. This sequence of events does fit in well with the story according to local folklore.

Since that expedition Richard Price has led others to the site. The Shetland Museum, owing to the foresight of curator Tom Henderson, has become the main repository of material from the ships sunk around the Shetlands. The museum has become highly skilled in the conservation of material from these wrecks and can provide almost immediate facilities.

Just before the end of the 1973 season on a Sunday the divers, who were looking for lobsters to supplement their diet, found two bronze cannon away from the *Kennemerland* site. One was a small breech-loader, the other a large muzzle-loader weighing over a ton. There was nothing else in the vicinity. Either they had found some jettisoned guns from a ship in trouble or else a new

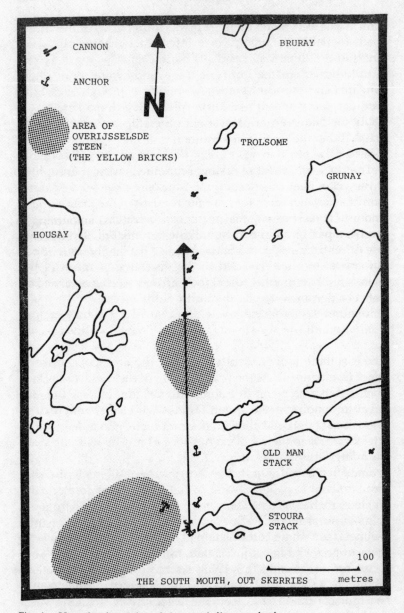

Fig. 4.   How the divers found the wreck *Kennemerland*

wreck. The inscription on the larger gun held some clues. It was made by Oudragge in Rotterdam and the date seems to be 1687. The site is to be investigated further soon.

In 1974 the team found a complete undamaged pocket sundial – an amazing discovery – and a compass card picked out with the cardinal points in red and blue paint. The extraordinary thing about the latter is that, though it is made of cardboard and has spent three hundred years under the sea, the markings are still clearly discernible!

The 1976 *Kennemerland* expedition proved just as exciting. The divers found large sea-boots, thousands of peppercorns, a section of a wooden bowl, ears of barley, carved ivory knife-handles and a new discovery – a large pile of lead ballast amounting to twelve tons of lead in two-hundredweight blocks. By ingenious use of oil-drums all the lead was raised for the museum.

Richard Price, who seems to have made the *Kennemerland* his own, says that the work on the ship is nowhere near finished. He believes that there are years of work in the scattered remains of this Dutch East Indiaman. And from the way he talks he will be going back there again and again and again.

The East Indies were not the exclusive preserve of the Dutch East India Company. There was of course the East India Company of England, but at the height of its fortunes it never possessed as great an empire as the Dutch built in the East. There was the Danish East India Company, which was later on the scene, having started operations in 1732. At first it did not do too well, losing ship after ship in the early years. One of these ships was the *Wendela*, a twenty-six-gun frigate, which was wrecked on a rocky headland on the east coast of the island of Fetlar in the Shetlands in December 1737.

As was usual with such a wreck, the locals and local gentry swooped to take what they could. And they did well, recovering silver ingots and coins in vast quantities. But finally the finds dried up – including those that could be reached by William Irvine, a famous diver of the eighteenth century, in his diving machine, another barrel contraption with holes for the arms made watertight by leather bands round the upper parts. How much they retrieved of the *Wendela*'s cargo of seventy-nine bars of silver and thirty-one sacks of coins, together with trade goods, it is difficult to calculate, but certainly it seems likely that a good part of the valuables were taken up.

And there the *Wendela* rested until her name caught the eye of Robert Stenuit, who had made such a magnificent job of excavating the remains of the Spanish Armada galleass, the *Girona* (see chapter 4). Stenuit had searched in archives in London and Edinburgh and Copenhagen for details of the missing ships of the Danish East India Company and finally made his choice of the *Wendela*.

So he arrived on the tiny island of Fetlar, just six miles long and four miles wide, with his old diving colleagues Maurice Vidal, Louis Gorsse and Andre Fassotte. They set to work, and they worked for weeks, not without success though. Stenuit describes the moment of triumph like this: 'As I swam down again to a circle of cliffs, someone pummelled my back. It was my colleague, Maurice, looking excited. With his thumb in his mouth, his hand around an imaginary bottle, he pretended to drink – it was our victory sign.' From the bootee of his diving wet-suit, Maurice Vidal produced a small plastic bag and Robert Stenuit saw gold and silver coins. Stenuit goes on:

Where had he found it? Maurice pointed to where bubbles indicated another member of our party, Louis. Above him was wedged a huge iron cannon, lying at an angle in a deep grotto under two vast rocks. I looked round and saw another, cut in two lengthways. I could see a third and Louis showed me two more. But the cannons were of no interest in themselves. 'The coins?' I asked Louis making a circle with my thumb and index finger. He took me to some fissures where the sand that he had disturbed had not yet settled. It was black, very deep and seemed almost inaccessible.

But the divers who had worked under appalling conditions on the *Girona* site were not to be put off by such things. They found more and more coins. Coins of both gold and silver, and under one cannon Stenuit describes seeing silver coins 'literally matted into the hollows of the rocks'! Ducatoons and patagoons from Holland, Scandinavian coins of all kinds, gold coins dating from 1609 to 1737 when the wreck took place; some with Danish kings on them; others with no dates and much older. Stenuit and his colleagues had done it again. Some of their coin finds are very rare indeed. In fact one of the gold coins from the *Wendela*, a 1730

Christian vi Danish ducat, was sold at Sotheby's in London for
£680.

Robert Stenuit has investigated many wrecks in the Shetlands
area, including the forty-four-gun Dutch warship *Curacao* which,
after successfully linking up with a homeward-bound convoy of
Dutch East Indiamen in 1729, lost them in fog. Currents took her
on to a rock needle on the east coast of the Isle of Unst and she
broke up and sank. Only five of the crew of two hundred were
lost. Stenuit and his diving team found her remains in ninety feet
of water at the foot of Ship Stack. Some coils of rope were
recovered complete! Forty large and medium-size iron guns were
found as well as five small breech-loading swivel guns bearing
the aa mark of the Amsterdam Admiralty, spoons, candlesticks,
navigation dividers, belt buckles, tobacco pipes, coin weights
and most amazing of all part of a book. It was only a small part of
the binding with the central part of forty pages, but when treated
the print was clear enough to be readable. It appears to be a Dutch
book on etiquette!

He found too among hundred of objects a copper tobacco
pipe-cover. This fitted over the bowl of the pipe and prevented
the tobacco from burning away too fast or being blown right out
of the pipe in a wind. A very necessary item for the sailor who
wanted to smoke – the only place it was allowed was on the deck
at the very bow and there is no windier or wetter place than that!

Another Stenuit investigation has located the wreck of the voc
ship the *Lastdrager*, which was sunk on 2 March 1653 off the Isle of
Yell in the Shetlands. This was another of those *Girona*-style
Stenuit operations where teams of divers spent up to five hours a
day every day for over two months breaking up concretion,
moving boulders weighing tons by means of lifting bags, all hard
back-breaking work. But it resulted in 2,746 items and fragments
being recovered from depths varying from 10 to 150 feet. Such
things as an important collection of navigational instruments, 407
silver coins, rings with coats of arms, jewels, shot linked together
for small arms and fragments of Bellarmine jars. And interestingly puddles of mercury were seen in many crevices under
water.

Anyone who wants to read more about these two superb

excavations should go to the *International Journal of Nautical Archaeology* (for the *Lastdrager* you want volume 3, no. 2 and for the *Curacao* volume 6, no. 2).

Up to now we have been looking at the wrecks of outward-bound East Indiamen. Loaded as they were with coin for the East, these shipwrecks obviously capture more of the attention that the inward-bound, laden more likely with spices, silks and textiles, though there might also be precious stones among the cargo.

The ship that concerns us this time belonged to the Swedish East India Company, the 690-ton inward-bound *Svecia*. She was 127 feet long and armed with thirty cannons. And she was wrecked on 18 November 1740 on the Reefdyke Shoal, off North Ronaldsay in the Orkneys, when homeward bound for Gothenburg. But the *Svecia*'s troubles had started long before this. She was carrying silks from Canton in China and had put into Bengal to pick up more cargo, mostly an Indian dye-wood called sanderswood, which is no longer grown commercially but was then highly valued for its sap and resultant red dye.

Once again we owe our knowledge of what happened to the *Svecia* to the research work of Rex and Zelide Cowan, this time in Sweden as well as in London and Scotland. In old documents they found out that while the *Svecia* was in Bengal one of her sailors shot a Bengali. This caused such a storm that the *Svecia* had to make a run for it, using one of the Nawab's ships as a hostage for their safe exit.

Then some tropical sickness struck the ship and spread in the cramped confines in which some 150 people had to live. She stopped at Guinea, apparently to off-load some who were ill, but by the time she reached Madeira forty people had died, including her captain. In command now was the former first mate Lanziell Agell. It may be that at some stage in the voyage Agell had a bout of sickness, for one of the passengers, Ninian Bryce of Glasgow, seems to have been in command for a while. But at the time of the wreck on 18 November Agell was captain. He would have been anxious to see the end of this ill-fated voyage – and it looks as though this urge to hurry home was the cause of the wreck.

It is difficult to blame him. He had kept his ship safe all the way up the west coast of Ireland. He had got her up past the Hebrides and when the Orkneys appeared he knew he was on the last leg for home. With a south-westerly gale behind him he turned into the obvious short cut between North Ronaldsay and Sanday to the south. It looks a natural shipping channel. It is not. The direct route is barred by jagged rocks of the Reefdyke Shoal, nastily hidden out of sight only a few feet below the surface. The *Svecia* was in the trap. Gusts of rain cut visibility and, by the time the look-outs screamed a warning of the white water ahead, it was too late. *Svecia* dropped two anchors, but both broke away and she struck. Boats were launched with orders to stand by, but the flood-tide which can reach five to six knots in the area swept them away into the murk. In fact a boat with thirty-one men on board reached Fair Isle, thirty miles away, and was smashed to pieces on the shore as they landed.

What life must have been like for those left aboard the *Svecia* one can only guess. They cut the masts away and worked for two whole days building a raft. This was then loaded with chests of valuables and the captain and about thirty of the crew set off for North Ronaldsay. Again the tide took over and swept the raft to the north where it broke up in a tide-race and no one on board made the shore. The storm now returned in even greater strength and the *Svecia* began to break up. Thirteen men got ashore on another raft. The reception they received resulted in calls for the islanders to be punished. One letter of the time refers to 'those Barbarous People . . . that let our friends perish when they could help them'!

Finally the ship broke up completely. The ship's parson was the last left alive on board. He tied himself to part of the ship hoping to be washed ashore, but was drowned.

As usual, the looters were on the scene within minutes on the shore and as soon as possible at sea. Some of these early salvors paid the price of their greed – they were swept away by the same tides that had killed the *Svecia*'s crew and were either smashed on the reefs or carried so far from land that they were never seen again.

The pickings were rich and the disputes bitter. It is natural that the Earls of Morton of Orkney and Shetland were involved in these wrangles again as they had been in the case of the *Kennemerland* and the *Wendela*. Mounds of silks were reported washed up on the shores around. One description of these says the mounds of silks were as high as houses, which is probably true if you remember that houses on the island were not likely to be two-storied affairs. Only eighteen chests out of five hundred said to have been on board were recovered. William Irvine and his diving machine appeared on the scene again recovering anchors and the ship's bell. The agents' official salvor, who arrived with a sloop, the *Dolphin*, salvaged little and was wrecked in a gale in 1741. The total loss was said to be some £500,000 – a colossal sum in those days.

How much was looted? How much did the Orkney folk and gentry get? We shall know more when Rex Cowan's team of divers have finished their work – because they found the wreck 235 years after she sank. This time the diving team was lead by Peter McBride, who was also director of underwater archaeology on the site. McBride of course is a wreck diver and underwater archaeologist of great experience and standing. It was he who was involved in such famous discoveries as the Royal Yacht *Mary* and the *Santo Christo de Castello* (see chapter 6), as well as many other important sites. He has written an excellent preliminary account of the first two seasons' work on the *Svecia* in the May 1977 issue of *Triton*, the monthly journal of the B S-A C.

The wreck was found, like the *Hollandia*, by use of Anthony Lonsdale's proton magnetometer, which detects magnetic anomalies on the sea-bed. Writes Peter McBride in *Triton*: .

At last the pen traced its ascending values, reaching a peak at 90 gammas, indicating a mass of equivalent to half a ton of iron at the depth we were searching. . . . Were we at last to be successful. . . . Or was this just another anti-climax in nine tedious days of searching?

After 15 minutes, the divers returned disappointedly from their sweep to the South of the buoy, complaining about the difficult kelp jungle through which they had to drag themselves. With air remaining they were directed to do a similar sweep to the North.

Within four minutes, Chris Rose hit the surface in a flurry of foam, his cry startling the surrounding seabirds for a quarter of a mile – the first solitary cannon had been found!

The following day the divers were on the site early and despite strong tides within twenty minutes Terry Hiron and Ron Lacey had found a scatter of cannons and a large anchor. Underneath one of the cannon was a piece of Indian dye-wood. The next day time was up and the divers had to leave.

But during that winter and spring of 1976 Rex Cowan and Peter

McBride planned the second expedition and tried to raise the money for it. Transporting all the diving gear and divers to a small island is no quick or cheap operation. For this expedition Rex Cowan calculates one month's work on site means an expenditure of £12,000 and the use of £25,000-worth of equipment.

On this second expedition there were twenty people in the party including a seven-man RAF diving team led by Bill Church and an advance party of Mike Pascoe and Paul Raynor; among the divers were McBride's two sons David, aged eighteen, and Godfrey, who was fifteen. They were to take part with Brian Ranner of the RAF in the proper archaeological survey of the site before any disturbance took place. But the first three days was spent cleaning the kelp over the site.

Then they found fifteen cannon, half of the number she carried and McBride saw in the positions of the cannon confirmation that the *Svecia* finally broke in half. They found iron ingots from the ship's ballast, some sherds of Chinese porcelain, a fine pair of navigator's dividers and a fine gold button, a lucky discovery by diver John Rose. And there was sanderswood everywhere, wedged into crevices, jammed under guns. They found too that the islanders collect the attractively grained hardwood when it is washed ashore after gales even today and turn it into beautiful objects such as spinning wheels. And the divers were able to have a nice crimson T-shirt each when they simmered some of the wood in alcohol and produced a splendid red dye.

So far no discoveries of great value have been made, but diving is continuing and the archaeological value of the site is growing with each dive.

Yet another Dutch East Indiaman wreck to have been investigated by divers is that of the *Adelaar*, which came to grief well off-course on Greian Head on the north-west coast of the Isle of Barra in the Outer Hebrides in 1728. The site was extremely exposed, artefacts were spread all over the place and the ship had been the subject of intensive salvage operations just after the wreck. Once again the objects remaining were found to be buried in an extremely strong concretion. The divers worked for a time with chisels and Colin Martin of the Institute of Maritime Archaeology became concerned when he saw that many objects were being damaged when the chisels cut right through them (including some silver coins!). So Colin Martin and another diving archaeologist Anthony Long decided to experiment with small explosive charges. And they worked so well that a three-ton concretion in a gully became soft and able to be hand-worked, and none of the artefacts in the concretion were damaged at all.

The idea of using explosives on any site makes some archaeologists practically swoon. But as Colin Martin pointed out in the ever-excellent *International Journal of Nautical Archaeology* (volume 4, no. 2), 'Explosives are a tool; in themselves they are neither "good" nor "bad",' and he goes on to point out the archaeologist responsible for the site is the only one who can decide when faced with the choice of using explosives or not. In the case of the *Adelaar*, the use of explosives seems to have provided the perfect answer.

TEN

'And many crying out for God's sake to save them which he could nott'

Lost at sea	On land
On the Scillies:	Queen Anne reigns
1707 Association	*Act of Union with Scotland*
Eagle	
Romney	
Firebrand	
with 2,000 men	

England was calling and Sir Cloudesley Shovell was anxious to get home. On 29 September 1707 his flagship the 90-gun, 165-foot-long *Association* led the way out of Gibraltar and through the Straits, and set course for disaster. Behind her came the 100-gun *Royal Ann*, the 90-gun *St George*, the *Somerset* and the *Torbay* each with 80 guns, the *Eagle*, the *Lenox*, the *Monmouth*, the *Orford* and the *Swiftsure* all with 70 guns, the 54-gun *Romney*, the *Cruiser* and the *Valeur* each with 24 guns, the *Weazel* with just 10 cannon, the *Griffin*, the *Isabella*, the *Phoenix* and the *Vulcan* with just 8 apiece and finally the *Firebrand*, a frigate which was so meagrely armed that no one bothered to note it. In fact the 54-gun *Panther* was the last to join the line, coming up alone from Tangiers as the fleet passed Cape Spartel.

A great deal of nonsense has been talked and written about the last voyage of the *Association* and those other ships. It has been left to Commander W. E. May of the Royal Navy to paint a true picture of what happened in his heavily researched article in the *Journal of the Institute of Navigation* (volume 13, no. 3). For this fascinating report he studied forty-four log books from the captains, masters and lieutenants of the ships involved, all of whom were required to keep logs while at sea.

But first let us look at the earlier part of the voyage to disaster –

because that is what is was. The weather was not good. First there were gales from the west for five days, then squalls and then as a relief two days of light winds. Such peaceful sailing was not to last and next the fleet was hit by easterly gales. On 18 October these gales died down, only to be replaced by another from the north-west. This was useful as the fleet now turned to run into the mouth of the Channel and home. On the twenty-first the sky cleared enough for some observations to be taken and the fleet hove to for a short while to take soundings. According to the log books these soundings varied between 90 and 140 fathoms and only told them that they were on the edge of the Continental Shelf.

And this is where the nonsense begins to be woven into the story of the *Association*'s last voyage. The fact that the ships hove to for soundings seems over the years to have been enlarged into a great meeting of Sir Cloudesley and his captains. The meeting was said to have been held on board *Association* in Sir Cloudesley's great cabin. All the sailing masters were present, and the question put to each one of them was, 'Where exactly are we now?' All except one were convinced that they were in the latitude of Ushant and right in the middle of the English Channel. The one voice against, was, according to the story, that of Sir William Jumper of the *Lenox*. Sir William insisted that they were well to the north and west and in three hours' sailing would reach the Scillies. Sir Cloudesley is said to have brushed this opinion brusquely aside and to impress Sir William with the error of his ways despatched him with the frigate *La Valeur* and the fireship *Phoenix* to announce their arrival to the authorities in Falmouth. So goes the story.

Let us see how that fits the facts. The fact is, according to the log books, that no such meeting took place. It is true that on 22 October, Sir William Jumper in *Lenox*, *La Valeur* and *Phoenix* were detached from the fleet for convoy duty at Falmouth. On that day Sir William noted in his log book the time of parting company from the fleet as 11 am and set off steering north-east by north. Sir William was not entirely sure where he was and sighting sail to the north of him set out after them to ask for exact bearings. By the set of the two ships' sails on the horizon he thought them to be English frigates. By two o'clock on that afternoon he was not near enough to speak, but knew that there was in any case no

point in trying to. He could see now the ships were not English
frigates but privateers, and they were clearly not stopping to
speak to him or his seventy guns. Visibility was dropping and the
weather thickening and Sir William began to fear that he was
about to run into the Cornish coast. So he altered course to
east-by-south. At four o'clock that afternoon he steadied on
east-south-east, and the three ships sailed on into the darkness.

Back to the main fleet. It is enough to know that the navigators
on board nearly all of those ships had placed their position as
miles and miles to the south and east of where they really were.
Commander May points out in his article that 'on one day the
officers of the *St George* differed by as much as 111 miles from
one another in their estimates of the latitude'! But, credit where
credit is due, Commander May also says that the master of the
Panther was very nearly correct in his position and must have
thought that the fleet was standing into danger. He points out too
that the *Panther* remained on the southern flank of the fleet and
was one of the few ships which did not have to alter course.

At 4 pm on 22 October the fleet hove to once again to take
soundings and then, not knowing that they were just to the east
of the Scillies, set course to the east again. Now with the wind
behind them their speed increased to nearly four-and-a-half
knots and they must have imagined that they were rolling happily home. In fact Sir Cloudesley and his fleet were on collision
course with the Scillies and heading for one of the biggest
maritime disasters that England has ever known.

At almost exactly 8 pm the ninety-gun, 165-foot-long *Association* struck the granite teeth of the Western Rocks. Within
moments the seas were breaking over her and she was a ship no
more. The *St George* following was luckier. She struck the same
rocks, but managed to get off. The *Eagle* was not so fortunate. She
went down like a stone with all hands. The *Romney* sank, and
only one man reached the shore. The *Firebrand*, a frigate under
the command of Captain Percy, sank too, but five of her crew
came ashore clinging to some wreckage, and Captain Percy and
seventeen of his men managed to get to land in a boat.

In a matter of moments it was all over. The ships had gone, and
Sir Cloudesley with them. Sir George Byng in the *Royal Anne* had
a narrow escape and, but for the presence of mind of his officers
and crew, would have joined Sir Cloudesley, drowning in the

sea. The handling of the *Royal Anne* was superb. She went about, and the rocks slid by less than a ship's length away.

From the four wrecks there were twenty-three survivors – in other words about two thousand men died in the space of a few minutes. The swiftness of the destruction was obvious to the crews of the Welsh fleet who the next day had the wretched task of collecting wreckage and bodies. There were seven men-of-war from the Welsh fleet in the Scillies at the time, and boats from the *Southampton*, the *Arundel*, the *Lizard*, the *Salisbury*, *Antelope*, *Hampshire* and the *Charles* were ordered about this task.

While all this ghastly work was going on, it is amazing to note that Sir William Jumper was upping anchor from the sheltered place in the Scillies where he had spent a few hours before daybreak, and heading back to Falmouth as ordered. Before he cleared the Scillies he did hear something about wrecks, but had no idea which ships were concerned.

What had happened to Sir William's *Lenox*, *La Valeur* and *Phoenix*? In fact he had sailed so far to the north after the privateers that it was not until three o'clock in the morning on 23 October that he was amazed to find himself among the Scillies. And he was coming down to them on a south-easterly course! *Phoenix* was holed on the rocks around Samson Island and had to be beached to save her. *Lenox* and *La Valeur* anchored safely until daylight when they continued on their way. His amazement at the navigational errors made by the fleet and his explanation for it is quite clear in a letter he wrote to the Lord High Admiral dated 29 October 1707 from 'Ye Downs'. This can be seen at the Public Record Office (Adm. 1 1981).

Was navigation really that bad? The answer is, yes, it was. But you must remember that often these navigators worked wonders with primitive instruments and unreliable or grossly distorted charts. The Scillies for example were shown to be about ten miles to the north of their true position, certainly up until the middle of the eighteenth century. In his book *Cornish Shipwrecks – The Isles of Scilly* (published by David and Charles), Richard Larn quotes two classic eighteenth-century navigational blunders. In 1703 a homeward-bound fleet of East Indiamen thought they were in the English Channel near the Isle of Wight. They were much surprised to find the land ahead of them was Lundy! In 1758 the 64-gun French man-of-war *Belliquex*, on passage from Quebec also sailed up to Lundy and into the British fleet. Her captain was convinced that he was about to enter Brest!

It was Rex Cowan who pointed out to me that Sir William Jumper's letter finally destroys the story of the meeting of navigators on board *Association* and the myth that Sir William's was the lone voice to protest that they were close to the Scillies. If the story were true, argues Rex Cowan, could Sir William have resisted saying, 'but, sir, I told them.' He is right. If the story were true then Sir William would never have written a letter like this:

I am extremely surprised for the bad news of ye Admiral . . . indeed fear I should have had the same fate if I had not parted with ye Adml that day and sailed away those hours to ye N to speak with two ships I took to be English Frigatts to know the bearings of the land butt they proved privateers, I should have steered to ye N'ward while daylight to make Scilly beleiving myself the length thereof; if it had not proved thick weather which made me keep my Luff and steer ESE & SE By E till I met with Scilly.

Indeed never so deceived in my life having come into the Channel above 100 times and very often when I had no observations of the sun for a fortnite or 3 weeks in the winter neither can I impute this extraordinary deviation from a serious consideration of my past works to anything but the age and deficiency of our Compass having had a very good observation two days before which agreed with the other ships and am pretty well satisfied this error has been in the age and def. of our compas since most or all the Fleet were a head of their ships which was reckon in Navigation a very good fault giving us cautions to look out early for Land or Danger.

Sir William's complaints about the wooden compass-boxes was acted upon and many compasses used in the fleet were found to be grossly defective. It was ordered that brass compasses should replace them and, although this order was not thoroughly implemented for another hundred years, it is perhaps the one good thing to come out of that day of disaster. For day of disaster it was. There were dead bodies everywhere on the beaches of the Scillies and one of them was that of Sir Cloudesley Shovell.

By the orders of Queen Anne there was an elaborate funeral for the admiral, and a fulsome memorial is still there in Westminster Abbey to mark his last resting-place. You will find it in the south aisle near the choir. It depicts Sir Cloudesley reclining, dressed as a Roman. And the inscription reads:

Sir Cloudesley Shovell Knt. Rear Admirall of Great Britain and Admirall and Commander in Chief of the Fleet. The just rewards of his long and faithful Services. He was deservedly beloved of his Country and Esteem'd tho' dreaded by the Enemy, who had often experienced his Conduct and Courage. Being shipwreckt on the Rocks of Scylly in his voyage from Thoulon. The 22nd of October 1707 at Night in the 57th year of his Age. His fate was lamented by all, But especially the Sea faring part of the Nation to whom he was a Generous Patron and a worthy example.

His body was flung on the shoar and buried with others in the sands, but being soon after taken up was plac'd under this Monument which his Royall Mistress has caus'd to be Erected to commemorate His Steady Loyalty and Extraordinary Vertues.

So Sir Cloudesley rests in the abbey, and this seems to be the right moment to investigate all the legends that concern his death. He was washed ashore at Porth Hellick, a sandy bay south of St Mary's, nearly seven miles from the scene of the wrecks. Legend number one says that he was still alive when washed ashore and was murdered by two women for the great emerald ring that glittered among others on his fingers. This story is embroidered to include the cutting off of the fingers to get at the rings. It is true that one Harry Pennick, who, searching the cover later found the body, did order it to be buried in the sand near the spot on which it came ashore.

Legend number two says that because Sir Cloudesley had had a sailor hanged from the yard-arm for daring to say that the ships were near the Scillies, grass would never grow on his grave, and never has done so to this day. And legend number three says that the woman who actually had the emerald ring could get no benefit from it – she dare not sell it, because it would have been recognized at once. On her death-bed she made a confession of her crime, and the ring was returned to Sir Cloudesley's family. Mr Roland Morris says that the emerald ring was made into a locket and is now in possession of Sir Cloudesley's family. He told me that he has seen the smaller ring – a gold band with a crest – after being sworn to secrecy about its present ownership. All he will say is that the ring's hiding-place is 'under a stone in a Cornish kitchen floor'.

Now the facts. We do know that Sir Cloudesley's body was washed ashore and that it was buried on the beach. We know that it was exhumed for the state burial. A letter of the time states that after his body was exhumed it was noticed that 'his ring was lost from his finger, which last however left the impression on his finger as also a second. His head was not at all swelled with the water, neither had he any bruises nor scars upon him, save for a small scratch over one eye as if by a pin.' And Dr James Yonge of Plymouth, who embalmed him, thought it worth while recording that he was paid £50 for the task, but made no mention of severed fingers or wounds. And a letter written by Addison, the Under Secretary of State, dated 31 October 1707 says: 'Yesterday we had news that the body of Sir Cloudesley Shovell was found on the coast of Cornwall. The fishermen, who were searching among the rocks, took a tin box out of the pocket of one of the carcasses that was floating and found in it the commission of an Admirall: upon which, examining the body more closely, they found it was poor Sir Cloudesley.'

At this moment it is important that we should swing forward in time to 1967 and chart the beginning of what can only be called the 'Scilly Shambles'. Let me stress at once that the blame for this description of what was to happen next does not lie with the two civilian and one Royal Navy teams which were granted contracts to search for the wreck of the *Association*, but can be explained by some strange lack of foresight in high places.

Be that as it may no one would, I think, argue that the credit for the relocation of the wreck of the *Association* must go to Dick Larn, who was at that time a serving petty officer in the Royal Navy. As diving officer of the Naval Air Command S-A C, a special branch of the B S-A C, he was the instigator of the navy's search for the remains of *Association*. He was ideally placed for such a search, as he was stationed at HMS *Culdrose*, the Fleet Air Arm's base near Helston. But he was not to know that two other civilian teams had had the same idea. The leaders of the civilian teams concerned were respectively Roland Morris, a former 'hard-hat' diver of great experience, and Bob Rogers and Mike Ross, who had little experience, but matched what they did have with a great deal of youthful enthusiasm.

Claims and counter-claims about who was first on the trail will go on until the end of time, but certainly it was the NACSAC (B S-A C special branch no. 66) that relocated the wreck in 1967. The NACSAC divers timed their expedition to the Scillies perfectly. The sun shone steadily day after day, and the sea around the

Western Rocks was mirror-smooth. Diving started on 2 July. That day the divers searched in the deep water to the west of the reef. They found nothing. The next day was the same.

But Tuesday, 4 July, was the day to remember. The divers rolled over from the Gemini inflatables that they were using as tenders and they landed on the sea-bed right on top of not one cannon, but dozens! They seemed to be almost in rows. Some were at a crazy angle tipped over in holes, others were clustered together in groups, as though they had rolled overboard in a heap. The area was, as the divers excitedly reported, covered in cannon – and at least three of them were bronze.

The navy divers, as you might expect, treated this as a team affair, but to be strictly accurate the first diver to see the cannon was Lieutenant Commander Jack Gayton, the then chairman of NACSAC. By the end of that week – the divers and the navy crewmen worked flat out, as they knew their time was limited – they had recovered in conditions of complete secrecy a bronze signal cannon, two breech-loaders, huge bronze rigging wheels, silver coins and the first gold coin to be found, a Portuguese 4,000-reis piece dated 1704.

They had tried to raise two huge bronze cannon, but failed. The lifting equipment at their disposal would not take the strain. The navy now gave the men an extension to continue their work. Bad weather at first held them up, but then with the aid of aircraft lifting bags with a capacity of ten tons each (airlifted from the Royal Naval Air Station at *Culdrose*) the first of these magnificent guns glowed its way to the surface. When HMS *Puttenham* put into St Mary's on the evening of Monday, 10 July, the two-and-a-half-ton richly decorated cannon was there for all to see hanging from her stern – and the secret was out.

The news of the naval diver's find spread swiftly and the newspapers gave it some splendid headlines. Sir Cloudesley Shovell was news again – 260 years after his death. Both the other contract-holders have recorded in print the way the news affected them.

Roland Morris, who had a non-exclusive contract with the Ministry of Defence for the *Association* in 1966 wrote: 'This news sent our blood pressure soaring, our anxiety complex became almost unmanageable, for this was exactly the area where we were intending to dive on our arrival in the Islands planned for the last week of July 1967.'

And Mike Ross of Blue Seas Divers, who also had a 1966 MOD contract for the ship, wrote in an article in *Triton*: 'No sooner had we set out on our plan than the news "Navy Sub-Aqua Club Locate Association" appeared. More reports followed: "Cannon, Gold and Coins found on wreck", "9 foot 6 inch Bronze Cannon Raised". We were stunned. We had a contract, but it was useless without money to support us. There was no other course but to get another partner with financial backing to join us.'

There is no doubt that at that moment the Scillies was the centre of attention of the European diving world. Everyone wanted to get in on the act. And many did. Though the contract-holders hurried to the scene and got down to the wreck site of the *Association* as soon as they could, the fact that they had contracts was not of great importance. The shambles had begun. The invasion of the Gilstone by divers of all sorts was not illegal. Anyone could dive on the wreck of the *Association* and bring up what they like, provided they hand what they recover to the Receiver of Wreck. In these circumstances the non-exclusive contracts handed out by the MOD afforded no protection.

But Roland Morris was not cheated of his dream of possessing a bronze cannon – in fact he and his team raised three beauties. But the best of all was the first to come up after he had blasted two rotten old iron cannon out of the way.

It is difficult to describe the thrill that looking at one of these ancient cannon recovered from the sea gives to you. I know that, when Roland Morris showed me that first prize of his in his famous Admiral Benbow restaurant in Penzance, my instinctive reaction was to reach out and stroke it. For these are no battered old guns, but highly decorated works of art. This first culverin of Roland Morris is without doubt the best of them all. The lifting eyes are two dolphins. And instead of the name 'Le Duc de Beaufort' that the NACSAC gun bears, this one has 'Le Comte de Vermandois' on it. The decorations gleam and wink in the light, and the sight for aiming this fine piece is a delicately worked lizard or salamander. If you are in Penzance go and see it at Roland Morris's museum.

If there was any doubt about the origin of these bronze guns it was all cleared up during the cleaning of them. Roland Morris would go down each night into the cellar where his men were working on the long task of removing the encrustation and verdigris of centuries under water to see how they were getting on. One night he could hardly believe his eyes, for there, in crude letters two-and-a-half inches high and cut three-eighths of an inch deep into the bronze of one of the guns, was the word VIGO.

'Good Lord!' exclaimed Morris, 'Why wasn't I told about this?' When the significance of the marking was explained, one of the men said: 'If it had been WIGAN we still wouldn't have known!' The reason for the marking was probably to make sure that the gun was identifiable as loot from the Battle of Vigo Bay in 1702 and to help with the later division of the spoils.

The divers who worked the wreck commercially were very conscious of the value of the items they were recovering. On several occasions they worked for hours to recover the intact sole of a leather shoe or a riding spur, or just a mangled 'something' because it looked interesting. It would have been all too easy to have ploughed through everything with hammer and chisel to get at the specie.

Some idea of the care taken by these men can be seen if you visit the Isles of Scilly Museum. On display are a matching pair of spurs, a silver ladle, a sand-box and seal and many other small items all carefully dug out from the marine growth of 260 years.

Dug out? What then is the site like? One thing is certain – it is no place for beginners. When the sea is calm everywhere else, it is still working on the Gilstone. Great waves have been known to erupt without warning from the 'calm' of the sea, and the divers – at one time there were five rival groups working the wreck – accepted them in the end as a normal hazard. As they all seemed to follow the same course, these waves were fairly simple to avoid with experience.

Mike Ross described the site under water as a canyon – a maze of gulleys, jumbled boulders and caves under these boulders. Tons of granite from rock falls have completely obliterated parts of the site. These are Ross's words:

There is no wreck as such to be seen, just the cannon and the anchors scattered over an area as big as two football pitches. Some cannon are 30 feet down in fissures in the rock. All manner of tools besides the usual hammers and chisels were needed. Coins and artefacts were usually covered with 'crud', hard layers of conglomerated iron oxide and pitch and had to be dug out with hoes, shovels and even pickaxes. Explosives were essential fairly often in the search to clear the rock-falls and crumbling iron cannon. But these were used with great care.

Dick Larn says: 'The most successful diver on the *Association* was the one prepared to work the hardest.' Coins on the Gilstone are hard won, but the rewards were high. One gold coin fetched £170 when sold at the July 1969 London auction.

Places on the wreck site acquired names recognized by each and every *Association* diver – 'Cannon Gully', 'Death Gulch' or 'Aladdin's Cave' were just a few of the names that could be instantly identified by any diver working the site. 'Aladdin's Cave' was the one which rated the most wordage in newspaper reports. It was in fact a hole under a boulder, from which Mr Morris's divers raised some fourteen hundred silver coins in six hard days' diving.

Coins, cannon, cannon-balls, gold wedding-rings (inscribed 'God above increase our love', 'True love is endless'), bronze pulley wheels marked with the broad arrow symbol of the British government, dividers for navigation, silver spoons, thimbles, a chamber-pot, a dagger-hilt – the divers found them all. Removing a huge iron cannon led Mike Ross and Bob Rogers to the strangest find of all. Preserved in pitch and iron oxide was a skeleton. Pieces of eight were stuck to the skull – pieces of eight that had come from a mint in South America.

But the divers were still tormented by the same question that worries archaeologists everywhere. All right, the coins were all the right date (there was not one later than 1707), the cannon and pulley wheels conformed to the theory that this was Sir Cloudesley Shovell's ship. But was it? There was no single item among all the treasures that the divers had brought up from the Gilstone that gave absolute confirmation that this was the *Association*. And for the contract-holders this was vital. Their agreements depended on the shipwreck being that of the *Association*. It was up to them to prove that it was.

In October 1969 Bob Rogers was diving with Terry Hiron, who now runs a diving firm in the Scillies, when they made a discovery that might be the clincher. Says Bob Rogers:

We saw it first buried 12 feet under a huge boulder. Only the breech showed when a torch was shone on it. We managed to lasso it with the help of a noose and ten-foot rod. Once we had the rope firmly around the breech we tied the other end to our chartered diving boat *Nemo* – then opened the engine full out.

The cannon came out with a rush, but it took the combined efforts of the skipper, Peter Thompson, and eight of us to get the cannon off the bottom and up to the surface.

The boulder that had trapped that cannon weighed at least a hundred tons, and the team could never have lifted it off, but the cannon came free fortunately – because it was unique.

Most of the other bronze cannon finds had been French, presumably the spoils of war, but this one was English. It was ornately decorated from breech to muzzle with such embellishments as the Prince of Wales's insignia and his motto *Ich Dien*, but it bore a Latin inscription on a plaque near the breech. In free translation the Latin read: 'Charles, Earl of Devonshire and Master of Ordnance, commissioned Thomas Pit to make it in the year 1604.' Perhaps this cannon was one of the admiral's favourite pieces. Who can tell? But one thing was certain: instead of confirming that the ship was the *Association*, it still left the question open to doubt.

What was really needed was the discovery of some piece of evidence that was absolutely impossible to deny, and in the winter of 1969 Roland Morris and his team of divers found it. To them goes the honour of the final identification of the wreck, a justifiable honour, because of all the teams they had been the most persistent. Identification came in the form of a solid silver plate. When it was cleaned the arms of Sir Cloudesley Shovell gleamed out clearly. Diver Mark Horobin had made identification certain with his find.

After eighteen months of consideration the MOD (Navy) announced that any items salvaged which were once the property of the government – that is, cannon, ship's fittings, other than personal property and coin, became the property of the finder – provided that the finders held MOD (Navy) contracts. This meant that the NACSAC team, Roland Morris and Blue Seas Divers could keep many of the items they had found. Objects found by non-contract holders would receive consideration according to their value. But all specie, coins, rings and other personal items were to come under the usual Board of Trade regulations and would be auctioned – the finder to receive one-third of the sale value. So that was that. Roland Morris by his discovery of the silver plate had clinched matters.

At the auction at Sotheby's on 15 July 1969 two bronze cannon were sold for £3,000 each. A Portuguese reis of 1707 made £160 and a French Louis of 1694 fetched £150. And the sale of coins and other items together brought a total of £12,354. At a second Sotheby's auction of items from the *Association*, on 28 January 1970, £310 was paid for a Peter II 4,000-reis of 1705 and a John V 4,000-reis of 1707, the year of the wreck, went for £190. Roland Morris bought back the plate which had identified the wreck for £2,100 and it can be seen today at his Museum of Nautical Art in Penzance. A pewter chamber-pot of about 1700, which had also been recovered, sold amid laughter for £270, as it seemed likely that this was the admiral's own. The laugh was on the spectators, for Roland Morris bought back the pot – only to find two gold coins encrusted under the rim! The total for the sale was £10,175, making the amount raised by objects from the wreck up to that date to £22,529.

This amount was in reality quite small. Roland Morris, who had been on the site for most of the time since the discovery of the wreck, has no doubts at all about what has happened. He believes that unauthorized diving has robbed the wreck of hundreds, possibly thousands of coins, which will never change hands in any official transaction. Could the Scilly Shambles happen again? It seems unlikely now that the Protection of Wrecks Act of 1973 can be invoked swiftly to guard such a wreck.

We have not heard the end of the *Association* though. Recently in the diving press, and particulary in *Triton*, the B S-A C magazine which goes individually to each of the twenty-five thousand active diving members of the club in Britain, and to other clubs in Europe and the world, the notice overleaf has appeared.

This notice is the work of Terry Hiron and Jim Heslin, whose names occur again and again in diving reports on wrecks in the Scillies. Terry Hiron put the reason for it to me quite simply:

The Ministry of Defence Contracts lapsed in 1972. We have been working the wreck since 1969, first with Blue Seas Divers and since 1971 we have been the only group working on the site. We have carried out an enormous amount of work and as the site is not protected we have found it necessary to use civil law to protect our interests.

For two-and-a-half years we have been preparing a site survey which

---

NOTICE TO DIVERS

Association

Notice is hereby given that the Isles of Scilly Underwater Centre is in possession as salvors of the wreck of the *Association* sunk off the Gilstone Ledges, Isles of Scilly in 1707.

The approximate co-ordinates of the centre of the site are 49° 51' 44" N 4; 06° 24' 30" W. The site is marked with two red marker buoys.

LEGAL ACTION WILL BE TAKEN WITHOUT NOTICE AGAINST ANY TRESPASSER

T. J. Hiron
Isles of Scilly Underwater Centre

---

has never been done accurately if at all. If divers are prepared to dive under our supervision we will be happy to allow them to dive on the site.

Is the treasure of the *Association* now long gone? Have the treasure hunters finally cleaned her out? Roland Morris once told me that he believed the divers had only just 'scratched the surface of what there is to be found on the site – in ten or twenty years' time there will still be pieces of gold coming up.' He said that in 1972.

Today Terry Hiron, speaking over six years later, says exactly the same thing: 'In my opinion, the *Association* has hardly been touched. This is based on research and my personal knowledge of the site. I think she is a wise old bird who will not yield up her treasures without a great deal more work on the salvors' part. We find the site is becoming more and more interesting as we find more and more of it. The odd coin can be found when the sea moves the boulders around.' However, he does not think that all that number of coins were looted from the site: 'If the lot totalled a thousand coins I would be greatly surprised'.

Terry Hiron and Jim Heslin are trying to negotiate a new

contract for the *Association* with the MOD. They report too that they have discovered a large area of timber, pottery and small items to the east of the present *Association* site. So far they are not able to say whether or not this is more of Sir Cloudesley's ship. Navigational instruments they have found there have been sent to the National Maritime Museum at Greenwich. Terry Hiron asks very tentatively if this new area of wreckage could be the *Romney*. And there starts another mystery – the mystery of Tearing Ledge.

Where are the rest of the ships that died with Sir Cloudesley and his *Association*? This problem is not yet completely solved to everyone's satisfaction. The trouble is that there are a lot of wrecks of wooden warships around the huge area loosely called the Western Rocks off the Scillies. Between 1630 and 1710 there are records of between thirty and forty wrecks that could have ended up there. If you add to that those ships that died suddenly in the night and left no trace of their dying then you have some idea of the identification problems that come with the frequent finds of cannon by divers in the area.

The site of one of these ships, either the *Romney* or the *Eagle*, could be out on Crim Reef. There in 135 feet of water one of Roland Morris's divers, Peter Grosch, found cannon, ship's brass navigation dividers and five silver coins. The site is a wild one – a reef top in twenty-five feet of water which falls away in spectacular sheer cliffs to the bottom at 130–150 feet. Atlantic rollers constantly bash at the six rocks which break the surface at low tide or the only two that show at high. A NACSAC team have surveyed the site. In that team again was Dick Larn. He reported that the divers found the remains nearby of two previously unknown wrecks, iron sailing ships of about 1875.

In 1969 a possible *Romney* or *Eagle* site was found on the Crebinicks Rocks and a large bronze bell and navigational slate were raised. Taking part in that expedition of Roland Morris was Paul Armiger, a staff photographer on the *Daily Telegraph* and one of the few Fleet Street photographers who can be told: 'The pic we want is a hundred feet down. Get it.'

Was the wreck that of *Romney* or was it *Eagle*? Surely the bell solved the mystery? Well, yes, it did and no, it did not. The bell which weighed two hundredweight was dated 1701 and bore the

Royal Navy's broad arrow mark. It was from a big navy ship all right, but the date did not seem to fit. The *Romney* came into service in 1694; the *Eagle* earlier in 1679. How did either get a bell dated 1701? Well, you have to be careful with bells, ships did tend to replace them if lost or damaged with any one that happened to be handy.

But we do know that the *Eagle* was rebuilt in 1699 and is missing from one navy list in 1700. So perhaps she was recommissioned in 1701. That would tend to indicate that the wreck on the Crebinicks at the place they call Tearing Ledge is the *Eagle*. No one is yet sure, for the 1975 Order No. 174, which came into force on 13 March that year designating the site under the Protection of Wrecks Act of 1973 says that this is a restricted area off Tearing Ledge near Bishop Rock, Isles of Scilly, round 'the site of the wreck of the vessel which is believed to be HMS *Romney*'!

Let us go back however to photographer Paul Armiger and his view of the site and the finds. He saw golden guineas from the reign of James II recovered by divers. He also was there when a plain gold wedding-ring, inscribed inside 'In thy sight is my delight', and a woman's diamond ring of great beauty were recovered.

Perhaps Tearing Ledge is the wrong name for the site. Perhaps we should call it 'Whispering Ledges'. Listen to Armiger: 'There are some forty cannon lying around the site. Four of us who have dived there have all heard whispering voices, probably due to the rock structure and the movement of the sea. But it is quite uncanny when you look up and find no one there.'

Working the site now is Rex Cowan. He and his team have done a great deal of original research into the final fate of Sir Cloudesley's lost ships. Once again the joint dive leader on the site is Roy Graham (with Terry Hiron). Other divers taking part were Harry Graham on a full-time basis, and part-timers Jim Heslin, Donald Bates, G. Brisby, Flying Officer Mike Cameron, Peter McBride, Tony Pike, Brian Ranner, Lieutenant-Colonel Walter Schob, D. Smith and Colin Thornley. The boat skipper was once again David Stedeford. Howard Pell and John Maloney were the archaeological assistants working on drawing and cataloguing finds in the archaeological unit in HMS *Belfast*.

Let us look first at our two ships. The *Eagle*, a third-rate, was built at Portsmouth in 1679 by Daniel Furzer. A big ship, the length of her gun-deck 151 feet 6 inches, her keel 125 feet, her breadth 40 feet 8 inches and her burden 1,065 tons. After her rebuilding she increased her tonnage to 1,099 but other dimensions were unaltered. She normally carried 70 guns.

The *Romney*, a second-rate, was built at Blackwall in 1694 by Sir Henry Johnson. She was smaller, the length of her gun-deck 131 feet and ½ inch, her keel 109 feet, her breadth 34 feet 4 inches and her burden 683 tons. She normally carried about 50 guns.

The number of guns will be important in later details of this detective story, but for the moment let us return to Rex Cowan and his research into the last moments of the ships. First of all let us take the *Firebrand* out of our calculations. There is good evidence that she struck a rock near the Bishop and Clerks, but managed to get into Broad Sound before sinking.

That leaves us with the *Romney* and *Eagle*. Remember that they struck in the dark. Add to that the fact that none of the survivors would have known the local names for rocks. All the rocks, now collectively called the Western Rocks, were at the time mostly known as the Bishop (named after the rock on which the lighthouse now stands) and the Clerks, which stand around the Bishop. The Gilstone on which the *Association* wreck was found is some way from the Bishop.

Every wreck diver loves a sunken ship puzzle. It gives him something to do in the winter days when diving is impossible. It drives him into research. The *Romney/Eagle* puzzle obviously fascinated Rex Cowan. So much so that his research turned up an original letter, once again from Sir William Jumper, in the Public Record Office. Dated 24 October 1707, it comes from the *Lenox* off Falmouth, and it gives an eye-witness account of the death-throes of some of those sailors from the wrecks. It conjures up only too well a ghastly picture of death in the dark. Sir William writes:

I am likewise to acquaint you that a small French prize laden with fish taken some days since by the Orford is arrived here.

The Master mate of the Orford who commands the said prize told me this at that ye 22nd instant in the evening lying about 8 o'clock he heard many guns fired as from a ship in distress, and about 9 his company cried out a Rock, on which he set his foresail and weather it but a very little, which he says was the body of a great ship wreck and many crying out for God's sake to save them which he could nott, but standing on then soon cried out Another Rock which bit he says was a wreck of a ship to butt standing a little further to ye South East about 10 o'clock they see the Bishop and Clerk two great rocks but weather all almost attaching the bigger rocks. . . .

Can you imagine the mate of the *Orford* having been given command of a prize not only finding himself weaving a twisting course in the dark through a sea littered with savage rocks, but also finding twice that he was not in danger of running on to rocks at all, but wreckage and men? And so close did he come to piling his own ship up on the wreckage that he could see even in the dark the faces and hear them calling out to him, 'For God's sake, save us.' But with the wind behind him and the heavy seas there was nothing that he could do but sail on and hope to save his own prize crew and the ship.

But, graphic as this account is, it still does not tell us which ship is which. The cannon survey carried out with Peter McBride revealed sixty cannon still on the site and it is known that two were removed by other diving teams earlier. There may be others hidden elsewhere as the site ranges from ledges near the surface right down to 130 feet. This number of cannon would seem to indicate that it could not be the *Ronmey* as there are too many for her fifty guns, and the calibre of several is larger than that of those she would have carried.

The divers' work goes on and positive identification will come. Cowan's divers thought they had it when they recovered a silver fork with a demi-griffon crest. A check through all the names of the crew of both ships – including captains, masters, officers, midshipmen, anyone in fact who might even faintly have a coat of arms – has proved negative. And the College of Arms has been unable to identify the crest. Was some eighteenth-century con-man trying to impress with his own faked coat of arms? Who knows? But there is a chance that we shall know soon which ship is which. As you read this, the divers are still about their pain-staking work on the sea-bed, where they know that nothing is too small or too ordinary not to be worth saving.

The bell of the *Fraumetta Catherina von Flensburgh*, sunk in December 1786, sits on the top table at Guildhall. Harry Secombe burst into song to evident delight of Prince Charles.
(See Introduction)
Picture by Brian Worth

The oldest evidence of a shipwreck ever found in British waters. These Bronze Age weapons were discovered underwater near the White Cliffs by Dover branch of the B S-A C. Divers (left to right) are Simon Stevens, Terry Dole, Keron Jaynes, Chris Osmond, Peter Harris-Mayes. (See chapter 1) Picture by Brian Philp of the Kent Archaeological Rescue Unit

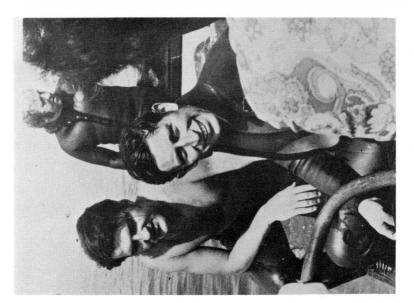

Phil Baker, BS-AC national coach for Yorkshire, found this Bronze Age sword while diving near Salcombe, South Devon. (See chapter 1) Picture by E. C. Walsh. And, *right*, Prince Charles chats to divers after his own dives to Henry VIII's *Mary Rose*, which sank off Portsmouth in 1545. (See chapter 3) Picture by Bob Field

This pewter flagon was recovered from the collapsed sterncastle of the *Mary Rose*. It is the earliest known pewter vessel to survive today. (See chapter 3) Picture by BP Chemicals. *Below*, some of the hundreds of coins recovered from the 'silver wreck' in Rill Cove, Cornwall. The coins are Mexican silver pieces of eight and, a rarity, a piece of two. (See chapter 6) Picture by Richard Larn

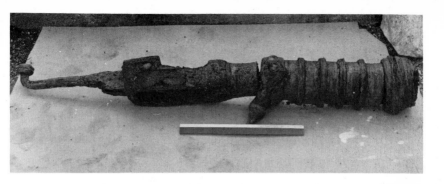

Is this cannon the clue to a shipwreck of 1509? Roy Wardle and the small bronze cannon he found sixty feet down off Challaborough, South Devon. (See chapter 2)

And, *top*, another rare sight, a banded cannon from the 'silver wreck' in Rill Cove, Cornwall. After conservation this one is on display in Southsea Castle Museum. (See chapter 6) Picture by Richard Larn

Treasures from the Armada galleass *Girona*, now in Ulster Museum, Belfast. *Top left*: gold cross of a Knight of the Order of Malta. *Top right*: a book-shaped receptacle of gold. It contained wax pellets made in Rome and blessed by the pope to give miraculous powers of protection!
Bottom left: one of eleven cameos of the Byzantine Caesars, carved in lapis lazuli and mounted in gold frames set with pearls. *Bottom right*: a golden salamander pendant set with rubies. (See chapter 4) Ulster Museum pictures

If anyone ever had any doubt that the Armada's main aim was the invasion of England, this picture should dispel it. Here, in the wreckage and amid the magnificent bronze guns of the Armada galleon *La Trinidad Valencera*, is one of the wheels, amazingly preserved, that were to trundle those guns into action on land against London. (See chapter 5)

Left: One of the earliest 'alarm clocks' figured among the recoveries from the *Santo Christo de Castello*, sunk in 1667. They include knife-handles, a knife-sheath, a religious figure – and two tiny brass cannon. The little brass cannon are from a sort of sundial alarm clock. The cannon were mounted under a magnifying glass. When the sun reached a pre-set point, the concentrated rays of the sun fired the cannon. You can see one of these clocks in the National Maritime Museum at Greenwich. (See chapter 6) Picture by Richard Larn

Right: Over three hundred years under the sea and still undamaged. A pocket sundial found in the wreckage of the East Indiaman *Kennemerland* sunk in the Out Skerries in 1664, must rate as one of the most amazing underwater finds of all time. (See chapter 9) Picture by Keith Muckelroy

This cannon from the Dutch East Indiaman *Hollandia*, sunk in the Scillies in 1743, has one of the two lifting dolphin broken off. It was found and replaced and the cannon is now on display in the Amsterdam Maritime Museum. Pointing out the damage in this picture to Receiver of Wreck Mr Eric Browne, is wreck hunter Rex Cowan. The diver, still in his wet-suit and underwater life-jacket, is Jim Heslin. (See chapter 8)

Lost and buried under sand since her wreck in 1686, the woodwork of the *Princesse Maria*, one of the Dutch East India Company's fleet, emerges as the airlift sucks the covering away. The diver handling the nozzle of the airlift is Lieutenant Roy Graham. (See chapter 8) Picture taken at a depth of forty feet by Paul Armiger

A remarkable under-water picture taken at a depth of 105 feet down on the wreck of the Dutch East India-man *Hollandia*. Lieutenant-Commander Jack Gayton (left) and Nowell Pierce have just unearthed a pew-ter plate. Pierce is actually astride one of the giant anchors of which the ring can be seen in the foreground covered with growths, which are called appropriately 'dead-men's fingers'. (See chapter 8)

The day they knew they had found the *Princesse Maria*. Rex Cowan is in the centre holding one of the yellow building bricks that the Dutch East Indiamen so often carried. The divers surrounding him are from his team led by Lt Graham and the RAF Coltishall branch of the BS-AC. Inset is the jar containing forty pounds of mercury which is now in the Amsterdam Historical Museum. (See chapter 8)

Real treasure! The Receiver of Wreck for the Scillies Mr Eric Browne examining some of the 7,500 silver coins recovered from the *Association* by divers Jim Hesslin (centre) and Terry Hiron, who are now 'salvors in possession' of the wreck. (See chapter 10) Picture by Paul Armiger

One of the most remarkable wreck diving pictures ever taken. Here, 110 feet down, divers Mark Horobin (left) and Colin Gregory recover a ship's bell dated 1701 from the site they call Tearing Ledge in the Scilly Isles. (See chapter 10) Picture by Paul Armiger

The largest jigsaw puzzle in the world. Here are just a few of over thirty thousand pieces of the broken vases from the collection of Sir William Hamilton, recovered by divers from the 1798 wreck of HMS *Colossus*. Standing at the back of this room in the British Museum studying the pieces from which they hope to rebuild the vases, is Dr Ann Birchall, the archaeological director of the recovery operation. (See chapter 11) Picture by Keystone Press

Ammunition was important. Diver Ann Morris looks at a lead shot mould she has recovered from the wreck site of the Dutch East Indiaman *Kennemerland* in the Out Skerries. (See chapter 9) Picture by D. Shaw

Ammunition and guns were vitally important to the Dutch East Indiamen – they never knew when they would be called upon to fight. So here, recovered from the wreck of the *Amsterdam* at Hastings are iron cannonballs, bronze measuring gauges to make sure the shot was the right size, reamer rods for cleaning out cannon touchholes, and lead shot, some of which seems to have been fired! (See chapter 8) Picture by E. J. Marsden

ELEVEN

'I have not yet begun to fight!'

Lost at sea	On land
1753 HMS Assurance *on the Needles*	*George II reigns*
	The Seven Years War
1779 Bonhomme Richard *off Flamborough Head*	*Wolfe at Quebec*
	George III reigns
1798 HMS Colossus *in the Scillies*	*American War of Independence*
	Ministry of William Pitt
	War with France

Captain Scrope in the dawn of 24 April 1753 was content. He had had nothing but fair winds from Jamaica, and even good weather after their stop at Lisbon. The crew had behaved well; so had his officers. In particular he was, he felt, blessed with his master, David Patterson, a sober, diligent and careful fellow. Such a master was indeed a blessing to any commander, judging by the tales his fellow-captains had told him of their troubles with less able men.

With the Isle of Wight coming closer and closer every moment, Captain Scrope felt that he would now leave the decision about HMS *Assurance*'s course to David Patterson. If they could get through the Needles Channel they would avoid the long haul around the island to their destination at Spithead. But he would abide by Patterson's decision, despite his anxiety to be home.

'Will you take her through?' Scrope addressed this question to Patterson, who stood by his side. Patterson nodded, but Scrope wanted to make sure that his question was understood. 'She's in your charge, then?' 'She is,' said Patterson.

The westerly wind looked ideal. Later Patterson was to say that the wind was west by north or west-north-west, but it made no difference to his decision to take HMS *Assurance* through the narrows. Patterson looked out over the bow, scenting the wind and noting carefully that he had Alum Bay open with the Needle Rock. A glance at the compass – north-east-half-east. Then aloft. He noted: 'All sails out, but the studding sails and the shore tack at the cathead.' The sails filled and the *Assurance* moved confidently ahead.

But for all his confidence Patterson had never taken a ship through that channel before. True, he had been part of the crew of many ships that had passed through, but he had never actually been in command himself. Still, he did not worry. In fact when one of the passengers, the retiring Governor of Jamaica Trelawney approached him, anxious in the early hours for a first sight of home, and asked how close to the Needles they would go, he answered a little boastfully that 'they would pass so close that the fly of the ensign might actually touch the rock'. Allowing for the boast, the truth is that David Patterson was more afraid of the Shingles on the port side. These great sandbanks appeared to Patterson to be unusually high out of the water. He feared too that they had shifted from their usual position. Not such a ridiculous fear either, for any Isle of Wight sailor will tell you today that the sands do shift this way and that a certain amount.

So Patterson then set his course closer to the Needles than he would normally have done, and relied on the tide 'horsing' the ship to the west. Not that he was afraid to take the ship through. When the captain had asked him if he would take the ship, he could have decided, with St Catherine's Point seven leagues away, to go the long way round. But David Patterson felt in good spirits, and quite confident. They were now almost up to the Needles themselves, and the 133-foot-long ship was still going well. Patterson's course took them very close to the Needles, but he had no inkling of the disaster that was about to overtake him – until the leadsman suddenly called, 'A quarter less five'.

Patterson realized his danger. 'Cast again – quick!' he shouted. But before the lead line even left the man's hand the ship struck with a grinding crash that stopped her as though she had run into a stone quay. The dismay that raced through Patterson's brain was tempered with complete and utter disbelief. There was no rock charted where they had struck. According to all the charts there was nothing but deep water at the point where *Assurance* had jerked to a standstill in helpless chaos.

Amid the pandemonium that broke loose above and below decks, David Patterson had only one thought – it ought not, could not have happened. A year and a half he had been master of *Assurance*, and never in all his service had he done the slightest damage to the ship. Now here she was on an uncharted rock near the Needles. At the moment of striking HMS *Assurance* had stopped dead. Her only movement after the crunch of collision was for her head to fall around towards the north. Patterson had no idea of how long she stayed poised on the rock. He felt that it was a century before the damage reports started to come in, but in fact within the hour the water was gaining fast on their attempts to pump her out. Captain Scrope knew his ship was lost. He spared only a glance of pity for the frozen figure of David Patterson before organizing the safe evacuation of his passengers and crew.

The *Assurance* did not go down like a stone. In fact there was plenty of time and Governor Trelawney had sufficient to supervise the loading of his savings – in pieces of eight – into the boats before there was any urgency about leaving the stricken vessel. In the end it was several hours before the water flooded in sufficiently for the *Assurance* (the fourth to bear the name in navy records; she was built at the Heather Yard, Bursledon, and launched on 29 September 1747) to sink most of the way beneath the surface.

After that it was only a matter of time before Captain Scrope found himself before a court-martial. By an Admiralty order dated 1 May 1753 'the Honorable Edward Boscawen, Rear-Admiral of the White Squadron of His Majesty's Fleet and Commander in Chief of His Majesty's ships at Portsmouth Harbour' was directed to 'assemble a court-martial for enquiring into the cause of the loss of His Majesty's late ship the Assurance the 24th April last, when, endeavouring to go through the Needles, the said ship struck in the Narrows and was lost, and into the Conduct of the Officers and Men on that Occasion'.

The court-martial took place on board HMS *Tyger* in Portsmouth Harbour on 11 May 1753 with Boscawen as president and the other judges Captains Robert Pett, George Bridges Rodney,

Jonathan Montague, the Hon. Sam Barrington, Roger Martin, Charles Catford, Julian Legg and Sam Marshall.

Admiral Boscawen was a stern but not unkindly man, an odd mixture of sea-dog and scholar, who could write letters to his wife before setting off on some voyage which contained such poetic sentiments as 'To be sure I lose the fruits of the earth, but then I am gathering the flowers of the sea.' With him as president there would be no hanky-panky. But the end of the affair was not in much doubt. Finally Boscawen turned to his fellow-judges. 'Is it your opinion that Captain Scrope was at all accessory to the loss of the *Assurance*?' 'No.' They were unanimous. 'Is it your opinion that the lieutenants were at all accessory to the loss of the said ship?' 'No.' 'Is it your opinion that the rest of the officers and crew were at all accessory?' 'No.' 'Is it your opinion that the loss of the ship was owing to the unskilfulness, negligence or carelessness of the master?'

Finally they sorted out a suitable form of words for the clerk to pen. 'No, we do not attribute the loss to the negligence or carelessness of the master, but we attribute it to his ignorance of the rock the ship run upon, which is generally said to be little known.'

'What article does the master fall under?'

'Under part of the 26th Article by running the ship unskilfully upon the rock.'

'What punishment do you award him?'

'In regard to the general good character of the master, the court are unanimously of opinion that he be imprisoned three months in the Marshalsea.'

So poor David Patterson went to prison. And no one would envy him his three months, for the Marshalsea in London was a diabolical place. It stood opposite Maypole Alley, in Borough High Street, Southwark, where there had been a prison since the fourteenth century. In the eighteenth century it became the county jail for felons, an Admiralty jail for pirates (and the likes of David Patterson) and a debtors' prison. The conditions there were so bad that in the same year that David Patterson was committed John Wesley described the building as 'a picture of Hell upon Earth'. It was the prison made famous by Charles Dickens in *Little Dorrit*.

So over two hundred years the remains of the *Assurance* lay on the bottom undisturbed by anything but the fierce tides and storm surges which are a feature of the Needles area. But in 1956 one man started on the road that was to lead to her rediscovery. Derek Williams is a draughtsman with an Isle of Wight hovercraft firm and he is a diver. But though Derek Williams and his fellow Isle of Wight divers derived a great deal of pleasure from straight-forward diving, he wanted something more. He wanted to find a wreck. A wreck of his own. For years he searched old records and old books for some ship that had been wrecked on the coast of the Island, and which he could be the first to find. Such dreams are rarely fulfilled, but one day he found a reference to an HMS *Insurance* wrecked off the Needles in 1753.

At first he drew a blank. No one, not even the navy, knew of an HMS *Insurance*, and it was not until he noticed that a Prudential brochure carried the words 'Prudential Assurance Company' that he realized he had probably been slightly off course. HMS *Assurance*. Now, that was different. Lots of people in charge of records could find him information about that ship. But all they could tell him about the position was that it was 'off the Needles', and that is a mighty big area. Then he learned about the mystery rock that the ship was supposed to have struck, and he would go up on the cliffs and look down on the sea and out over the lighthouse and wonder just where she was. And his every spare moment was spent searching through old records, until at last Derek thought he knew – roughly – where the old ship lay.

For weeks after that [says Derek Williams], the weather wouldn't come right. But then it did – have you ever noticed how the weather and sea are perfect for diving all week and just when you're free at weekends the weather breaks up? – and off we went. We anchored close to the rock where I thought the ship was, and over the side I went. Within moments of hitting the sea-bed I suddenly realized I was over a big heap of cannon. I was so excited I just surfaced straight away. And I remember shouting 'She's there, she's there!' The wife and family were all in the big boat we were using at the time and back down I went again. I began scrabbling around picking up things like copper nails. The feeling was really quite something. It was unbelievable really – my dream had come true.

Copper nails shone bright green all around him, and he had thoughts immediately about lifting the cannon. However once back in the boat with his trophies – some of the first turned out to be cheap standard-issue marlin spikes all clearly marked with the navy's broad arrow – he had second thoughts. If he arrived back on shore with a cannon swinging from under the boat his discovery would immediately be common knowledge – and Derek wanted to keep this one to himself for the time being.

Subsequent dives proved that all the cannon were iron – there were twelve in all and Derek had them assessed as nine-pounders. The cannon were all jumbled together in a pile and cannon-balls made up part of the same heavily concreted heap. Was this the wreck of HMS *Assurance*? On almost the very next dive Derek thought he had found the final proof. On the site he found three pieces of a ship's bell. Some quite clearly had lettering on them, but it was not until he cleaned them up and put them together that he found to his horror that the wording on the bell read 'DREAM 1838'. For a time he was shattered.

Back he went to his wreck detection. Was there such a ship as HMS *Dream*? He could not find one. But there was a schooner called *Dream* of 162 tons built in Yarmouth, Isle of Wight in 1837 and lost somewhere around the island. What had more than likely happened was that *Dream* had been wrecked near the same spot, and her pieces had joined those of HMS *Assurance*.

So Derek went on with his underwater work. The wreck site was an extremely exposed and shallow area and, though he could expect thirty to forty feet visibility, on neap-tides he had only twenty minutes of slack water before the Solent tides bore down on him. And 'bore down' is the right description of what happened under water when the tide turned. First of all the visibility would disappear as all the gunk and muck from the Hampshire coast was swept through the Narrows. The force of the tidal waters was impossible to resist. It was just possible to cling on to some object on the bottom when it started, but Derek describes that sort of position as most uncomfortable, and even says that the waters give you a physical battering.

The wreck site itself measures about 200 feet long by 50 feet wide, and is pretty well concentrated. Derek Williams has searched around the site, and there seems to be nothing further out. Near the cannon is a mortar, and it looks as though the bomb is still in position in the muzzle. He recognized the mortar immediately, as it is very similar to the one which is outside the museum at Southsea. The mortar is quite short, about 4 feet long and 18 inches in diameter, in comparison with the cannon, which are all about 8 feet long. All the cannon seem to be the same size and are heavily encrusted, and rather worn round the muzzles. All are iron.

What else has he found? Clay pipe bowls, which fit the date, and a thin gold wedding-ring with some marking inside, but when I looked at it with Derek Williams it was impossible for us to decipher the meaning of the marks.

Down the starboard side of the probable line of the wreck are masses of big copper pins that were used to hold the timbers together, and then, close to the jumbled pile of cannon he found a sounding lead. The base of this – normally a hole filled with wax to pick up traces of the bottom and tell the leadsman what sort of sea-bed the ship was travelling over – has been rounded and battered by the sea so that the hole is gone. It is interesting to think that this is the lead whose last cast told Master David Patterson that he was in dead trouble. It is close to the probable position of the bow, and it is tempting to say that this was the very one, but such surmise is too romantic for the cold facts demanded by marine archaeologists.

Right beside the sounding lead Derek found a beautiful brass weight. Polished now, it gleams beautifully in the light, and beside the avoirdupois sign is the figure 8. Yet oddly enough the weight weighs exactly six pounds. A close study of the actual figure 8 may well expose a cheating eighteenth-century ship's officer. The top loop of the 8 does look as though someone has scratched it in, thus turning a 6 into an 8. The possibility that there was 'fiddling' in the issue of rations is obvious.

The diving has continued year after year and the wreck is now designated under the 1973 act. But Derek Williams has his problems, because coins and other items he has found on the site indicate that not only is the *Assurance* there, but so is the *Dream* and so is another ship, the *Pomone* of 1811. And it may be that Governor Trelawney did not get all his fortune off the ship when she sank. Some coins that Derek has discovered are dated 1749.

To say that Commodore John Paul Jones was looking for a fight is putting it mildly. In his *Bonhomme Richard*, the name he had given to the old *Duc de Duras* which Louis xvi of France had given him to raid British shipping in their home water, he sailed from Lorient on 9 August 1779. With him were *Pallas*, *Cerf* and *Vengeance*. At Ile de Groix he was joined by the frigate *Alliance*. Now the American Continental Navy was in action and the most important naval battle in the American Revolutionary War was only a month away.

You could hardly say that John Paul Jones had been given a fine ship. Quite the reverse, for the *Duc de Duras* had been long in the service of the French East India Company. She was slow. Her length was 154 feet and her beam 40 feet. She was designed to carry twenty guns, but Jones had her sides pierced to take an extra twenty-four pieces.

Even so Jones created havoc among shipping heading in and out of British ports, and took many prizes. In September Jones deliberately invited battle off the Humber, but no one took up the challenge, though he knew by now that a large English naval force was bound to be after him soon. On 23 September, near Flamborough Head, Jones sighted forty-one ships. It was not a naval force, but a convoy of merchant ships homeward bound from the Baltic. Between Jones and the convoy stood two English naval ships. One was the new fifty-gun frigate *Serapis*, commanded by Captain Richard Pearson; the other the twenty-gun sloop *Countess of Scarborough*.

Jones had with him now the 36-gun frigate *Alliance*, the 32-gun *Pallas* and the 12-gun cutter *Vengeance*. The odds were obviously against Captain Pearson, but he did have the advantage of a faster ship and naval crews. Though of course Pearson was not to know it, Jones had a mixed crew of Americans, French, English, Irish, Scots, Swedes, Norwegians, Portuguese, Italians, Swiss and East Indians.

In the evening the battle was joined. Pearson soon proved his superior handling qualities and within a short time Jones's ship was badly damaged by several broadsides, two of his eighteen-pounder guns exploded killing the crews and those handling the four-pounders. But Jones pressed on. His only chance now seemed to be to grapple and board. This he finally did when Pearson lost way, as Jones closed in taking the wind out of his sails. Optimistically at this stage Pearson called out, 'Has your ship struck?' To which Jones replied in words that are now part of American naval history, 'I have not yet begun to fight!'

As the two ships crashed together Jones seized the broken

forestay of the *Serapis* and lashed it to his mizzen mast. There then began one of those pounding matches that boggles the modern mind. With gun-muzzles literally touching the opposing vessel's side, they poured shot into one another. The English gunners elevated their gun-barrels to fire up through the *Richard*'s sides and up through her decks, thus almost eliminating the American broadside guns. Then they depressed their guns and fired through the American ship below the waterline. Pearson's naval gunnery training was paying off.

After two hours of this Jones had no guns on the *Serapis*'s side still working so he ordered others to be trundled across from the port. It would seem that Jones was finished. But a French tactic was to save the day. Diving archaeologist and naval historian Syd Wignall puts it like this:

The English displayed what was to be their Achilles heel in naval warfare right through to the end of the Napoleonic Wars – their predilection for broadside gunnery and neglect of accurate, well-disciplined musketry fire from the fighting tops. In this the French had always excelled, adding to their ships' complements scores of sharpshooting marines, who, in a close engagement, shooting from fore, main and mizzen tops could clear the enemy's decks of guns' crews. The heavy loss of life to English crews at the Battle of Trafalgar in 1805 was due in the main to the French marines musketry fire. It was a French marine, shooting from the tops of the *Redoutable*, who took the life of England's greatest admiral, Horatio Nelson.

Unsporting though this type of warfare may have seemed to English seamen, it was to win the day for Jones, for he had on board 137 French marines. Their fire cleared the *Serapis*'s upper deck of men and soon her ten-pounders were deserted except for dead and wounded around them. Among the bodies lay the English gunners' sail-cloth cartridges of black powder. A few well-aimed hand grenades and *Serapis* was ablaze.

But the *Bonhomme Richard* was sinking. Even so Jones refused to strike his colours and when the chief gunner ran aft to do so, Jones threw his pistol at the man and sent him tumbling unconscious to the deck. Both ships it seemed would soon explode. Finally though it was Pearson who struck, pulling his colours down with his own hands. He had done his job, the English convoy had escaped and any further bloodshed was pointless.

Jones made every effort to save the *Bonhomme Richard* but at 11 am on 25 September 1779 she sank bow first and the last thing to be seen was Jones's pennant flying at her stern. Within seconds that too was gone. John Paul Jones's remains are buried in the crypt of the US Naval Academy at Annapolis. His ship lies on the sea-bed off Flamborough Head.

But with the growth of diving techniques, in particular search techniques, in 1976 the idea of raising at least the guns from the ship gained great support in the United States of America. Which is where Sydney Wignall comes in once again. He is now executive director of the Atlantic Charter Maritime Archaeological Foundation of Austin Texas and leading the search for the *Bonhomme Richard*. The Decca Survey Group put their search vessel *Decca Recorder* to work in a 'high-probability' area some four miles offshore from Flamborough Head and discovered three wrecks. One proved of particular interest. Sonar traces showed that the wreck in 150 feet of water was roughly the shape one would expect the ship to be in after nearly two hundred years under water, with a spread of ballast stones in the shape of a ship and about nine feet high. An appeal for volunteers from the B S-A C to act as divers was totally oversubscribed and diving work will start shortly.

None of the ordinary crew members aboard HMS *Colossus* knew that one of the crates loaded aboard her contained the dead and embalmed body of an English admiral. If they had they would have blamed any shift of the wind against them on to the bad luck that every eighteenth-century sailor knew was bound to come from carrying such a cargo. So nobody told them. But *Colossus* collected her bad luck all the same.

Not that *Colossus* had been an unlucky ship up till to then. She was built at Gravesend in 1787 and took part in the Battle of Cape St Vincent, in which though she was disabled she gave a good account of herself against much larger Spanish ships. This resounding English victory, in which Admiral Jervis and his Mediterranean fleet defeated a Spanish battle fleet twice his size on 14 February 1797, enabled Nelson to show his daring by leading a boarding party from his own damaged ship, HMS *Captain*, and capturing two huge Spanish ships. He reached the second Spanish warship by using his first capture as a bridge to get across to her!

HMS *Colossus* stayed on in the Mediterranean fleet and took part in the blockade of Malta as well as patrolling off Cadiz and Lisbon. By November 1798 she was ordered home. But first she was to go to Naples to load stores bound for England. Most of the crates that were swung aboard the *Colossus* were the private property of Sir William Hamilton, our envoy in Naples. The crates contained a part of his second collection of ancient Greek vases – he had sold his first collection to the British Museum for the then princely sum of £8,400. They were being shipped out hastily because of Sir William's fear that Napoleon's invasion of Italy would snap up Sir William's vases too. Sir William obviously had some influence to be able to get his goods shipped home this way, but then you must not forget his wife Emma was already more than 'just good friends' with Nelson! So eighteen crates of Sir William's collection were loaded into *Colossus*.

Next stop for the *Colossus* was Lisbon where she was to take charge of a homeward-bound convoy. This is where the body of the admiral came aboard in a perfectly innocent-looking wooden crate. The admiral in the crate was Lord Shuldham, who had died in Lisbon. Whether or not the body brought bad luck, *Colossus* had a hard time of it. She was long overdue for a refit after almost two years' active service in the Mediterranean fleet. She carried not only her crew but also sick men and the wounded from the Battle of the Nile. And she ran into contrary winds on the way home. Finally a north-easterly forced her to seek shelter in the Roads off St Mary's in the Scillies. With her at anchor were eight smaller vessels of the convoy.

Here on Friday, 7 December 1798 her Captain George Murray might well have thought that his seventy-four-gun ship would be safe, riding to her main anchor cable, almost out of the wind. And so she was for nearly three days. But in the afternoon of 10 December the weather changed dramatically.

The wind had swung completely round to the south-east. Even so Captain Murray must have still felt that the shelter of St Mary's would protect him. And it did until late in the afternoon when the winds increased to a full gale. Whether it was because the *Colossus*'s ropes and cordage had been weakened by two years of salt and Mediterranean sun, or because of some major fault in the main anchor cable, we shall never know, but the fact is that at four o'clock in the afternoon that cable gave way. *Colossus* started drifting to the north-west and the further she went from land the more the gale got a grip. Down went her bow and sheet anchors, but they failed to bite. Murray ordered his topmasts to be struck to offer less resistance to the wind, but by now she was moving fast in front of the violent gusts.

At 8 pm she struck the Southward Wells Rocks nearly a mile from her anchorage point and due south of the Island of Samson. At first Murray hoped to get her off, but during the night the constant buffeting of the gale thumped her again and again on the granite rocks. Her rudder was smashed and she began to fill with water. At dawn Captain Murray knew she was finished and started abandoning ship. By the afternoon everyone, the sick, the wounded and the crew, was off safely, with one exception. This man, a quartermaster, was the only casualty from *Colossus*. He leaned out too far to try and sound the edge of the rocks and see if there was any deep water close by. In doing so he fell from the ship into the sea and was swept away.

In the night that followed *Colossus* started breaking up and was a total wreck. And in the shattered hull the cold Scilly waters closed over Sir William Hamilton's crates of vases. But not all the crates on board were lost. One we know was hauled up together with some of the ship's stores in salvage operations. Unfortunately this salvaged crate contained not vases but the body of Admiral Lord Shuldham. This was the last straw as far as Sir William Hamilton was concerned. In a letter still in the British Museum he wrote: 'I have learnt that the body insolvent of Admiral Shuldham has been saved from the wreck. . . . damn his body, it can be of no use but to the worms, but my collection would have given information to the most learned.'

But Sir William must have been happier about further salvage during the following week because ten crates containing some of his collection were recovered, which left eight. Salvaging the ship was not too difficult a task – the depth of water in which she had been broken was mostly only forty feet. Certainly many of her cannon were recovered, but then over the years interest in her waned.

Did any of Sir William's vases remain intact on the bottom? Certainly finds of hundreds of intact amphora after hundreds, even thousands of years under the sea in the Mediterranean have shown just how tough pottery is. Given the right conditions, that is. But you could hardly call the boiling seas and great under-water surges around Southward Wells Rocks the right con-ditions. Still, with things that have sunk in the sea, you never know, and if other divers thought the chance of finding anything was so remote that it was not worth bothering about the *Colossus*, one man could not get her out of his mind. That man was Ronald Morris. Indeed, when he started hunting for Sir Cloudesley Shovell's ships, he had also named *Colossus* in his application for a contract from the MOD.

Another man with *Colossus* on his mind was diver film-maker Slim Macdonnell. He had first heard about *Colossus* when on underwater assignment for Independent Television News to cover the *Association* story. Slim had filmed since then with all the great names in wreck diving, including of course Roland Morris and his team of divers, and had found himself many times back in the Scillies. It always seemed when he was there that someone would mention *Colossus*, but never, except for Roland Morris, very seriously.

In 1974 Slim Macdonnell was once again in the Scillies, work-ing this time for the BBC on a documentary about Rex Cowan. The route back from the Scillies generally used must take in Penzance and this time was no exception. So Slim called in on his old friend Roland Morris at his superb Admiral Benbow restaurant and Museum of Nautical Art in the town. The talk got round to wrecks of course. Mark Horobin, one of Roland Morris's diving team, joined in and then up came that name again – *Colossus*.

In an article in *Triton* (volume 22, no. 1) in January, 1977, Slim Macdonnell described what happened then like this: 'Maybe I should have known better – the outline script looked good, but no-one had written an ending. "Why don't you boys spend a few weeks looking. I'll meet all the expenses," Roland said. Perhaps it was the ghost of Sir William Hamilton or Johnny Walker that prompted us to agree.' That was the start of a saga of wreck diving that is probably the most amazing of all in British waters because of what the divers recovered.

Mark Horobin and Slim Macdonnell found the top of the reef covered in a carpet of weed with the rock of the reef meeting the sand at about fifty feet. The weed was a damned nuisance, but even so on a random search they found three anchors all with their stocks pointing into the reef. And then under the weed the 'hallmarks' of the shipwreck of a large naval ship – cannon-balls, large bronze pins used for fixing the timbers, glass fragments, but no sign of any of Sir William's treasures.

They had found a large shipwreck. But was it that of *Colossus*? Roland Morris plunged again into that essential part of all wreck diving, research, and during the winter of 1974 applied for the site to be designated under the 1973 act. This was done and in the spring of 1975 the diving started again. Soon the divers had discovered seventeen cannon of Admiralty pattern, two carronades and numerous other items, including a very encrusted but well-preserved pistol and some sword scabbards. But still no Hamilton vases.

The divers worked on. In three months' diving, spending three hours each day under water, they covered hundreds of square yards of sea-bed. Cold was their real enemy and this was what really limited their bottom time in the shallow water. The time allotted to them to find the wreck was running out too. So was the money to keep the work going. The licence to excavate the site would come up in mid-July and if nothing was found would presumably expire. Things looked grim. They extended the search by another hundred yards. Roland Morris gave the divers another ten days and then that would have to be that.

Slim Macdonnell was desperate, but his desperation did not influence his methodical searching. On 4 July, he saw the small face of a satyr looking up at him from between two rocks in the new extended search area. 'It was just waiting to be found, looking up at me – a sherd of pottery measuring eleven centimetres by eight. It was perfect!'

On 16 July in London at the British Museum came the real test. Was this really a sherd from one of Sir William's collection? Dr Ann Birchall, assistant keeper of the Greek and Roman Antiquities section and an expert on Hamilton and his vases, had no doubt. Yes, she said, it was. She could go further – the satyr's head with horses ears came from an ancient vessel used to mix wine and water.

The British Museum had shown the divers the sort of thing they were looking for – vases or pieces of them with red and black figures dating back to 700 BC and ranging in size from six inches to three feet. And now that the British Museum were sure that the vases did exist even if in sherd form, they supported the expedition, lending money against the eventual sale of the pieces to them. In other words when the collection is put up for sale by the Receiver of Wreck, the British Museum will have first refusal. Otherwise the pieces will go to the highest bidder.

The expedition was now given a full excavation licence for the wreck site and within days had discovered thousands more sherds – the position of each one being carefully logged by reference to the grid which was now covering the site. By the end of the 1975 season the divers had recovered 8,500 sherds. And pictures from the sides of vases that Sir William had had drawn by an artist before shipping them could be matched with the pottery pieces.

In 1976 after the winter growth of weed had been removed the grid lines were re-established over the site. The divers knew that it was vital that not one shred should be missed and they were getting right down to bedrock to make sure that none were. They lifted four hundred tons of rock out of the way with inflated lifting bags and sifted through the exposed sand. Thousands more sherds were found and the divers' spirits were high. Even more so when they read newspaper reports of the value of their discoveries using phrases like 'priceless' and quoting unnamed art experts as valuing the sherds at 'around a million pounds'.

By the end of the 1976 season the divers had raised some thirty thousand pieces of 120 pots, vases and the like and at the British Museum under the expert eye of Dr Ann Birchall, who was appointed the archaeological director of the *Colossus* excavation, the mammoth task of putting together the biggest jigsaw puzzle in the world got under way. It must be awful to be an archaeologist and sit in a boat on the surface and listen to divers talking about the amazing things they have seen on the wreck below. Some can take it. Some do the only sensible thing and learn to dive – Margaret Rule of the *Mary Rose* did it at the age of forty. Now Dr Birchall has done it too. She has taken a course in aqualung diving at Fort Bovisand, Plymouth to prepare herself for dives to see the remains of *Colossus* for herself.

The diving is still going on at the time of writing this chapter. Will the divers and Roland Morris share out a great sum for all their work? Are those sherds really worth £1 million? Neither the divers nor the British Museum can answer those questions just yet. For one thing they do not know how much money the excavation will have cost by the time it is finished. Nor do they know what price the sherds as opposed to intact vases will fetch.

All you can say for certain is that an old quip about Sir William Hamilton – that he shared his wife with an admiral and his treasure with the sea – now lacks a lot of its bite!

APPENDIX I

Unknown Ships and How to Name Them

The ship which struck the Farne Islands off Northumberland some time between 1650 and 1750, left no record of her passing – except that her guns gave the name to a small group of rocks near Staple Island. Gun Rocks dry at times as much as eleven feet at low water. At high water the only sign that the rocks are there is a little patch of foam where the sea breaks on the highest tip.

Bill Smith, a former diving officer of Tyneside branch of the B S-A C, was the man who was so intrigued by the name of the rocks that he led his branch to dive there. Slightly to his amazement they found on that first dive not only bronze pulley wheels but also nine cannon. They went on diving and found at least thirteen cannon, sword-handles and other artefacts but no real clue to the ship's identity. The trunnions of some of the cannon bore the letters G, S and F. Pieces of pottery were identified as being part of late seventeeth-century Bellarmine stone jars. The sword-handles may have been of Dutch manufacture. That and the Bellarmine jars point towards a Dutch ship, but there is as yet no real proof.

Recently Bill Smith and Peter Napp have however found a report of a diver being asked to work on a forty-gun Dutch frigate in the area in 1704–5. The ship was described as lying in large pieces. But tantalizingly the old document says no more about the ship, nor does it name her. The diving however goes on. One day perhaps a diver will discover a tiny fragment that will solve the mystery. Until then she stays unknown.

Unknown too is the wreck that the divers of Croydon branch of the B S-A C found on the Great Mewstone Rock off the estuary of the Yealm near Newton Ferrers in South Devon. Dick Middlewood was the first man to see the cannon. On a Whitsun dive, he reported: 'I was following a gully when I came across some peculiarly shaped rocks. They struck me as being a bit too straight for rocks, perhaps they were logs, but then . . . no, not logs! I suddenly realized they were two six-foot cannon. And on the way back to the boat I saw a third.'

Then the divers of three branches of the B S-A C, all interested in underwater archaeology, joined together to explore the site. The divers most deeply involved were Dick Middlewood, Dennis Hinchcliffe and Nick Parrott of Croydon branch of the B S-A C, Martin Dean and Dick Johnstone of Slough S-A C and John Smart of Gwynedd branch of the B S-A C. Many members of all clubs joined in the work. The ten iron cannon together with the pottery found on the site indicate a wreck of the eighteenth century.

But the divers cannot put a name to her. Matters are complicated by the fact that the site of the wreck appears to overlap the site of the sinking of the steamer *Ajax*, which was lost on the Mewstone on 13 October 1854.

The area around the Mewstone was to lead to an even greater mystery. Plymouth Sound branch of the B S-A C, which you will remember from the beginning of this book located the *Fraumetta Catherina von Flensburgh* in the Sound itself, took its families to the beach at Wembury one late September day in 1970. This was quite a regular dive spot for the branch. The sheltered shallow waters inside the Mewstone meant that novices could enjoy their training dives in calm conditions while their wives and families could enjoy a day on the beach.

Wilfred Jenkin was to take Joe Naysmith on his first boat dive and Bruce Ogden was to assist. Shallow water had been chosen for this and the three divers made their entrance down the anchor line to a plateau of rock and thick kelp at fifteen feet. They then moved south-east to the edge of the reef and dropped on to a large sand patch. The depth was now thirty feet. They then began exploring the gullies which led to the north-west off the sand into the face of the reef. The gullies were carpeted at first with coarse sand, then shingle. Around them the kelp swayed in the ground swell.

At one moment when the weed parted in the swell Wilf noticed a wheel-like object, blending almost perfectly into the mottled background of sea growths. Wilf debated whether to pick it up. Talking about that moment he says: 'At thirty feet leading a dive with a novice in the group, my first thought was – should I bother to pick it up? It was probably only a piece of scrap metal, probably a wheel-head from a valve. . . . On second thoughts and second looks, there was this green staining in places suggesting bronze. Well, it was easy to carry, but I could hear my wife saying, 'More junk for the garage.'

The dive was completed successfully with no other incident and back on the beach Wilf looked more closely at his find. 'The first thing I noted was that the wheel was not symmetrical. It was lobe-shaped with a ring at the top. This suggested to me that it was designed to hang up and was possibly part of an instrument, perhaps used to check list on old ships.'

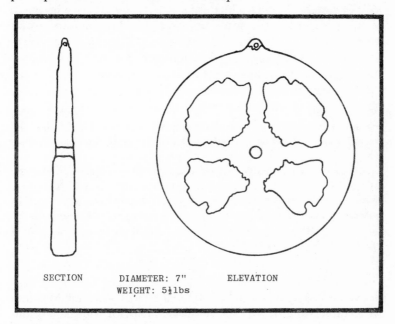

SECTION   DIAMETER: 7"   ELEVATION
WEIGHT: 5½lbs

Fig. 5.   Wilf Jenkin's astrolabe

During the next six months Wilf Jenkin found himself too busy training new divers and with other diving activities to do much about his find. He did carefully clean one side, but he preserved the other side in its original condition as found. Then diver Mike Spencer pointed out an article in an old issue of a magazine illustrating an astrolabe discovered in Bermuda and noted as only the twenty-fourth known to be in existence in the world. Wilf Jenkin then knew that he was holding in his hands number 25! (In fact it was number 32 but he was not to know that at the time.)

The astrolabe was one of the early instruments used in the navigation of ships. In its simplest form it was a circle of metal marked with a scale of degrees. This hung from a ring which you slipped on to a finger or held in your hand. In the middle of the circle was a ruler or sight which you pointed at a star or the sun to determine its elevation and so knew, hopefully, where you were. In practice of course it was not as simple as that on the deck of a heaving, rolling ship, or in a howling wind. But some remarkable feats of navigation were carried out with such primitive aids.

Wilf caught the bug which infects so many divers who make discoveries under the sea – he wanted to know more. So he contacted Mr D. W. Waters, head of the Department of Navigation and Astronomy at the National Maritime Museum at Greenwich. He sent him sketches, notes and a photograph of his find. In April 1971 Mr Waters wrote back:

My diagnosis of the instrument is that it is almost certainly English because the diameter is 7.1 English inches, which is near enough to the round figure of 7 inches which the craftsmen of those days liked to work to.

. . . the fact that it is wedge-shaped suggests that it is of the period of the last quarter of the 16th century and the first quarter of the 17th century, while its rather decorative design suggests again that it is of the 17th rather than the 16th century. . . . I am inclined to date it therefore to the first quarter of the 17th century. After that time the Sea-Astrolabe passed out of use amongst English seamen in favour of the Davis Backstaff, though the use of astrolabes did continue at sea into the last quarter of the 17th century.

Later the astrolabe was taken to the National Maritime Museum where it was registered as on temporary loan for safe keeping and further research.

Before that happened though the Plymouth Sound branch set to work to see if they could find further evidence of a wreck. Under the wing of their Advanced Diving Group headed by the Diving Officer, Ian Skelton, they combed the area. In all the Plymouth Sound divers searched thousands of square yards of sea-bed without any other dramatic discoveries. The team was headed by Wilf Jenkin and Ian Skelton, Alan Coates and Colin Hannaford and Ken Metcalfe took part, with help from Paul Andrews, Arthur Ball, Andrew Borne, Mel Bowen, Alan Gibson, Andrew Keast, John Martin, Alan Mitchell, Joe Naysmith, Bruce

Ogden and Mike Spencer. Was there a wreck or did some clumsy navigator let his astrolabe fly from his hands over the side?

The diving goes on, and so does the research. In 1974 Wilf Jenkin added another sheet to his research file when divers from Chester s-a c found a bell on the opposite side of the Mewstone to the place where he found his astrolabe. The bell was dated as probably from a vessel of the seventeenth or eighteenth century. Is the bell from the same ship as the astrolabe or from the ship from which the Mewstone cannon came? Are they one and the same wreck? At the moment both must be marked as 'unknown'.

Another unknown wreck was discovered in 1976 when the Port of London Authority were carrying out one of their routine sonar surveys of the shifting mudbanks of the Thames Estuary some ten miles north of Margate. A channel had shifted through a mudbank and when divers went down they found to their amazement that the ship seemed to have been sucked virtually intact into the mudbank.

The National Maritime Museum were informed and they called in Colin Martin and the St Andrews Institute of Maritime Archaeology. In a joint operation, during which the Royal Navy supplied a ship, the institute divers went down to survey this new find. Difficult tides and almost zero visibility made a conventional survey impractical, but the divers were able to discover that the wreck was almost intact. Much of her and her cargo stand hazardously proud of the sea-bed. And the cargo is intact! It includes bottled wine, anchors and iron in 'bundles'. As a result of their discoveries the ship, which appears to be of the late eighteenth century, has been scheduled under the 1973 Protection of Wrecks Act. Even so at the time of writing no further work is planned on this unknown wreck in the South Edinburgh Channel of the Thames estuary.

Identification of ships from a cannon or two and maybe a few pottery sherds close by on the sea-bed will always present enormous problems. And only a lunatic will expect too much. For example I do not expect to find – and I doubt that anyone else will ever find – any written clue to the reason why I found a piece of Roman pottery on the sea-bed well out to sea off Pagham Harbour in Sussex.

But there is more chance of identifying a wreck which has

recently emerged from the sea-bed near Teignmouth, Devon. Fifteen-year-old Simon Burton made the discovery in quite shallow water. While snorkelling he saw an eleven-foot-long cannon, or sacre. It has since been raised. It weighs twenty-two hundredweight and has a bore of three-and-a-half inches. Early identification says that it was cast in the same Venetian foundry of Sigismunde Alberghetti in the sixteenth century as one of the cannon found on the *Trinidad Valencera* Armada shipwreck site in Ireland. There are other items nearby and work on the site is being carried out by divers of the South Devon Technical College branch of the B S-A C. They believe that the wreck has emerged from the sea-bed because of man's interference with nature, in other words that the groynes recently put in position in the area have changed the sea-bed. Sand has shifted and the wreck has emerged. Is it an Armada wreck? Only further work on the site will give us the answer. The site is now protected as that of a wreck of historical importance.

Even as I am in the closing stages of writing this book, discoveries are being made. Such is the boom in skin-diving with its daily discoveries that one just has to stop a book somewhere and leave later finds to the next. But I just have time to squeeze into this section about unknown wrecks the latest discovery by divers of Bournemouth and Poole branch of the B S-A C. In some thirty feet of water off Swanage they have found evidence of a wreck of the 1700s – cannon and cannon-balls are among the seaweed-covered remains.

Every time a diver finds some wreckage he will want to try to find out what ship she was and how she came to sink. Indeed putting clue together with clue until the picture becomes clear can be almost as satisfying as finding the wreck itself. I say 'almost' because nothing can be as exciting as that moment of discovery of a previously unknown wreck. Do not forget wreck research can work the other way round – from the research to the wreck, not from the wreck to the research. Here then, whichever way your research goes, are some invaluable sources of information which no serious wreck diver can afford to be without:

The Public Record Office, Chancery Lane, London, WC2A 1LR
This is one of the biggest sources of information for the wreck detective. The staff are incredibly helpful and should be treated

with the respect their knowledge deserves. The office contains millions of documents relating to the actions of the government of Britain and its courts of law from the eleventh century, and included in all those documents are hundreds of thousands which concern ships and their wrecking.

But it is no use just going along and expecting to be shown exactly what you want without some preliminary work on your part. First of all, just to get inside the building, you must fill in an application form for a reader's ticket. Write to the Keeper for the form. You will be sent with this a useful *Information for Readers* leaflet. You should also note that a large part of the records has recently been moved to a new PRO at Ruskin Avenue, Kew, Richmond, Surrey. Read the advice in the leaflet, but it would be worth a telephone call to check the exact position of the records you want to see. For Chancery Lane ring 01-405 0741; for Kew 01-876 3444. You will receive general guidance, not details, over the telephone.

The search rooms are open from 9.30 am to 5 pm, Monday to Friday. Do not take a biro or fountain pen with you. Their use is forbidden. Pencils only, but there is some accommodation (limited) for those who want to use tape-recorders or typewriters. Ask about this at the office.

On your first visit you may well find it all a bit awe-inspiring, but do not let it put you off. The staff are there to help you, and they will. But do have a clear idea in your mind of what you expect to find. Mr E. K. Timings, head of the Search Department, gave all wreck researchers a first-class tip when he told me that you 'should look further than the wreck itself. . . . think who would have been affected by it.' With this in mind here are some of the sources you will find in the PRO files.

If the wreck of a naval ship and there were survivors it is likely (though not always certain) that someone will have been court-martialled. Sometimes these courts-martial were used more as a method of getting at the cause of the loss of the ship than of apportioning blame, and so you can expect to find a deal of information from them. In one that I read for example the actual rock the ship hit is named and a little research would have saved at least two groups of wreck hunters a great deal of useless diving! So your ship may be in the 'Digest of Courts-Martial', which covers the period from 1755 to 1806. The index number is

4779. From the Digest you can go to the actual report of the court-martial. These come under the Admiralty 1 series (5253 onwards) and are mostly in the beautiful copperplate hand of some long-dead clerk, who quilled away as the court-martial was actually being held in the great cabin of some anchored man-of-war. The court-martial records run from 1680 right up to one hundred years ago. More recent court-martial documents are not available as a hundred-year rule is applied before the papers pass into the public domain. (Do not despair here – in many cases the Press was present, although not at secret sessions. For press accounts try the British Museum Newspaper Library at Colindale. See under British Museum.)

If your ship was likely to have been involved in an affair of some consequence from the time of Henry VIII onward (the Spanish Armada is a good example), then you should find something about her in the State Papers (Domestic) in the Round Room. For the Spanish ships wrecked in Ireland you will want the State Papers (Irish). There is a printed calendar to guide you towards both of these.

Still no luck? Do not despair yet. All the 'In' letters to the Admiralty are preserved (there are gaps of course, but there are a great number left), and here you will find the letters from the Port Admirals and the Port Agents, and even from the officers in charge of look-out points around the coasts. These were often concerned with reporting losses to the Admiralty. You will find them under Admiralty 1 and List and Indexes 18. There's an Admiralty Digest subject index there with a key to all Admiralty papers. All wrecks too are listed per year. You will find this under Wrecks (Cut No. 31 in the Digest).

And if the log survived it may well be in the PRO. Even if it did not (I have noted that, in some cases where a ship was lost by what can only be called 'demned carelessness', even though there was plenty of time to get everything else off, the log mysteriously drowned), the logs of any ships in the area can be revealing. Captains' logs are under Admiralty 51 and the logs of masters under Admiralty 52.

Was there any salvage done on your ship? Was there a legal squabble about her? Try the High Court of Admiralty records or the records of the Admiralty Division of the Supreme Court (from 1873).

And do not think that if you do strike lucky you have to copy out all the details laboriously with a pencil. The PRO has a fine photocopying service at reasonable prices.

You will find in your research that one thing leads to another. For example if it is a treasure ship that you are after there may well be a great deal of information about her in the Treasury records for that period. This is what is meant by looking 'further than the wreck itself'. If the treasure was State money its loss will not go unrecorded among papers that on the face of it have nothing to do with ships. But these records may not be at the PRO but at the new repository at Kew.

Did your ship carry troops? Then the military records at the PRO may well give you information. After all, if a whole troop was lost, someone was going to have to report it to someone higher up the chain of command.

So, there is a pretty good chance that the PRO can find you something about your ship. But do not expect them to give you a map and mark the spot she sank with an X. Though come to think of it, that is what happened to Roland Morris during his research – he found a map that said, '*Association* lost here.' And that is in the PRO too!

Hydrographic Department, Ministry of Defence, Beadon Road, Taunton, Somerset

Old charts can give vital clues. The classic example of this is, as already mentioned, that Roland Morris found an old map which actually named the rock on which the *Association* was lost. Remember that the names of rocks and headlands have changed a great deal over the years. So see if the Hydrographic Department can give you a copy of a chart that was in use at the time of the loss of your ship.

Write to the Curator, who will tell you what is available. Basically they have a large number of manuscript documents from which the charts were compiled. These date from the early 1800s. Earlier material than this is very limited, but there are some surveys from the late 1700s, and a few hand-drawn charts from earlier dates. Photographic copies of sections of them can be obtained at reasonable prices. Write to the Wrecks Section at the address above.

The Wrecks Section set up a card index in 1913 in which every known wreck was allotted a card. This was not to help divers with their searches, but so that a record could be kept of wrecks that were, or might become, a danger to navigation. Their records now hold details of every known wreck from 1913 onward – such as the name, tonnage, date sunk and depth of water over wreck. If it was dispersed (i.e. because it was a danger to navigation) this is on record also.

They have a handy leaflet available (Wrecks Section Booklet RL/69) giving some sources of information, and which also stresses that their wreck records are of little value for: (a) historical wrecks and wrecks sunk prior to 1913 (in general information on wrecks prior to the twentieth Century is very scant and positions are frequently unreliable); (b) ownership (a very important point when intending to recover articles from a wreck); (c) wrecks in areas for which the Admiralty chart is not the primary authority; (d) the law relating to salvage, acquisition of wrecks etc.

It should be pointed out that many wrecks exist, the names of which are not known, and many more which have never been located. It is therefore of great value if salvage concerns, sub-aqua clubs and similar bodies send details of wrecks found to the Hydrographic Department, giving as much information as possible. In order to provide a better service than hitherto, it is present policy to add to the wreck records details of ownership, voyage and cargo at time of loss, and any other information which may be of general interest.

A person interested in obtaining information from the index cards is advised to use the following procedure: (i) buy a *Catalogue of Admiralty Charts* (Home Edition, price 5p; World Edition, price 67½p) from any chart agent and from this select and buy the largest scale chart available for the area concerned; (ii) take off the position of any wreck of interest in latitude and longitude, or decide on the area of interest (e.g. 'All wrecks within twenty fathoms between Burmouth light and Castle Head'); (iii) write, giving these details, and a brief statement of the reason for the inquiry, to the address given at the beginning of this section.

A search fee is charged that is commensurate with the work involved in producing the information required. However in the case of an inquiry of an academic nature, or where the provision of new information leads to the enlargement of the wreck records, all or part of the search fee may be waived.

It is interesting to note here that the deep-draught super-tankers of today have forced the Wrecks Section to increase the danger depth of wrecks (it used to be forty-eight feet in 1963) to 90 feet. So many 'harmless' wrecks of the past may in future have to be dispersed as a danger to navigation, and wreck divers will have lost another chance to explore these sunken ships.

Board of Trade (War Risk Insurance Office), Parliament Square House, 34–36 Parliament Street, London, SW1A 2ND
They will help with details of Allied merchantmen lost (due to enemy action) during both World Wars. They can also give details of ownership and cargo.

Director General of Defence Contracts (Naval) Section 85, Ensleigh, Bath, Somerset
These are the people to contact if you want to buy a Navy wreck!

Lloyd's Register of Shipping, 69–71 Fenchurch Street, London, EC3M 4BS
They have brief details of the ship and how she was lost from their Quarterly Returns since 1890. Write to the Principal Clerk in charge of the Statistics Department, giving the ship's name and the date of her loss.

Trinity House, Tower Hill, London, EC3N 4DH
In return for name and general position of wrecks in home waters, they can give details of dispersal, position, buoyage, cargo etc. But unfortunately their pre-1940 records were destroyed by fire.

The British Museum, Bloomsbury, London, WC1B 3DG
I do not propose here to try to tell you everything that is in the British Museum! But early newspapers and maps are of particular interest to the wreck detective, and this is where they are.

To use the facilities of the British Museum Reading Room and associated libraries, you must have a ticket (a long-period one lasts for a year and the short-period one for six days only). Applications for either have to follow a certain form, because the

British Museum is there to provide readers with 'facilities for research and reference which are not readily available in other libraries normally accessible to them'. Write to the Director's Office (readers' tickets) and they'll send you a form telling you how to apply.

London newspapers printed before 1801 are kept at the British Museum itself, and there is a file for *The Times* from 1809 to the present day. For most of the others you will have to go to the British Museum Newspaper Library, Colindale, London, NW9 5HE (where again you will need a Reader's Ticket). The Newspaper Library is opposite Colindale Underground station, and there you will find all the newspapers in the National Collection, including of course English provincial newspapers, but the London, Edinburgh, Belfast and Dublin *Gazettes* are kept at Bloomsbury. To save time, and to find out exactly what you can see, write to the superintendent. *Lloyd's List* is also kept at Colindale.

Old maps are kept at Bloomsbury.

Imperial War Museum, Lambeth Road, London, SE1 6HZ

This can supply information only about the date and location of British merchantmen and Royal Navy ships lost by enemy action in World Wars I and II. The lists do not include ships lost during those wars due to storms or other causes. But official histories and ship histories are available in the museum's Printed Books Section, and you can get photostats of documents.

Customs House Library, Kings Beam House, 39–41 Mark Lane, London, EC3R 7HE

This has ship registers dating back to the early eighteenth century.

The National Maritime Museum, Greenwich, London, SE10 9NF

This museum has many experts and is a mine of information. They prefer you to write to them first (to the Director) and not just drop in if you have any specific query. This is not because they are trying to complicate life – they are all keen to help – but because unless you do write the expert in the field in which you require help may not be available.

Basically then, here is how the National Maritime and its extensive collections can help you. When you write, your letter will be guided to the right department, which could be one of the following:

(i) The Navigation Department, which holds an extensive collection of charts from the sixteenth century onwards, together with a fine range of nautical instruments from the same period.

(ii) The Manuscript Department. Here are the builder's plans of Admiralty ships from the eighteenth century (and if they have not got them for your particular ship there is the chance of finding those of a sister ship, or one of her class). Commercial builder's plans date mostly from the late nineteenth century, both steam and sail, iron and wood, to the present day.

(iii) The Library. If you know the name and the approximate date of the wreck it will help, but here are just a few of the sources open to you: Lloyd's *Register of Ships*, from 1764; *Lloyd's List Reprints*, 1741–1826; *Lloyd's Lists*, 1869–1953; Lloyd's Manuscript Wreck Registers, 1855–95; Lloyd's *Dictionary of Disaster during the Age of Steam*, 1824–1962; *Mercantile Navy List* from 1857; reports of wrecks and courts of inquiry in the *Nautical Magazine* (March 1832 to date); a collection of books on individual shipwrecks, shipwrecks in general and wrecks of particular areas; articles and notes on wrecks past and present, and many other books and papers.

Just for a moment, let us suppose that you have found a ship fitting that you cannot recognize. That unidentifiable piece of material may well be instantly recognized by one of the museum's experts. Write first, and send a photograph if you can. Found a cannon or any kind of armament? Send measurements, photographs, and all details you can. They will do their best. Do you know what your ship looked like – or the captain or admiral? Try the Museum's picture library. They have an extensive collection of prints, oil paintings, water-colours, engravings, portraits and photographs, and will let you have copies very reasonably.

The Science Museum, South Kensington, London, SW7 2DD
Very good source for constructional details of ships and their equipment. Mr B. W. Bathe, Assistant Keeper of the Department of Water Transport, is very helpful.

Lloyd's, Lime Street, London, EC3M 7HA

They have brief details of the vessel at time of loss, cargo, and the way she was lost, and usually have ownership at time of loss, but not after any claims have been settled. These reports have appeared (and do appear today) in the marine casualty columns of *Lloyd's List*. The earliest copies date from 1741, and can be seen at the offices of the shipping editor. Records are world-wide, and if you want them to find your ship they will charge you a search fee, depending on how much searching they have to do.

The Committee for Nautical Archaeology, Institute of Archaeology, 31–4 Gordon Square, London, WC1H 0PP

Not so much a source as a source for sources. For the CNA will help, advise and guide you to people who can assist you, if you are undertaking a serious survey of excavation of a sunken ship. Founded in 1964 to develop and guide underwater archaeology, its aims are: to promote research in nautical archaeology; to promote underwater training in this field; to provide contact between divers, archaeologists and historians; to safeguard the archaeological content of underwater sites; to safeguard the rights of divers co-operating with the CNA.

The committee publishes a journal, the *International Journal of Nautical Archaeology*, which contains superb research articles and full reports of finds. It is a must for any wreck diver. Subscription inquiries to Seminar Press, 24–8 Oval Road, London, NW1.

The British Sub-Aqua Club

The B S-A C has formed a Wreck Register sub-committee which is in close liaison with the Hydrographic Department and the Salvage Association. The aim is to supply club members with information about wrecks around the coasts of Great Britain. Their register grows daily and it would be well worth contacting them, even if you are not a member of the club, before deciding that you have made a brand-new discovery. It may well be on their files. To contact them you should write to the Wreck Register Committee at B S-A C HQ, 70, Brompton Road, London, SW3 1HA.

The B S-A C also has a diving archaeologist Keith Muckelroy as its archaeological adviser. He reports regularly to the club's National Council, which can and does allocate money for wreck research and survey. Write to him if you need help with your wreck.

Divers are great ones for finding cannon. Indeed discoveries of cannon are a regular occurrence during each diving season. Finding the cannon is one thing; dating and identifying the ship through them is another.

Two of Britain's top experts on cannon have agreed that I should give them here as sources for the identification of cannon. But before you write to them – or stagger with your precious find in your arms into their offices! – I think I must stress one or two points. Firstly if you write do include a stamped addressed envelope for their reply. Secondly do give them the proper information.

For example expert Austin C. Carpenter of the Department of the Environment, 1–3 Albert Road, Devonport, Plymouth, Devon PL2 1AA says this:

I should like to point out that for many years I have on occasion been sent approximate sizes of guns lying on the sea-bed, which are encrusted with marine growth and concretion, and have been asked to identify same. This is impossible. Occasionally one may find a bronze gun which has remained clean and, with good underwater photographs and good detail of dimensions, one could give a pretty near date and provenance etc. But unless guns are raised from the sea-bed and in most cases cleaned, one cannot honestly give good and genuine identification.

Cast-iron guns are normally better left and not raised as they will, unless put through costly preservation treatment, break down in structure and disintegrate. However, I see no reason why a cast-iron gun could not be raised, cleaned, identified and then returned to its last resting place.

The basic points to note in trying to identify a gun, cast-iron, bronze, or wrought-iron, are as follows:

(1) Length of piece.
(2) Diameter at muzzle.
(3) Diameter at breech.
(4) Size of bore.
(5) Number and position of mouldings.
(6) Shape of cascabel (knob at the breech end).
(7) Length of trunnions, and size, their position on the gun in relation to the bore.
(8) Markings on end faces of trunnions.
(9) Coat-of-arms, Iron founders' marks, weights and shot poundage are also in the 'first reinforce', in other words in the region of one to two feet up the barrel from the breech end.

Another man who is available to divers for cannon aid is H. Blackmore, Esq., Keeper of Firearms, The Armouries, HM Tower of London, London, EC3, Mr Blackmore is a great expert and will willingly help any diver with cannon identification problems.

APPENDIX II

How to Stop the Rot

If you have found your wreck and you have had to raise an object for identification or dating, then you have got a problem on your hands. That object, which has survived in the sea for centuries, can literally fall to pieces after being exposed to air for a short time. What should you do? Here I am indebted to underwater archaeologist Margaret Rule and *Triton* magazine for permission to concentrate her articles about conservation into this appendix. She points out that too often, finds are brought to the attention of museums several weeks or even months after their recovery from the sea when deterioration has already occurred. A cast-iron shot fissured by a network of deep cracks, or badly shrunk and distorted waterlogged wood, cannot be recovered, and clearly the responsible diver wants to preserve the object as it was when he first found it on the site.

The legal requirement to deliver an object salvaged from the sea to the Receiver of Wreck can often be waived by arrangement, if the finder can show that the object requires urgent 'first-aid' treatment if it is to survive. But obviously an expensive conservation process cannot be undertaken until the legal ownership of the object is decided. And since the Receiver has to have the object in his legal, if not his physical, custody for a year before the question of ownership can be decided, it is clear that some interim treatment will be essential.

Let us look at the problems and see how they can be solved. Waterlogged organic material sealed beneath sands, silt, clay or ballast mounds often survives well-preserved in a state of chemical and microbiological equilibrium. This equilibrium is quickly destroyed when the object is recovered and brought into the surface air.

Contamination by airborne mould spores and aerobic bacteria and fungi can rapidly reduce waterlogged rope and leather to an evil-smelling mess if left bagged in soggy paper within a polythene bag. Too rapid drying out causes shrinkage and distortion at an alarming rate if the object is left for long periods on a breezy deck while the inevitable photographs are taken.

Conservation must begin on the bottom. Fragile objects do not survive the journey to the surface tucked inside a diving jacket or clutched unfeelingly in icy cold fingers. Divers working on archaeological sites must, like boy scouts, be prepared, and a selection of lidded plastic storage boxes, plastic seed trays and wire-mesh cages will cope with most small items. Larger items need purpose-made lidded boxes which support and enclose the object while it is being lifted.

Whenever possible, fragile items should be raised in their supporting matrices of clay or sand and the final 'excavation' should take place underwater in the rigidly controlled environment of the kitchen sink or the family bathtub. A header tank, such as a plastic wine-container with tap, available from most grocers selling 'loose' sherry, connected by its tap to a length of plastic tubing, can be used to direct a controlled current of water around the submerged object gently to remove the surrounding matrix.

A mounted needle, small brush and hand lens are often needed to tease away the last vestiges of the enclosing mud. Finally, after fully recording the object with drawings and photographs, it can be stored in a lidded plastic box containing fresh water and a suitable preservative.

Final conservation treatment using water soluble polyethylene glycol or dewatering solutions is basically a job for a professional conservator, but careful excavation, recording, cleaning and storage by the diver will ensure that the conservator has a good chance of doing his job successfully when the object eventually reaches him.

The preservation of wood recovered from the sea is a long and expensive process and a great deal of research is currently going on in Britain and other countries to improve and speed up techniques. Most museums have only limited facilities and can cope with only the most important items. The diver is therefore faced with the problem of preserving waterlogged wood after he has found it until someone makes up their mind whether it is important or not!

Ultimately the decision may be to record the timbers and then rebury them in the sea-bed, but on an exposed site the diver has often only two alternatives when he has exposed loose timber: either to recover the timber and preserve it for expert examination, or to allow it to remain *in situ* where, without protection, it will inevitably deteriorate. The basic requirements necessary to preserve timber long enough for examination and evaluation are simple. The timber has to be cleaned with a sponge or brush and copious quantities of fresh water, drawn and photographed, and care must be taken to ensure that the wood does not dry out and distort during this work.

Mary Rose timber is stored in cellars beneath Brunel's Blockmills in the Royal Naval Base at Portsmouth where the constant low temperature and constant high humidity is ideal, but a damp cellar will do. The wood is stored in polythene-lined tanks of water with 1 per cent boric acid and sodium borate, in a ratio of 7:3 as an inhibitor to prevent the growth of micro-organisms. Cheap and serviceable storage tanks can be made of 'hammocks' of 1,000-gauge polythene supported in a cradle of 2 square inches of timber, and storage tanks of this type have been in use at Fishbourne Museum for eight years.

Eventually it may be decided that the timber concerned is not important enough to justify long term conservation treatment and it may be considered sufficient to cast a plaster replica in a silicone rubber mould taken from the timber, or even to rebury the timber in the sea-bed and retain only the drawings and the photographs. The important thing is that the timbers are recorded and photographed and their importance is properly evaluated. In order to do this it is necessary to prevent shrinkage, distortion and micro-biological degradation. All of these operations are well within the scope of the amateur, who should follow the guide-lines just described.

Cast- and wrought-iron objects are frequently found preserved in a cocooning accretion of iron oxides, carbonates and silicates – the result of chemical and biological degradation. Preserved within the accretion may be evidence of the fauna on the sea-bed when the accretion was being formed and also of organic material, rope and wood, 'entombed' within the accretion.

The accretion around iron objects recovered from the *Mary Rose* is liberally bespattered with oysters which must have abounded in the eastern part of the Solent when the accretion was forming on the sea-bed, but which now are much more common at the western end of the Solent. One of the iron 'built-up' guns recovered from the *Mary Rose* in 1971 yielded evidence of two baulks of timber and a bag of wood shavings preserved in the accretion underneath the gun.

Environmental and technical evidence of this nature is well worth recording, so care should be taken when removing accretion. Within the accretion the iron is usually in a state of equilibrium and it would probably remain so as long as it was left in the sea-bed environment. Once it is raised and allowed to dry out, a process of mineralization can rapidly occur in the oxygen-rich atmosphere to which it is now transferred.

As long as chlorine from the sea-water is present within the structure of the metal, this process will continue and cast iron which may appear to be immaculate when first removed from its protective cocoon of oxides can disintegrate into meaningless fragments at an alarming rate. It is essential that the chlorine is removed from the metal as soon as possible and this can be done quite simply by storing the iron in a bath containing a solution of 5 per cent sodium sesquicarbonate in de-ionized water, such as that which goes into car batteries.

Once more simple polythene-lined storage tanks can be constructed within a light timber framework and in these tanks the iron objects can be washed in many changes of the sesquicarbonate solution. If the iron object is transferred to these tanks immediately after removal from the sea, the object will not suffer deterioration caused by the mechanical stresses of drying out.

The wash solution should be changed at monthly intervals and the process continued until the wash water is found to be free from chlorides. Testing for chlorides is simple and only basic chemicals available from any chain of chemists are needed. A 10ml sample of the wash solution is acidulated with a few drops of dilute nitric acid in a narrow test tube. This solution should be bright and clear when viewed against a black background. Five drops of silver nitrate solution (1.7 grammes per 100 millilitres distilled water) are added to the test solution and the presence of one part per million of chloride will be detectable by a milky opalescence.

Blank tests should be carried out on the de-ionized water used to wash the iron and on the sodium sesquicarbonate solution. If iron is stored in 5 per cent sodium sesquicarbonate solution which is changed at monthly intervals, it will ultimately be washed free from chlorides and, although the process is lengthy, often taking a year or more, it is relatively cheap and effective.

Treatment by electrolytic reduction is more rapid and by this method corroded iron is reduced to metallic iron by the action of nascent hydrogen evolved at the cathode in an electrolytic tank. Small guns can be treated in tanks made from mild steel off-cuts of piping with welded-on bottoms. The gun is suspended freely within the cylinder and it forms the cathode while the tank becomes the anode. A solution of 5 per cent sodium sesquicarbonate or 2 per cent sodium hydroxide is used as the electrolyte and a current of between 10 and 50 volts is passed between the anode and the cathode at a density of 10 amps per square metre. The electrolyte has to be changed at frequent intervals and electrolysis continues until no further chloride is detected in the solution.

Laboratory processes for the treatment of iron include reduction by hydrogen in an oven! Obviously a hazardous process if it is not rigidly controlled, and certainly not recommended for the 'do-it-yourself' man. One of the *Mary Rose* guns was treated in this way by EM-Varian Ltd. The gun was heated very gradually to 1,050 degrees Centigrade in a continuously flowing atmosphere of 10 per cent hydrogen and 90 per cent nitrogen, and after several hours the gun was allowed to cool. As a result of this process, the corrosion layer was reduced back to metallic iron, but in the process the metallographic structure of the iron was changed. Obviously therefore it is advisable that any metallographic study of the iron takes place before this rather radical conservation process is undertaken.

The method has been in use for some years with great success in the *Vasa* conservation laboratories in Stockholm and a hydrogen reduction furnace is currently being installed in the conservation laboratories of Portsmouth City Museum which will be capable of dealing with iron objects up to 2.5 metres long. Although these facilities will in theory at least, only be available for material destined for museums through the Area Museum Service, they will provide a service which at present is sadly lacking.

With the inevitable expansion of underwater archaeology in this country it is essential that funds are made available to expand museum conservation facilities which in many cases are little more than a sink and a tap. In the meantime the amateur can often manage a good 'holding operation' for his own finds. Although laboratory conservation facilities are hard to find for treating privately owned antiquities, it is still possible for the diver to ensure that his finds do not deteriorate before professional advice can be obtained.

Most of the processes of decay are rapid and irreversible and it is essential that finds receive treatment as soon as possible after they are removed from the sea. Silver objects are frequently well preserved although they may be very fragile and their beauty may be masked by unsightly accretions of carbonates and silicates.

Professional advice should always be sought before any chemical 'stripping' technique is used to remove these accretions as radical chemical or mechanical stripping can destroy surface detail and reduce the value of the object. Well-preserved objects should be cleaned with a soft brush and warm water containing a few drops of a wetting agent such as Lissapol NDB.

Resistant area of accretion can be removed by soaking the object in 30 per cent (w/v) formic acid and then washing carefully in several changes of water, but care must be taken to remove any copper which may be redeposited on the surface of the metal and the operation should be watched throughout. Formic acid, which is volatile, is safer than citric or tartaric acid as any minute residual traces are moved from the silver by volatilization at room temperature.

Bronze guns and small objects of bronze are frequently recovered in superb condition and after superficial washing and drying they sometimes survive without any obvious deterioration. However in other cases active corrosion may occur and the occurrence of bright green spots on the outer surface of the metal is a sure sign that urgent attention is required. Sometimes, when an object has been cleaned, dried and lacquered for display, an outbreak of these green spots (bronze disease) can be masked until the corrosion is extensive and serious, and for this reason I prefer not to lacquer bronze objects until they can be shown to be stable for at least two years in normal storage conditions.

Bronze objects can be stabilized, without changing their appearance, by impregnating them with a 3 per cent (w/v) solution of benzotriazole in industrial methylated spirit. If this can be done under vacuum using a waterjet vacuum pump and a small desiccator, so much the better, but soaking in an aqueous solution 3 per cent (w/v) of benzotriazole at 60°C will give some protection until the object can receive professional treatment.

It should be remembered that heavily corroded bronze may be literally held together by the corrosion products. In that case it is better to stabilize the object by storing it in 'super dry' conditions in an airtight box, with a little silica gel which has been oven dried as a desiccant, than to atttempt to remove the corrosion products and end up with a lot of little pieces.

Well-fired pottery is usually stable, although glazes, painted decoration and burnishing may have been almost completely removed by solution and mechanical attrition during the time the pot was on the sea-bed. Any evidence of surface decoration is best seen when the pot is still wet, immediately after it has been recovered from the sea, and if such traces are seen it is best to note them carefully and take a colour photograph before the vessel dries out.

If you want to have the pot identified by an archaeologist, it is best to keep it damp in a polythene bag with moist tissue paper until it can be examined. Often pots are covered with marine growth and other calcarious deposits and these are extremely difficult to remove once they have dried out and hardened, so it is best to keep such vessels moist until they can be treated.

Careful local application of hydrochloric acid (10 per cent v/v) will remove carbonates from the surface, but the pot should not be immersed in the acid if there is any possibility that the clay body may contain a lime-rich 'filler'. Silicates are more difficult to remove and frequently it is better to leave them on the vessel than to risk damage by removing them mechanically with a mounted needle or miniature electric drill.

Broken pottery can be repaired using UHU or HMG adhesive, but first the broken surfaces should be thoroughly cleaned and dried. Care should be taken not to scrape down the edges of the sherds or it will be difficult to get a good join. The fragments can be supported in a box of sand while the adhesive dries and it is best to stick only two or three pieces at a time working upwards from the base of the pot.

Small bags of sand and straps of sellotape are useful to keep the sherds exactly in place while they dry. The jigsaw-puzzle technique is a challenge and it is rewarding to see the pot grow, but I recommend that a start is made by 'restoring' a broken flower-pot before attempting to tackle a treasured seventeenth-century olive jar.

Fungicides are necessary to prevent the growth of micro-organisms on damp organic material when it is stored, and it is necessary to select and use them with care. Many fungicides are strong irritants and care should be taken to avoid contact with the skin or eyes. Dowicide (a sodium ortho phenyl phenate) is frequently used to inhibit mould growth on damp material and at low concentrations (0.1–0.01 per cent) it is relatively non-toxic.

Timbers from the Swedish warship *Vasa* and the Tudor ship *Mary Rose* have been stored in tanks containing a 2 per cent (w/v) solution of boric acid and borax in a ratio 7:3. This comparatively weak fungicide is innocuous and it has effectively prevented mould growth for several years. It is also relatively cheap to buy!

Taking impressions and casts can be worth while in many ways. Firstly there is the obvious pleasure in making replicas of coins and small objects to give to your friends. Then there is the simple fact that it is often easier for an expert to identify a founder's mark on a gun or a coin from an impression than from a photograph. Lastly there is the exciting possibility of learning something about early craftsmen from iron objects which have vanished leaving only negative casts or 'ghosts' of their original shape.

Fortunately modern casting materials, available from any good hobby shop, make it possible for us to make replicas quickly, simply and cheaply. Wrought iron often disappears completely. Mineralization of the metallic iron leaves only the cocoon of concretion which formed around the iron object as a result of its delay. This cocoon often retains minute detail of the shape of the lost object and it can be used as a mould to make casts which perfectly reproduce the original object.

The clean, dry, negative casts are treated with a separator to ensure that they come away easily without tearing the replica. An aerosol furniture polish containing silicon is ideal for this purpose. The hollow cast is filled with successive layers of silicone rubber or polysulphide rubber and allowed to cure at room temperature. Care must be taken to allow each layer to 'go off' before adding the next and to avoid entrapping air bubbles within the latex. After curing, the concretion is broken away with a small chisel and a hammer and the replica released. This replica can be used to make a two piece mould of dental plaster from which other replicas can be made as required.

In the early sixties, Michael Katsey and Van Doorninck used a polysulphide rubber, 'Smooth-On Mould Compound 100 and 300', to cast replicas of Byzantine tools found on a seventh-century shipwreck at Yassi Ada in Turkey and today we are using silicone rubber to cast lost iron fastenings from the *Mary Rose*. A study of the varying sizes of wrought-iron spikes and nails used to construct the ship is being made from casts made from these negative concretions.

Coins can be used to make one-piece moulds of silicone rubber and from these moulds replicas can be made in epoxy or polyester resins. Great care must be taken to avoid entrapped air and dust as every imperfection will be reproduced by the mould. Single-surface moulds can be made in small fences of plasticine but 'dip moulds' can be made by fastening stiff card to half of the circumference of the coin and then casting the whole object in a small box leaving only the card protruding to form a slit from which the coin can be extracted. Again it is necessary to apply a separator such as 'Pledge' furniture polish to ensure easy release from the original coin.

Vinagel 118, a polyvinyl chloride moulding material, can be used to take accurate impressions of coins or founder's marks for identification. The Vinagel, a putty-like substance, is softened in the hand and then well talced before applying it to the surface of the object, which should also be dusted with talc to ensure easy release between the object and the moulding compound. The impression can be permanently cured in an electric oven by baking it for half an hour at 140°C. These impressions are often more use to experts than photographs or rubbings.

Where to buy the chemicals? Many of the chemicals can be bought in major chain-store chemists, but Frank W. Joel, at 9 Church Manor, Hertford, Hertfordshire, specializes in supplying small quantities. Many moulding and casting materials are available at hobby shops throughout the country. Alec Tiranti, of 21 Goodge Place, London W1 stock Vinagel, cold casting resins and many other useful materials for the cast-maker or pottery restorer.

Two essential books are fortunately inexpensive, and should be on every club bookshelf. *First Aid For Finds*, published by Rescue, price 75p, is a useful handbook, although unfortunately does not have much to say about the special problems of finds from the sea. *Conservation in Field Archaeology*, by Elizabeth Dowman, published by Methuen at £1.50, is essentially a practical book for land archaeological expeditions, but much of the advice is relevant for underwater expeditions as well.

Hopefully the situation will change in the next few years and conservation facilities and advice will be available for all important finds from the sea. But at present it largely rests with the finder, the diver who recovers the object, to ensure that the object survives the drastic change of environment when it is raised. If you have any doubts about it, do not raise it! If you do raise it, please do not let it rot.

APPENDIX III

Protecting a Wreck

The Protection of Wrecks Act 1973 enables the Secretary of State to designate by order the site of any wrecked vessel lying on or in the sea-bed in United Kingdom territorial waters if he is satisfied that it ought to be protected from unauthorized interference on account of its historical, archaeological or artistic importance. A designation order is made by statutory instrument whenever such a site is designated. It identifies the site of the wrecked vessel and specifies the extent of a restricted area around it. Within that area it is an offence without the authority of a licence granted by the Secretary of State to tamper with, damage or remove any part of the wrecked vessel or anything contained or formerly contained in it, to carry out diving or salvage operations, to use diving or salvage equipment or to deposit materials so as to obliterate or obstruct access to the site or to damage the wreck.

A committee of expert advisers under the chairmanship of Viscount Runciman of Doxford assists the Secretary of State in selecting sites to be designated and the persons to be licensed to carry out diving or salvage operations on designated sites. Diving interests are consulted regarding the extent of the restricted areas, which are kept as small as possible. Other departments, for example the Scottish Office and those concerned with the control of dumping at sea and with fishing, and lighthouse and harbour authorities, are also consulted, as appropriate.

The intention to designate a site and its surrounding restricted area is advertised in the national and local press. Time is allowed for consideration of objections before an order is made and the advertisements indicate the procedure for notifying objections. When a site needs immediate protection a designation order may be made without prior consultation or advertisement but the making of the order will be advertised and the order may be modified or revoked in the light of representations received. The designation orders are publicized and are also notified in 'Notices to Mariners'. Where practicable the designated sites will be marked with buoys and/or in some other suitable way marked on Admiralty charts.

Licences to carry out diving or salvage operations in a restricted area are subject to conditions or restrictions necessary for the protection of the archaeological value of the site. The advisory committee is consulted regarding the conditions or restrictions to be imposed, which are kept to the minimum necessary to secure their object. In cases where the owner of a designated wreck is known, arrangements would be made to safeguard his interests and the interests of any salvor working on it at the time of designation. In exceptional cases, and especially where the vessel and its contents may be largely intact, the site might need to be kept undisturbed until full-scale archaeological survey and recovery operations could be organized.

The act places no restriction on navigation, anchoring, fishing or bathing in restricted areas provided that authorized salvage operations are not obstructed. No offence is committed under the act by actions taken in an emergency, in the exercise of statutory functions or out of stress of weather or navigational hazards.

Information about the discovery of wreck sites which may be of historical importance should be given, in confidence if desired, to the Receiver of Wreck at the Custom House in the nearest port, or to the Department of Trade, Marine Division, Branch 1c, 90/93 High Holborn, London, wc1v 6LP (telephone 01-405 6911, extensions 492 or 495). That is the Department of Trade's general guidance for divers concerned about the protection of an historic wreck. It is interesting to note that the Secretary of State is also enabled under the provisions of the act to designate dangerous wrecks for protection from unauthorized interference. At present only one dangerous wreck site, that of the *Richard Montgomery* near Sheerness, is designated.

The *Richard Montgomery*, a United States Liberty ship, sank in the Thames Estuary in 1944 after running aground less than four thousand yards off Sheerness. She was carrying some three thousand tons of high explosives and bombs. The explosives are still dangerous and experts say that if she was disturbed in any way they could explode and do colossal damage.

APPENDIX IV

A Diver's Guide to Wrecks around the Coasts of Britain

5000 BC	Not exactly a wreck, even though found 60 feet deep but evidence of man raising stones beside the sea. (See chapter 1.)
1200 BC	Bronze Age arms-trader cargo, found by Dover branch of the B S-A C. (See chapter 1.)
100	Roman barge sank in Thames. Excavated by Peter Marsden at Blackfriars.
100	Roman ship. Part of amphora found off Seaford Head, Sussex. (See chapter 1.)
160	Roman vessel, wrecked off Whitstable. (See chapter 1.)
851	*Drakkar* (the 'Serpent'), Viking ship lost in Thames.
1439	*Grace Dieu*, warship built by Henry V in 1418. Accidentally burnt in 1439. Timbers still to be seen in River Hamble. (See chapter 3.)
14 January 1494	*St James of the Croyne*. This could be the Tudor ship in the Cattewater. (See chapter 2.)
1509	The ships of a fleet taking the King of Castile back to Spain were caught in a storm in the English Channel and off South Devon. (See chapter 2.)
20 July 1545	*Mary Rose*, lost in full view of King Henry VIII. Located by Alexander McKee. (See chapter 3.)
18 August 1588	*El Gran Grifon*, wrecked on Fair Isle, Shetlands. Some salvage done in 1970. (See chapter 5.)

September 1588   *Duque de Florencia*, possibly the Tobermory galleon. A big puzzle because no one is sure what ship this is. (See chapter 4.)

16 September 1588   *La Trinidad Valencera*, foundered at anchor. Site discovered by City of Derry divers. (See chapter 5.)

16 October 1588   *Girona*, Spanish Armada casualty, wrecked in the Giant's Causeway. Almost totally salved by Robert Stenuit. (See chapter 4.)

21 October 1588   *Santa Maria de la Rosa*, wrecked in Blasket Sound. Located by Sydney Wignall. (See chapter 4.)

1 November 1588   *San Pedro el Mayor*, Spanish Armada hospital ship, wrecked in Hope Cove, Devon. (See chapter 5.)

1590   *Santa Catarina*, galleon lost near Colliestow, Aberdeenshire. Searches have been made without success.

1617   The 'Great Silver Wreck', found by Mike Hall and Ken Simpson. (See chapter 6.)

15 June 1640   *Reiger*, sunk in Lerwick Harbour by Spaniards. Located by diver. (See chapter 9.)

2 March 1653   *Lastdrager*, Dutch East Indiaman, wreck in Shetland located Robert Stenuit. (See chapter 9.)

1656   *Primrose*, twenty-two-gun vessel, wrecked at Seven Stones.

1664   *Kennermerlandt*, Dutch East Indiaman sunk in Shetlands. (See chapter 9.)

7 October 1667   *Santo Christo de Castello*, found at Mullion by Peter McBride. (See chapter 6.)

28 May 1672   *Royal James*, burnt at Battle of Solebay. Divers searching for her. (See chapter 7.)

25 March 1675   *Mary*, eight-gun Royal Yacht, wrecked off the Skerries. (See chapter 6.)

11 January 1679   *Santa Cruz*, lost galleon off Pembroke, Wales. Said

to be a treasure ship. Local searches made without success.

February 1686 — *Princesse Maria*, Dutch East Indiaman, wrecked on Silver Carn, Scillies. Located by Rex Cowan. (See chapter 8.)

5 July 1690 — *Anne*, badly damaged at Battle of Beachy Head. Beached. (See chapter 7.)

9 October 1690 — *Dartmouth*, sunk by a storm near Oban while putting down the Scottish clans. (See chapter 7.)

1 September 1691 — *Coronation*, caught in storm while trying to enter Plymouth Harbour. Great loss of life. Located by Plymouth divers. (See chapter 7.)

1 September 1691 — *Harwich*, 70 guns. (See chapter 7.)

12 September 1691 — *Exeter*, blown up by accident at Plymouth. (See chapter 7.)

7 January 1701 — *Michael*, merchantman, wrecked off the Casquets, Alderney.

27 November 1703 — *Stirling Castle*, 70 guns, *Mary*, 70 guns, and *Northumberland*, 70 guns, all three lost on the Goodwins.
Vanguard, 70 guns, sunk at Chatham.
York, 70 guns, lost near Harwich; all lost but four men.
Resolution, 60 guns, coast of Sussex.
Newcastle, 60 guns, at Spithead, 193 drowned.
Reserve, 60 guns, at Yarmouth, 173 perished.
(Great storm caused loss of all the ships above.)

30 October 1706 — *Nassau*, third-rate, 80 guns. Wrecked off the Kent coast.

22 October 1707 — *Association*, 70 guns, wrecked off the Scilly Isles with the other vessels listed below. Scene of Britain's first real underwater treasure discovery. Located by navy divers. (See chapter 10.)
Eagle, 70 guns.
Romney, 50 guns.
Firebrand, fireship.

Hundreds of men died in minutes. (See chapter 10.)

15 October 1711   *Edgar*, 70 guns, blew up at Spithead, all on board dead. (See chapter 3.)

1711   *De Liefde*, East Indiaman, sunk Shetlands. (See chapter 9.)

7 December 1721   *Hind*, twenty-gun, wrecked off the Channel Isles.

1728   *Adelaar*, Dutch East Indiaman, wrecked Outer Hebrides. Colin Martin investigating. (See chapter 9.)

1729   *Curacao*, Dutch warship, wrecked Scotland. Robert Stenuit investigation. (See chapter 9.)

December 1737   *Wendela*, Danish East Indiaman, wrecked Shetlands. Excavated by Robert Stenuit. (See chapter 9.)

18 November 1740   *Svecia*, Swedish East Indiaman, wrecked in Orkneys homeward bound. Located by Rex Cowan. (See chapter 9.)

13 July 1743   *Hollandia*, Dutch East Indiaman. Treasure ship. Excavated after location by Rex Cowan. (See chapter 8.)

21 September 1744   *Colchester*, 50 guns, wrecked on Kentish Knock, fifty men lost.

5 October 1744   *Victory*, 100 guns, near the Isle of Alderney; all drowned.

26 January 1749   *Amsterdam*, Dutch East Indiaman, near Hastings. (See chapter 8.)

24 April 1753   *Assurance*, on the Isle of Wight. Site located and dived. (See chapter 11.)

14 February 1760   *Ramillies*, 90 guns, second-rate. Twenty-six ratings only survived her storm wrecking on Bolt Tail, Devon. Property now of Mike Borrow and David Langfield. Debris on bottom – cannon, cannonballs etc. – is theirs. Divers have been warned!

15 February 1760   *Conqueror*, lost on St Nicholas's Island, Plymouth.

3 November 1760   *Ann*, Frigate, wrecked off Caernarvon Bay, Wales.

1772   *Chantiloupe*, vessel returning from West Indies wrecked close to Bantham. All lost except one man. On board was a woman, who put on her richest gems and clothes, hoping that if she was washed on shore her appearance would help. Locals, however, waiting for loot, seized her, stripped her of clothes and gems. Even cut off fingers for rings, mangled her ears for earrings, and left her to die. Proved at inquiry that she was alive when she reached shore and was deliberately murdered.

1774   *Driad*, schooner, wrecked near Raven Rock, Bantham, in the great storm of 1774.

23 September 1779   *Bonhomme Richard*. Paul Jones and all that. Located by Sydney Wignall. (See chapter 11.)

2 March 1782   *Britannia*, storeship, 20 guns. Wrecked Kentish Knock.

29 August 1782   *Royal George*, about nine hundred drowned. (See chapter 3.)

1785   *I. A. Juno*, merchantman, disappeared until found recently by Steve Burrows in the Scillies.

6 January 1786   *Halsewell*, East Indiaman wrecked Seacombe, Isle of Purbeck. Sometimes known as the 'ship in the cave', as some people escaped into cave when ship sank. 182 died. Bob Campbell has dived in search of her. Found very few traces.

10 December 1786   *Die Fraumetta Catherina von Flensburgh*, being excavated by B S-A C Plymouth Sound branch divers. (See Introduction.)

10 December 1786   *Christian Hendrick*, ashore in Deadman's Bay, Plymouth. (See Introduction.)

18 December 1795   *Catharine*, trading vessel, wrecked near Fleet, Weymouth.

	Thomas, merchantman, wrecked near Fleet. *Venus*, merchantman, wrecked near Fleet.

4 May 1795   *Boyne*, by fire at Spithead. Man-of-war, of 98 guns, destroyed by fire at Portsmouth by the explosion of the magazine; 14 killed. Portions were recovered in June 1838 when she was blown up as a danger to navigation. Alexander McKee discovered shingle mound covering wreck in May 1965.

29 December 1795   *Amethyst*, 38 guns, wrecked near Alderney, CI.

26 January 1796   *Dutton*, East Indiaman, wrecked Plymouth Hoe, Devon.

15 July 1796   *Trompeuse*, brig sloop, 16 guns, wrecked Kinsale Head, Southern Ireland.

1798   *L'Amitié* or *Amité*, French ship intended to aid Irish rebellion in Londonderry, wrecked near Belfast. The site known as 'Cannon's Hole' was investigated by Robert and Maureen Trouton of Belfast Branch of B S-A C, who found eight cast-iron cannon there. One raised identified as a demi-culverin.

10 December 1798   *Colossus*. Wrecked on Scillies. Thousands of fragments of pottery recovered. Located by Roland Morris's team. (See chapter 11.)

10 February 1799   HMS *Weazle*, lost with all hands on Baggy Point, North Devon. Ilfracombe divers have located and raised her cannon.

9–10 October 1799   HMS *Lutine*, 32 guns, was wrecked off Vlieland, coast of Holland; only one saved, who died before reaching England. The *Lutine* was a former French ship captained by Admiral Duncan. She contained much bullion and money, belonging to merchants; a great loss to the underwriters at Lloyd's.

19 October 1799   HMS *Impregnable*, Captain Jonathan Faulknor, struck near entrance to Langstone Harbour after convoy duty from Lisbon. Salved. Cannon found by Southsea diver John Eberhard. More by Alex McKee and Maurice Harknett.

2 November 1799   *Guernsey Lily*, lost at entrance to Solent in Yarmouth Roads. Described as an ordnance transport; all saved.

16 November 1799   *Espion*, 36 guns, wrecked off Goodwin Sands.

9 July 1800   HMS *Brazen*, sloop off Newhaven. Fred Baldwin of Bromley BS-AC has located cannon.

16 March 1801   *Invincible*, 74 guns, wrecked Harborough Sands, Yarmouth. Captain J. Rennie and crew drowned, 126 saved.

10 January 1803   *Active*, 350-ton West Indiaman from Greenock. Carried £67,000 in gold. Sunk in storm at Margate. Most of gold salvaged.

12 January 1803   *Hindostan*, East Indiaman, off Westgate, Kent. Silver bullion on board in 13 chests, 11 recovered.

16 November 1803   *Circe*, frigate, 32 guns, off Yarmouth.

13 October 1804   *Firebrand*, fireship, wrecked near Dover.

24 November 1804   *Venerable*, 74 guns, at Torbay; lost 8 men.

6 February 1805   *Earl of Abergavenny*, East Indiaman foundered Weymouth. Has been located by Ron Parry.

20 October 1806   *Athenienne*, 64 guns, wrecked off Scillies.

17 November 1807   *Glasgow*, mail packet vessel. Wrecked Farne Islands

28 November 1807   *Boreas*, 28 guns, wrecked on Hanois Rocks, Guernsey. Wreck located by Richard Keen and Dave Archer.

29 December 1807   HMS *Anson*, 44 guns, wrecked on Loe Bar, near Pothleven; many lives lost. Located. Some cannon raised recently.

21 January 1809   *Dispatch*, transport carrying men and horses of the 7th Dragoons from Corunna, on Lowland Point, The Manacles, Cornwall. 7 men survived.
Primrose, brig on Manacles, one boy saved out of 126 on board. Pintle found.

14 October 1811   *Pomone*, 38 guns, wrecked off Needles, IOW.

14 January 1814   *Queen*, transport on Trefusis Point, Falmouth, over three hundred and fifty dead. Some diving.

17 December 1814   *British Queen*, packet, wrecked on the Goodwin Sands, and all on board lost.

21 January 1817   *Telegraph*, schooner, 14 guns, wrecked Mount Batten, Plymouth.

23 October 1817   *William and Mary*, packet, struck on the Willeys rocks, near the Holmes lighthouse, Bristol Channel, nearly sixty persons perished.

8 August 1821   *Earl of Moira*, on the Burbo Bank, near Liverpool; forty drowned.

26 December 1821   *Juliana*, East Indiaman, on the Kentish Knock; forty drowned.

3 February 1822   *Thames*, Indiaman, off Beachy Head.

14 December 1822   *Racehorse*, brig sloop, 18 guns, wrecked off IOM. Located.

17 August 1831   *Rothsay Castle*, wooden steamer, wrecked in Dutchmans Bank, Menai Strait.

15 October 1833   *United Kingdom*, West Indiaman, with rich cargo; run down by the *Queen of Scotland* steamer off Northfleet, near Gravesend.

6 September 1838   *Forfarshire*, steamer, on its passage from Hull to Dundee, was wrecked in a violent gale, and 38 persons out of 53 were drowned. Lighthouse-keeper James Darling and his heroic daughter Grace ventured out in a tremendous sea in a coble, and rescued several of the passengers. Wreck located by divers.

4 January 1841   *Thames*, steamer, Captain Gray, from Dublin to Liverpool, wrecked off St Ives. Captain and 55 persons lost.

30 March 1850   *Royal Adelaide*, steamer, wrecked on the Tongue Sands, off Margate, four hundred lost.

24 December 1852   *Lily*, stranded and blown up by gunpowder on the Calf of Man, thirty lost.

29 September 1853   *Annie Jane*, of Liverpool, an emigrant vessel driven on shore on the Barra Islands, on the west coast of Scotland; about 348 lives lost.

19 October 1853   *Dalhousie*, foundered off Beachy Head; the captain (Butterworth), the passengers, and all the crew except one – about sixty persons in all – drowned.

30 November 1853   *Marshall*, steamer, foundered off mouth of Humber.

1 December 1854   *Nile*, screw-steamer, struck on the Godevry Rock, St Ives Bay; and all drowned.

3 May 1855   *John*, immigrant ship bound for Quebec, on The Manacles, Cornwall. 196 men, women and children drowned.

2 June 1857   *Northern Belle*, a large American vessel, was wrecked near Broadstairs. The American Government sent 21 silver medals and £270 to be distributed among the heroic boatmen of the place, who saved the crew.

25–6 October 1859   *Royal Charter*, screw-steamer, Captain Taylor, totally wrecked off Moelfre, on the Anglesey coast; 446 lives lost. The vessel contained gold amounting in value to between £700,000 and £800,000; much of this was recovered. Some diving has taken place.

19 February 1860   *Ondine*, steamer; lost through collision with the *Herione* of Bideford, abreast of Beachy Head; the captain and about fifty lost.

28 February 1860   *Nimrod*, steamer, wrecked on rocks near St David's Head; forty lives lost.

April 1862   *Mars*, Waterford steamer, struck on a rock near Milford Haven, about fifty lost.

20 December 1862   *Lifeguard*, steamer, left Newcastle, with about forty-one passengers, never since heard of, supposed to have foundered off Flamborough Head.

14 January 1865   *Lelia*, steamer, foundered near Great Orme Head, Mersey.

23 March 1866   *Spirit of the Ocean*, steamer, wrecked on Start Point, all lost except 4.

10 July 1866   *Amazon*, screw sloop, and screw steamer *Osprey*, sunk by collision near Plymouth. Several passengers and sailors drowned.

19 August 1866   *Bruiser*, steamer, sunk by collision with the *Haswell*, off Aldbrough, about fifteen lives lost.

5 January 1867   *James Crosfield*, iron ship, wrecked off Langness, IOM; all on board lost.

25 March 1867   *Jonkheer Meester van de Wall Puttershock*, East Indiaman, wrecked Poldhu Cove, Cornwall.

23 May 1868   *Garrone* on Buck Rocks, near Lamorna Cove. Many lost. Dennis James has located some wreckage.

28 January 1869   *Padarn*, brigantine, wrecked Mothercombe, Devon.

1 February 1869   *Amalie*, brig, wrecked Chesil Cove, Portland Bill.

13 February 1869   *Jane and Margaret*, sloop, foundered Ramsey Bay, IOM

28 August 1869   *Anne Longton*, full-rigged ship, foundered Goodwin Sands.

12 September 1869   *Oneidi*, brigantine, wrecked three hundred yards west of Langley Point, Sussex.

13 September 1869   *Caravan*, barque, wrecked Walton Bay, Somerset.

13 February 1870   *Sea Queen*, steamer, wrecked North Scroby Sand, Norfolk.

7 March 1870   *Normandy*, steamer, by collision with the steamer *Mary* off the IOW; the captain and 33 others lost.

27 October 1870   *Geneva*, full-rigged ship, wrecked Stones Reef, Cornwall.

31 January 1872   *Manitobah*, barque, wrecked Buck Rocks, Cornwall.

25 November 1872   *Royal Adelaide*, iron sailing ship of 1,320 tons driven by gale on to Chesil Beach. Cargo of spirits, six crew drowned, but twenty 'salvagers' died on beach from 'excessive drinking'! Dived by Bournemouth and Poole branch. Very broken up.

22 January 1873   *Northfleet*, frigate rammed by steamship *Murillo* at Dungeness. 293 people drowned. Dived by Folkestone branch B S-A C who now own her.

1 March 1873   *Boyne*, barque, wrecked off Mohilo Bay, Cornwall; about twenty lost.

March 1873   *Lalla Rookh*, from Shanghai, bound London. Wrecked March 1873 on Prawle Point. Cargo 1,300 tons of tea and sixty tons of tobacco. All crew except Chief Mate saved by rocket apparatus. Tea washed in and left in ten-foot-high wall at high-tide mark.

21 October 1874   *Chusan*, trading vessel; wrecked Crinan Rocks, Ardrossan, west Scotland.

17 February 1875   *Strathclyde*, Glasgow steamer, sunk by collision with the Hamburg ship *Franconia*, in Dover Bay in daylight; about seventeen lost. (Verdict of manslaughter against Kuhn, captain of *Franconia*, quashed on appeal; 7 judges against 6 decided against British jurisdiction, 13 November 1876.)

1 September 1875   *Vanguard*, battleship; collision off Wicklow.

6 December 1875   *Deutschland*, Atlantic steamer, from Bremen to New York, went on sandbank, the Kentish Knock, at the mouth of the Thames during a gale; about seventy lost (many emigrants).

5 January 1877   *Oscar*, steamer, wrecked Whitby Rocks, Yorks.

18 August 1877   *Commodore*, brigantine, wrecked Encombe Ledges, Kimmeridge.

14 September 1877   *Irishman*, steamer, wrecked Burial Island, Ballyhalbert, County Down.

19 September 1877   *Blackwatch*, full-rigged ship, wrecked West Point, Fair Isle.

31 October 1877   *Pauline*, brigantine, wrecked Rickham Cove, Devon.

10 November 1877   *Anger H. Curtis*, brigantine, wrecked west side Walney Lighthouse, Irish Sea.

28 December 1877   *Fairy Queen*, steamer, wrecked North Carr Rocks, Fifeness.

4 January 1878   *Balmoral*, steamer, wrecked on rocks one mile north-west of Hartlepool, Heugh Light, Durham.

23 January 1878   *Pioneer*, steamer, wrecked Puffin Islands, Menai Strait.

26 January 1878   *Myrtle*, steamer, wrecked Ballycastle, County Antrim.

22 February 1878   *Moldavia*, steamer, wrecked Nash Rock, Glamorgan.

3 September 1878   *Princess Alice*, by collision with the screw-steamer *Bywell Castle* in the Thames near Woolwich; between six and seven hundred lost.

25 November 1878   *Pomerania*, Hamburg-American mail-steamer sunk off Folkestone by *Moel Elian*, iron barque, of Caernarvon a little after midnight. 162 saved by boats, about forty-eight missing.

11 January 1879   *Loch Sunart*, full-rigged ship, wrecked Skullmartin Reef, Ballywalter Bay, County Down.

13 January 1879   *Schiehallion*, iron barque, wrecked three-quarters of a mile east of Blackgang Chine, iow.
Don Quixote, brigantine, wrecked North Arran, Galway Bay.

27 January 1879   *Edith Owen*, steamer, wrecked Coal Rock, Anglesey.

26 June 1879   *Gleanen*, brig, stranded Gunfleet Sands, Thames.

13 August 1879   *City of London*, Aberdeen steamer, run down and sunk by the *Vesta*, in the Thames.

17 July 1880   *Hydaspes*, sailing-ship, sank in collision with *Centurion*, screw-steamer, off Dungeness in a fog, both blamed; no lives lost.

16 January 1881   *Edith Morgan*, schooner, wrecked Black Rocks, Sound of Islay.

18 January 1881   *Sainte Ann*, schooner wrecked Penarth Head, Bristol Channel.

27 January 1881   *Claremont*, steamer, wrecked Atherfield, iow.
Ruperra, steamer, wrecked near Bolt Head, Devon.

4 February 1881   *Bremen*, full-rigged ship, Levenwick, Shetland Isles. Surveyed by Gilbert and Norman Dinesen.

19 February 1881   *Caledonia*, steamer, wrecked Oyster Rock, Jersey, CI,

6 March 1881   *Essen*, steamer, wrecked half-a-mile west of St Catherine's Light, iow.

29 April 1882   *Alexandrovna*, Liverpool ship, wrecked off Swanage; all crew lost.

16 October 1882   *Constantia* and *City of Antwerp*, steamers, sunk by collision off the Eddystone, about fourteen lost.

26 November 1882 *Cambronne*, steamer, sunk by collision with *Marion*, near Lundy.

27 January 1883   *James Gray*, steamer, wrecked Tuskar Rock, near Porthcawl.

7 February 1883   *Silksworth*, steamer, wrecked River Weir entrance.

30 March, 1883   *Norman Court* lost off Anglesey. Located by Peter Salmon.

24 April 1883   *British Commerce*, sunk by collision with *County of Aberdeen* off Selsey Bill; 25 lost.

9 May 1883   *Strathenerick*, steamer, wrecked off Linney Head, Pembrokeshire.

10 May 1883   *Mercury*, steamer, wrecked Blackpool, Lancashire.

7 June 1883   *Lively*, steamer, wooden. Wrecked Chicken Rocks, Stornoway Harbour.

21 July 1883   *Priscilla*, barquentine, wrecked Redcar Rocks, Yorkshire.

1 September 1883   *Christiane*, barque, wrecked Chesil Cove, Portland.

2 January 1884   *Bentuther*, barque, wrecked Grassholm Island, Pembrokeshire.

12 January 1884   *Hilda*, schooner, wrecked five miles south of Bridlington, Yorkshire.

2–3 August 1884   *Dione*, steamer, sunk by collision with *Camden*, steamer, near Gravesend; about seventeen persons drowned (captain of the *Dione* punished for reckless navigation).

2 April 1885   *Queen Victoria*, barque, wrecked Swallow Bank, New Romney.

15 October 1885   *Nordstjernen*, brig, wrecked the Binks, Spurn Point, Yorkshire.

1 November 1885   *Eleanor Dodson*, barque, wrecked near Orford Haven, cg Station, Suffolk.

25 November 1885   *Aurora*, steamer, wrecked off Hartlepool, Durham.

1 March 1886   *Missouri*, screw-barque, lost off Anglesey and found by divers in 1963.

15 May 1886   *Pala*, steamer, wrecked Kimmeridge Ledge, iow.

30 August 1886   *Belfort*, steamer, wrecked Selle Rock, Guernsey, ci.

15 October 1886   *Malleny*, Liverpool iron steamer, foundered on the Tuskar reef, Bristol Channel, all 20 hands lost in the gale.

Teviotdale, steamer, of Glasgow, lost on the Carmarthen coast; 18 lives lost.
Ben-y-Gloe, iron ship, stranded near Nash Point, Glamorganshire.

25 November 1886   *Strathpeffer*, steamer, stranded near Workington, Cumberland.

10 December 1886   *Balnacraig*, steamer, foundered off North Foreland, Kent.

2 September 1887   *Avenir*, brig, wrecked Maplin Sand, Essex.

27 October 1887   *Flying Hawk*, steam tug, wrecked Maiden Rocks, Dalkey Island, County Dublin.

30 October 1887   *St Lukas*, brigantine, wrecked Portlet Bay, Guernsey, CI.

1 November 1887   *Mayo*, steamer, wrecked St Alban's Head, Dorset.

2 December 1887   *Capri*, steamer, wrecked Kentish Knock, Essex.

8 March 1888   *Lanoma*, iron barque, wrecked near Weymouth; 12 lives lost.

9 March 1888   *City of Corinth*, sunk by collision with *Tasmania*, near Dungeness.

7 October 1889   *St George*, full-rigged ship, wrecked near Peel, IOM.
Heros, barque, wrecked Hare Island, County Galway.

5 November 1889   *Göteborg*, wooden steamer, wrecked Salt Scar Rocks, Redcar.

29 December 1889   *Cleddy*, steamer, sunk after collision with *Isle of Cyprus* steamer, off St Catherine's Point. About thirteen lives lost.

17 January 1890   *Arbutus*, steamer, wrecked Goldstone Rock, Holy Island, Durham.

19 January 1890   *Penthesilea*, iron full-rigged ship, wrecked Baggy Point, Devon.

25 January 1890   *Irex*, full-rigged ship, wrecked Scratchells Bay, IOW.
Thorne, iron barque, wrecked Douglas Bay, Isle of Man.

19 February 1890   *Highgate*, steamer, and *Sovereign*, ship, both sunk by collision off Lundy Island; 12 lost.

21 April 1890   *Brankelow*, steamer, wrecked Loe Bar, Porthleven, Cornwall.

16 June 1890   *Hermine*, lost Anglesey; very broken up, says Bill Butland, who has dived on her.

23 November 1890   *Uppingham*, Cardiff steamer, bound for China, struck on a rock below Hartland Quay, Cornwall; about seven drowned.

18 December 1890   *Oregon*, eight-hundred-ton barque, lost near Thurlestone. Located by Kingston branch divers.

1891   *Marana* in snowstorm struck the Blackstone Rocks off Start lighthouse. Went to pieces in minutes. Some thirty crew took to boats, but only 4 reached shore; they were Swedes. Located by George Tessyman. Very broken up.
Dryad, barque, possibly Blackstone Rocks, a few hours after *Marana*.

26 October 1891   *Charlwood*, barque, sunk by collision with the *Boston*, near the Eddystone lighthouse; 15 lost.

11 November 1891   *Benvenue*, full-rigged ship, bound for Sydney and wrecked off Sandgate; 27 persons suspended in the rigging for sixteen hours; were saved with great difficulty by the Sandgate lifeboat and taken to Folkestone; Captain James Moddrel and 4 men drowned.

21 February 1892   *Fratelli F.*, barque; lost near Land's End. Found by divers recently.

24 February 1892   *Forest Queen*, steamer; sunk by collision with the *Loughborough*, steamer, near Flamborough Head; about fourteen lives lost.

| 1 July 1892 | *City of Chicago*, Inman Atlantic liner, run ashore near Old Head of Kinsale, during a fog; passengers landed 1 July; totally wrecked 7 July. Ship broke in two. Divers have located badly broken-up wreckage. |

14 August 1892 — *Thracia*, barque, capsized near Port Erin, IOM, 17 lives lost.

18 November 1893 — *Hampshire*, steamer, of London, owners Messrs MacBeth and Grey of Glasgow (Captain Weir and 22 men) sunk off St Ives, Cornwall, all lost except Mr James Swanson, chief officer.

1894 — *Theodora*, brigantine from Hamburg, ashore on Thurlestone Sands during gale in February 1894. Cargo of cotton seed and dye woods. Captain and 2 hands lost. Mate and lads saved.

15 April 1896 — *Elbe*, North German Lloyd steamer, from Bremen to New York, sunk in collision with the *Crathie* of Aberdeen, off Lowestoft, about 6 am. 334 lives lost, including Captain von Gossel.

16 June 1897 — *Susannah Kelly*, steamer, sunk in a gale in Belfast Lough; captain and 9 men lost.
HMS *Foudroyant*, 80 guns, wrecked near Blackpool.

1 February 1898 — *Channel Queen*, steamer, from Plymouth, wrecked on the Black Rock off Guernsey; 12 passengers and some of the crew drowned.

14 October 1898 — *Mohegan*, Atlantic Transport Company steamer, wrecked on the Manacles, off Cornwall by error of navigation; Captain R. Griffiths and 106 drowned. Located by Roy Davis and Bernard Rogers. Well dived.

11 February 1899 — *Arno*, steam collier, wrecked near Selsey Bill; 13 deaths.

30 March 1899 — *Stella*, excursion steamer from Southampton to Guernsey (SWR), wrecked at 4 pm while going at full speed in a fog on the Black Rock near the Casquets, eight miles off Alderney. Out of the 140 passengers and the 40 members of the crew, 105 persons were drowned, including Captain Reeks.

Great heroism was shown, and there was no panic; the ship sank in eight minutes.

16 September 1900   *Gordon Castle*, Glasgow steamer, and the Hamburg steamer *Storman* sunk by collision during a fog in Cardigan Bay; Captain Casey and 19 others from the *Gordon Castle* lost.

28 December 1900   *Primrose Hill*. Iron barque, lost near Holyhead. Dived by Bill Butland. Very broken up.

14–15 January 1903   *Manchester Merchant*, steamer, with seven hundred bales of cotton on fire, scuttled in Dingle Bay, Kerry.

18 March 1904   Submarine A1 off Spithead; 11 lost.

18 August 1904   HMS destroyer *Zephyr*, rammed in Portsmouth Harbour.

23 January 1905   A7 submarine, foundered Whitesand Bay, Cornwall.

4 April 1905   Destroyer *Spiteful*, in collision off Yarmouth (IOW); 2 drowned.

8 June 1905   Submarine A8 off Plymouth; 15 drowned.

16 October 1905   Submariné A4 sunk in Portsmouth Harbour after explosion.

1906   *Blesk*, Russian oil-tanker, came on shore in a cove a little above the Greystone in thick fog. As she broke up oil floated up to Kingsbridge, South Devon.

18 March 1907   *Djebba*, four-thousand-ton West Africa mailboat, ran aground Bolt Tail. Boilers and plates still remain.

2 October 1907   *Alfred Erlandsen*, of Copenhagen. St Abbs. No survivors despite search by Eyemouth lifeboat. Located by Edinburgh branch of the B S-A C.

7 November 1910   *Preussen*, at Dover, the largest steel sailing-ship – five-masted – of her time. 4,768 tons, she was in collision with the cross-Channel steamer *Brighton*.

Preussen badly damaged, finally sank despite salvage attempts in Crab (or Fan) Bay. Has been visited by many B S-A C branches, including a Bromley branch team under Malcolm Todd and Reg Dunton. Very broken up.

13 November 1911   *Angele*, brigantine, wrecked Doom Bar, Padstow, Cornwall.
Hansey, full-rigged ship, wrecked Housel Bay, Lizard.

11 February 1912   *Pindos*, barque, wrecked near Coverack, South Cornwall.

28 December 1912   *Cecil Rhodes*, spritsail barge, foundered half a mile off Margate.

1 January 1915   HMS *Formidable*, battleship torpedoed by U-24. Has been found by Silas Oates salvage team. Is a war grave.

7 May 1915   *Lusitania*, Cunard liner, torpedoed by U-20. Has been dived by John Light.

28 October 1915   *Argyll*, HM Cruiser, wrecked Bell Rock, Arbroath. Has been located and dived by Scottish divers.

27 March 1916   *Empress of Midland*, steamer, mined North Foreland, Kent.

11 July 1916   *Kara*, steamer, mined Gorton, Norfolk.

23 January 1917   *Laurentic*, 14,892 tons, sank three miles north-west of Dunaff Head, Northern Ireland, after hitting a mine. 100 feet to wreck, which shows only some twenty feet above sea-bed now. Was carrying £6 million in gold. Almost all recovered in epic salvage operation. Boilers there, proud in the middle of what looks like a scrapyard.

23 March 1917   SS *Maine*, torpedoed, sank Bolt Head, Devon. All saved. Heavily dived. Property of Torbay branch B S-A C. Some salvage work done.

24 May 1917   *Greltoria*, steamer, torpedoed; Flamborough Head.

2 October 1917   HMS *Drake*, cruiser of 14,100 tons. Abandoned
                       safely after torpedoing off Rathlin Island, Northern
                       Ireland. Capsized and sank. Belfast branch B S-A C
                       have dived on her frequently. *Drake* rises from
                       sea-bed at 50 feet to within few feet of sur-
                       face.

4 December 1917   *Riversdale*, 2,085 tons. Upright in 150 feet of water.
                       Is the property of Torbay branch B S-A C, who dive
                       her often.

30 December 1917   *El Toro*, Admiralty oiler, wrecked Blasket Island,
                       Southern Ireland.

25 January 1918   *Folmina*, steamer, torpedoed, near Sunderland.

25 March 1918   *Hercules*, steamer, torpedoed Filey Bay.

26 May 1918   *Kyarra*, hospital ship, torpedoed off Durleston
                       Head. Owned by Kingston branch of B S-A C.

24 July 1918   *Pincher*, destroyer, wrecked Seven Stones reef.

28 July 1918   *John Rettig*, steamer, torpedoed Bridlington Bay,
                       Yorks.

10 August 1918   *Bretagne*, steamer; sunk after collision with French
                       ship. Owned by Bristol Aeroplane Company spe-
                       cial branch.

17 August 1918   *Eros*, steamer, torpedoed near Filey.

18 August 1918   *Clan MacVey*, armed British merchant ship, 3,710
                       tons, torpedoed off Poole, Dorset. Cargo coal. At 45
                       feet, very broken up.

8 October 1923   *City of Westminster*, steamer, wrecked Runnelstone,
                       Cornwall.

12 November 1925   M1 HM Submarine, lost off Start Point. Located by
                       diver.

19 September 1931   *Lyminge*, steamer, wrecked Gunnards Head, North
                       Cornwall.

26 January 1932   M2 HM Submarine, off Portland. Dived by many
                       B S-A C branches.

25 March 1936	*Herzogin Cecilie*, famous grain-race four-masted clipper, struck Hamstone, finally sank in Salcombe Estuary. Much dived; very broken up.
13 April 1937	*Island*, two-thousand-ton steamer ran aground off the Isle of May in the Firth of Forth. Bought for Perth Branch of the B S-A C by diving officer Phil Rogers, 163 passengers and 39 crew saved, but ship later slipped off rocks and sank in 60 feet of water. Had been royal yacht of King Christian x of Denmark.
17 September 1939	HMS *Courageous*, aircraft carrier, torpedoed.
14 October 1939	HMS *Royal Oak*, battleship, torpedoed. Has been dived.
13 November 1939	*Blanche*, steamer, mined and sunk, Thames Estuary.
8 December 1939	*Louis Shied*, 5,945-ton Belgian cargo vessel ran aground a hundred yards from Links Hotel, Thurlestone, South Devon. Very broken up, but still a dive for beginners.
3 May 1940	*Kyle Firth* went ashore, Anglesey. Located by Bill Butland.
1 November 1940	*Placidas Farroult*, gate vessel to Salcombe Estuary boom. Hit Blackstone Rocks in gale. Much dived. On even keel. Still ship-shaped.
1 December 1940	*Empire Politician*, sank after going aground in the Sound of Eriskay, South Uist, Scotland. This ship was the inspiration for Sir Compton Mackenzie's novel and the film *Whisky Galore*. Lieutenant George Wookey, the record helmet diver, was one of a team who relocated her. The whisky was just drinkable, even if it had a tendency to turn green after opening!
25 March 1941	*Somali*, cargo ship, set on fire by German bomber near Seahouses. Salvage divers in possession.
17 March 1942	*Adept*, HM Tug, wrecked Hebrides, West Scotland.

23 June 1942   *Leny*, Dutch motor vessel of 343 tons, sunk by mine off Poole, Dorset. Very broken up and scattered at 45 feet.

31 March 1943   *Caulonia*, Admiralty trawler, foundered Rye Bay, Sussex.

6 April 1943   *Golden Gift*, Admiralty trawler, collision, Oban Bay, West Scotland.

20 March 1944   P715, submarine, wrecked west side of Islay.

18 June 1944   *Albert C. Field*, steamer, aerial torpedo, St Catherine's Point.

1 February 1945   *Persier*, torpedoed, wreck near Challaborough, South Devon. Still an exciting dive. Owned by Colin Hopkins.

21 March 1945   *James Eagan Layne*, seven-thousand-ton Liberty ship, torpedoed and sunk in Whitesand Bay, Devon. Mast shows above water, and keel is at 75 feet on sandy bottom. Much dived. Cargo: trucks, tractors and agricultural machinery.

19 September 1945 *Minerve*, submarine, wrecked Portland Bill.

3 November 1962   *Jeanne Gougy*, trawler, wrecked Land's End, Cornwall.

17 November 1962   *Green Ranger*, Admiralty tanker, wrecked Hartland Point, Devon.

24 October 1963   *Juan Ferrer*, motor vessel, Carn Boscawen, near Land's End.

18 March 1967   *Torrey Canyon*, super-tanker struck the Seven Stones Reef. Later bombed to stop oil pollution. Has been dived.

2 January 1969   *Ceta*, motor vessel sunk by tanker off Rye. Found by Malcolm Inch and Bromley branch divers.

26 April 1970   *Glen Strathallen*, 330 tons, steam yacht, scuttled outside Plymouth Sound to carry out dying wish of her former owner. 50 feet deep, she is used as a training wreck for the School of Nautical Archaeology.

Further Reading

about the technique of diving

A practical manual is the *British Sub-Aqua Club Diving Manual*, available from the BS-AC at 70 Brompton Road, London SW3 1HA.

about underwater archaeology

BASS, GEORGE F. *Archaeology under Water*. Penguin 1970

BLACKMAN, D. J. (Editor). *Colston Papers* no. 23. Butterworth 1973

FLEMMING, N. C. (Editor). *The Undersea*. Cassell 1977

MCKEE, ALEXANDER. *History Under the Sea*. Hutchinson 1968

—— *King Henry VIII's* Mary Rose. Souvenir Press 1973

MARSDEN, PETER. *The Wreck of the* Amsterdam. Hutchinson 1974

MARTIN, COLIN. *Full Fathom Five*. Chatto and Windus 1975

STENUIT, ROBERT. *Treasures of the Armada*. David and Charles 1972

TAYLOR, JEAN DU PLAT (Editor). *Marine Archaeology*. Hutchinson 1965

WILKES, BILL ST JOHN. *Nautical Archaeology*. David and Charles 1971

SHIPWRECKS SERIES. David and Charles, *continuing*. Authors include LARN, DICK; CARTER, CLIVE; WYNNE JONES, IVOR.

Note: Underwater swimming can be dangerous. The way for amateurs to learn is for them to be properly trained by a branch of the British Sub-Aqua Club. Details of the nearest of the Club's eight hundred branches to you can be obtained from the BS-AC headquarters (at the address above).

Index